German Library
bibliographical information

The German Library has a catalogue record of this book in the German National Library: detailed bibliographical data is available on the internet at http://dnb.ddb.de.

First edition ©2004 and second edition ©2005 published in Germany by **FN**verlag der Deutschen Reiterlichen Vereinigung GmbH, Warendorf

Third edition ©2007 by **FN**verlag der Deutschen Reiterlichen Vereinigung GmbH, Warendorf (ISBN 978-3-88542-358-4)

English translation ©**FN**verlag der Deutschen Reiterlichen Vereinigung GmbH, Warendorf, 2008

Translated by:
HippoTranslation Carol Hogg, Osnabrück

Revised by:
Gertrud Anna Rüggeberg, Herborn

Cover picture:
Ute Schmoll, Wiesbaden (photo)

Photographs/Illustrations:
See page 254

Layout and cover design:
Ute Schmoll, Captain Pixel, Wiesbaden

Printed by:
Media-Print Informationstechnologie Paderborn

ISBN 978-3-88542-444-4

Table of Contents

The Training ◄
of the Rider

Equipment ◄
of the Horse

Table of Contents

> The Training
of the Horse

Table of Contents

Riding of ◄
Exercises and
Movements

Participation ◄
in Dressage
Competitions

Breaking-in ◄
– Basic
Education
for Horses

Klaus Balkenhol, one of the most successful German dressage riders and trainers ever, has been coaching the US Team for some years now

It is indeed a great pleasure for me to be given the opportunity to write the foreword to the book "Riding with Understanding and Feeling" by Michael Putz.

I see this book as a necessity because, sadly, the training of riders has not managed to keep up with the improvement in quality of the horses as a result of progress in horse breeding over the last decades. And this situation has arisen despite the fact that success is based 75% on training and only 25% on the natural abilities of the horse. This is why numerous horses of over-average talent disappear into oblivion as a result of incorrect and over-hasty training whilst other difficult horses of rather average talent become successful horses as a result of considerate, well-structured and patient training.

Many riders and trainers, however, have also never had the opportunity of developing their sensitivity on a well-ridden horse and, unfortunately, in spite of theoretical training, there is frequently also a serious lack of theoretical knowledge.

In my capacity as a head instructor on courses, I have often asked myself whether or not it is possible to "retrain" the way riders feel when in fact some of them are sitting on totally tensed up horses, and then to effectively convey to them how this feeling should really be. Riders often resort quickly to draw reins in order to simplify their work and speed it up. Auxiliary reins of all kinds should, however, be superfluous in the context of correct training. Very few people actually realise that it is usually a question of incompetence on the part of the rider.

Additionally, however, horses also confront experienced riders and trainers with new, difficult predicaments, which should also be a good reason for the rider and/or trainer once again to examine the riding theory closely and in particular the German training scale.

I was very fortunate myself to have had a trainer from the Cavalry School in Hanover, an excellent rider and trainer who adhered to all the rules of the classical school. He made me realise that sound fundamental training must precede everything else. He taught me how to feel what it is like when the horse begins to relax and when the horse is ready for collection. He also taught me that the rider may accept the collection, even in the case of young horses, provided this happens without any coercion – and that coercion can lead to tenseness in the rider as well as the horse. It was always possible to see how his horses became more beautiful in the course of training. He taught me that success is not everything and we have a responsibility for the horses in our care which are consequently dependent on us.

This applies in equal terms to the competitive rider as well as to the happy hacker. Training successes are fundamentally based on the rules of classical training, which are to be found in the "Guidelines for Riding and Driving Volume 1 + 2" of the German Equestrian Federation (FN).

This book can be an enormous success in the implementation of these equestrian rules in practice. Mr Putz conveys and explains the principles of equestrian theory in a style which can be well understood and, above all, put into practice. he is able to substantiate what he writes by his decades of experience as a trainer, judge and rider, during the course of which he has been confronted by numerous training problems, for which he has always found a solution by means of careful investigation of the causes and reference to the principles of classical horsemanship.

I can recommend every rider and trainer to take a look at this book. Preferably before problems occur and fundamental mistakes are made. This instructional book should be a companion for riders and trainers throughout their entire training – from the initial fundamentals through to advanced level.

Klaus Balkenhol

Klaus Balkenhol

For some years now Michael Putz has been writing numerous articles for the magazine "Pferdesport international" on "all kinds" of equestrian subjects. He particularly emphasises fundamental principles in the training of horse and rider from novice to advanced level.

These short articles are highly esteemed in equestrian circles. M. Putz knows exactly how to explain the important and essential elements of training of horse and rider in concise and comprehensible terms. After reading these articles many enthusiastic riders therefore expressed the wish that Mr Putz should publish these articles, appropriately edited and ordered and embellished with good pictures and subtitles, in book form. Although there is nothing fundamentally new in equestrianism and indeed many new books only put different emphasis on the good old principles, this book by Michael Putz has its own special significance. Numerous questions relating to horse management and the training of rider and horse are discussed with great care in concise terms in a style which is easy to understand and applicable for practical riding and training – practical information based on practical experience. Reading the Table of Contents it becomes clear that the author is not simply addressing the principles of training in a narrower context but rather he is giving meaningful explanations which are relevant to the entire wide-ranging area of equestrianism and dealing with horse and training.

Wherever it is appropriate the theory of training which has been handed down from generation to generation is emphasised in clear terms. Also the reasons for these principles which have been compiled over the decades by important equestrian experts, riders and trainers are presented in a convincing way. It is made clear in the book that indeed over the course of the last 30 to 40 years the conformation, sequence of movement and riding qualities of the horse have improved significantly. This situation, however, should not give riders, trainers and even judges any reason to believe they may deviate from this well-founded equestrian doctrine which has been passed down over the decades.

Following conclusion of studies to become a teacher and experience in student riding teams, Michael Putz took over management of the dressage yard of the successful rider Josef Neckermann, experienced there the agreeable but logically consistent training of that exemplary dressage rider and also participated himself in numerous horse shows, in the context of which he acquired the "Goldene Reitabzeichen" (Golden Badge). After running the well-known Landesreitschule in Vechta for four years, Mr Putz – following a period of thorough familiarisation – took over the management for approx. 15 years of the successfully functioning Westfälische Reit- und Fahrschule in Münster, an establishment which is very closely linked with the names Stecken and Klimke. At this important training centre the author gained valuable experience in the training of horse and rider, in instructing and in the execution of training courses for riders and instructors as well as in the responsible running of a large equestrian establishment. At the present time Michael Putz – also qualified as a competition judge up to Grand Prix level – works increasingly in short clinics held all over Germany and abroad.

Extensive equestrian experience with great success in important positions, particular pleasure in writing and precise explanations of equestrian connections are optimum qualifications for writing with intricate care about interesting subjects concerning the training of rider and horse for all riders, irrespective of age, as well as for trainers in a comprehensible style which is as concise as possible, in a book with good pictures and graphics.

Paul Stecken
22nd April 2004

Paul Stecken, Director of the Westfälische Reit- und Fahrschule from 1950-1985, has instructed many well-known riders, trainers and judges, and is himself a former international judge.

Preface

Michael Putz
with Lancelot

Throughout my twenty years of activity, initially at the Landesreit- und Fahrschule Weser-Ems in Vechta (Weser-Ems Regional Riding and Driving School) and subsequently at the Westfälische Reit- und Fahrschule (Westphalian Riding and Driving School) in Münster – both located in Northern Germany –, I have constantly been involved in training riders from the entire range of equestrian disciplines. Whilst the training of amateur and professional instructors, including successful riders up to the highest level, was of principal importance, I was nevertheless also occupied on a regular basis with lessons for complete beginners of all ages.

Thus my intention in this book is to provide practice-related assistance to riders virtually from preliminary to advanced level and to offer tips for the training of these riders, as well as of their horses. I included some concrete suggestions about how to solve all important problems which occur in dressage work. And in this context I always try to recognize and deal with the actual sources of the problems rather than simply treating the symptoms.

Although I may seem to be somewhat unorthodox in some details, I nevertheless adhere very strictly to the so-called classical riding theory as it is summarised in the "Guidelines for Riding and Driving Volume 1 + 2" of the German Equestrian Federation (FN).

During my activity, particularly in the last 10 to 15 years, I frequently had opportunities to find out about other ways of riding, to become involved in them in somewhat greater depth and, in some cases, to be able to discuss the common elements as well as the differences with well-known representatives of the various fields. The more insight and knowledge I acquired concerning these different ways of riding, the more confirmed I became in my conviction that the German way of riding is absolutely correct and suitable for horses and that no other way is superior in this respect. The core content of its system and theory based on the doctrines of Pluvinel, Guérinière, Hünersdorf, Seidler, Seeger, Kegel, Steinbrecht, Bürkner, v. Heydebreck, Lauffer, v. Redwitz etc., indeed we could almost say its philosophy, is to train rider and horse so that both have pleasure in their mutual sporting activity together for as long as possible.

Nevertheless it is a sad fact that many riders and trainers, whilst making reference to this theory, indeed work in a way which is not good for their horses, in some cases even to the extent of inflicting pain, because they lack the genuine knowledge, feeling as riders and also ability to exercise self-criticism. To make matters worse these people sometimes actually try to teach other people to ride in such a way.

A horse which is brought on honestly and seriously according to our training scale, in other words correctly schooled and trained, has the best prospects and chances, in spite of its service under the saddle and the exertion this involves, of actually staying fit for longer than a horse living wild and in complete freedom.

A rider who has learned according to our training scale and has developed himself, can best do justice to his horse and enjoy long-term pleasure with it, regardless of the level at which he is involved with horses.

For all those smitten by a love of horses, riding is certainly the most enjoyable way of taking exercise. For every genuinely horsy person the pleasure in riding only achieves its true quality when the two individuals have adapted to each other to such a degree that they work together in as perfect a way as possible – in other words when the pleasure of the human being is in no way detrimental to the well-being of the animal.

Anyone who believes this harmony is easy to achieve, however, risks serious disappointment. A rider will only be able to do this if he is prepared to become seriously involved in the subject of equestrianism; and this requirement concerns leisure riders to exactly the same extent as riders in competitive sport.

The more demanding, perhaps even complicated, an area of interest – in this case riding – is, the more the degree of success to be achieved is dependent on the approach and attitude to the subject in the first place. This applies particularly when it is a question of changing habits or even putting an end to some faults which have managed to creep in. Only someone who has fully understood for himself the reasons why something can function in one particular way and not in another, or why it is important to eliminate a particular mistake, will be able to be fully motivated and successful.

Really good riding, which naturally also means riding in a way which is good for your horse, is only possible, however, when the rider also has enough ability as well as will to pursue our sport with feeling. In the first place this concerns the rider's own feeling for himself, for his own body and then, of at least equal importance, for the physical and mental sensitivities of his horse. This so-called rider's feeling also has to be trained and constantly perfected.

The object of this book is that more riders become real horsy people. I sincerely hope the application of what is taught in it can make a contribution here.

I have quite consciously omitted the subjects of piaffe and passage from this book.

On the one hand, these are exercises for which relatively few horses have the potential required to learn to do them properly.

On the other hand, it also requires great experience and a very finely tuned feeling on the part of the trainer and also rider to teach horses to perform these tasks without inflicting any pain. The danger of making serious mistakes is significantly greater here than it's the case with other lessons.

This, however, does not exclude the possibility of anyone who can sit in balanced posture on a horse having the experience of doing a piaffe and, with certain restrictions, also passage on a suitably trained "schoolmaster horse" – although this should be done with the full guidance and assistance of an experienced trainer.

By way of conclusion to this introduction as well as an opening to the book itself, I should like to make you familiar with a quotation which I personally consider to be an important equestrian motto:

"A good rider has a critical mind, great feeling and a sensitive hand." (Tu Yu, 72 B.C.)[1]

Michael Putz

Michael Putz

Indications are given at the end of each chapter about where to find further information in this book about the subject matter in question. Furthermore, points which the author considers to be of particular importance are mentioned in several chapters in order to avoid the reader having to refer constantly to earlier or later pages.

A very detailed Table of Contents also makes it easier for the reader to refer quickly to specific subject areas.

Indication ◄

---

[1] Taken from: Wanless, Mary, Reiten in Vollendung, CH-Cham. 1999

Acknowledgements

The following riders and their horses exercised great patience and perseverance in preparation of the photos:

- Dominik Buhl with Rivondo and Moonlight
- Dorothee Schmid with Lucky the Man
- Corinna Schultze with Balou
- Falk Stankus with Lancelot
- Monika Ulsamer with Bowie, Piano Forte and Palisander
- Christoph Vente with Chivas and Dorissima
- Anja Wilimzig with Condillac
- Linda Birkhahn with Whitney
- Andrea Huber with Mists of Avalon
- Horses from the Westfälischen Reit- und Fahrschule: Albert, Gladness
- Horses from the Essing yard: Colossal, Lancelot and Rossini

The deliberate presentation of mistakes was an especially difficult as well as a thankless task, therefore I am particularly grateful to the riders for their support here!

I should like to thank

- in particular all those people who familiarised me with good riding when I was still a very young rider and at the same time impressed on me the importance of good theoretical knowledge and introduced me to appropriate books on equestrian subjects,

- additionally all horses and pupils who enable me to continue learning more every day and enjoy some successful and enlightening experiences,

- the patient and competent reader, the never-tiring photographer as well as the imaginative, experienced and reliable graphic designer,

- Mr Stecken, who finally encouraged me to add yet another book to the enormous number of equestrian books already on the market,

- Carol Hogg for the translation into English. In addition to the actual translation work, I should particularly like to thank her for the great patience she invested in dealing with an author whose consistently high ideals sometimes made him rather pedantic and hard to please, as well as her efforts to maintain as much of my style of language as possible in the English version.
  Translation of such a detailed and specific equestrian text is an extremely demanding task. In parts a direct translation was not even possible and it was necessary, in close collaboration, to use innovative license and attempt to create new expressions and turns of phrase.

- and last but not least my dear wife, without whom my entire professional development would not have been possible in this form and who, with her patience and good eye, was also an enormous help to me in taking the photographs.

The Training of the Rider

Part 1

1. The Rider's Training Path

An essential element of German riding theory is the well-known and much-discussed scale of training for the horse.

Somewhat less well-known, although already described in the Guidelines of the German FN, is a similar arrangement for the rider, The Rider's Training Path, which consists of four sections:

- **Seat and training of the seat**
- **Application of the aids**
- **Feeling**
- **Influence**

In recent years increasing importance has been placed on including and using knowledge acquired in the field of sport education and in particular also the theory of movement in the training of riders, therefore it seems a good idea to develop this rather meagre framework somewhat further and expand its content.

In this connection it is well worthwhile taking a more precise look at the "Ethical Principles of the True Horseman"[1] compiled and published by the German Equestrian Federation (FN) (published for the first time in 1995). Accordingly all riders – whether beginners, more advanced or even active competition riders – repeatedly have to be reminded about what a great responsibility the human being takes on if he wants to become actively involved in equestrian sport:

Breeders have been increasingly successful in recent decades in making horses available to riders which are particularly suitable for use under the saddle on account of their conformation as well as their inner qualities; it was possible to achieve this particularly by means of appropriate selection according to riding horse points and characteristics. Nevertheless, it is important to remember that it is only as a result of competent, careful training and ongoing schooling that a horse becomes able to actually carry a rider on its back and not simply to bear him. In this connection everyone involved in the training of horses, whether as a rider or a trainer, must acquire as good knowledge as possible and also try to put this into practice in their daily work and continue to do so even on a medium and long-term basis. Judges also carry a lot of responsibility here because they prescribe what is either honoured positively or judged negatively, thus playing a very significant role in determining values, at least concerning competition riders.

Before dealing with the training aims for the rider in detail, it is worth thinking about the mental attributes which make it easier to deal with horses and in some cases are indeed essential pre-requisites for doing so:

The Ethical Principles
Taking over of responsibility
Adapting to natural requirements
Health is of utmost significance
All horses are to be respected equally
The history of the horse is a historico-cultural heritage
Particular significance in the development of personality
The objective is optimum harmony
Orientation according to nature, ability and willlingness to perform
Responsibility for the end of the horse's life

- **Genuine respect for the creature and love of the animal**
- **Considerable empathy and willingness to understand**
- **Great patience and perseverance**
- **Absolute honesty towards oneself and willingness to admit to one's own mistakes**
- **Curiosity and a constant willingness to learn**

[1] The German version of the brochure "Ethische Grundsätze des Pferdefreundes" is available free of charge from the Deutsche Reiterliche Vereinigung e.V. (FN), Abteilung Mitgliederservice, 48229 Warendorf, Tel. 0049 (0)2581 6362-222, Fax 0049 (0)2581 63 62 333, E-Mail: pschaffer@fn-dokr.de

- **Good concentration ability**
- **Reliable powers of observation, particularly for sequences of movement**
- **Discipline and self-control**

These attributes will be stimulated and probably also further developed in the course of a correspondingly systematic and well supervised training.

Anyone who would like to practise our wonderful equestrian sport, whether as a "happy hacker" or a top performance rider, has the moral obligation to subject himself as well as his horse to training, at least to such an extent that both participants can enjoy this sport to the full for as long as possible without it ever being to the detriment of the horse.

Many people believe that riding is a form of sport in which performance comes principally from the horse and therefore that only the horse has to fulfil the relevant conditions. Obviously this is completely wrong! Also a happy hacker, whose sole aim is to enjoy riding his horse out in the countryside, has to be in a position whilst sitting on his horse to be well-balanced and make circumstances for the horse as easy as possible.

Before any training can actually start on the horse, the learner-rider must have good basic fitness. Otherwise it is absolutely essential to work on this at the same time. Modern lifestyles unfortunately mean that nowadays even children and teenagers often suffer from a lack of physical fitness. The same applies for the knowledge already referred to briefly above. Because riding involves a connection between two living beings which should harmonise as well as possible, this is one of the most demanding and complicated forms of sport. Precisely for this reason, in order to have enjoyment and success it is important to acquire as much knowledge as possible about horse and rider – in particular about inter-connections and dependences between them – and to be prepared to continue learning for as long as one continues to ride. This knowledge first ac-

quires its full value, however, when it is carefully thought about, understood and filled with personal riding experience. Ideally theoretical and practical learning go hand-in-hand and complement each other in a positive way.

The diverse training aims on the way to becoming a good rider can be summarised in the following eight points. Here, just as in the training scale of the horse, it is important to realise that they do not represent individual stages which are entities in themselves and are finished with once they have been achieved, it is rather the case that, despite a prescribed sequence of succession, some of them must be aimed for on a parallel basis:

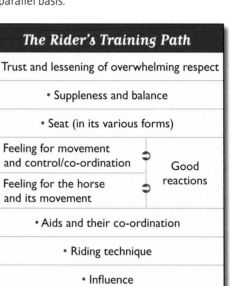

The Rider's Training Path

- Trust and lessening of overwhelming respect
- Suppleness and balance
- Seat (in its various forms)
- Feeling for movement and control/co-ordination
- Feeling for the horse and its movement

Good reactions

- Aids and their co-ordination
- Riding technique
- Influence

1.1 Trust and lessening of overwhelming respect

Particularly people who have not grown up with (large) animals, perhaps not had any form of closer contact with animals whatsoever, will initially have overwhelming respect for horses. This is perfectly natural but it is also the reason why, before beginning any actual riding training as such, a certain degree of trust has to be developed, in-

1. ➤ The Training of the Rider

Even grooming is a good opportunity for developing and strengthening a relationship of trust between rider and horse

- typical characteristics and features of its nature,
- the development and training of its sensory organs based on its history,
- its naturally innate requirements which are important concerning how it is kept etc.

How this knowledge is best acquired, whether in theory lessons, by means of books and videos, or explanations given by the instructor in the context of dealings with the horse, depends entirely on the pupil's individual learning circumstances; however an ideal solution would be a combination of all possibilities.

1.2 Suppleness and balance

Suppleness and balance are essential requirements for enjoyable and good riding. Both are intrinsically linked as well as inter-dependant:

A rider who has serious balance problems – for whatever reasons this may be – will never be able to relax properly, either physically or mentally (see also "Suppleness of the Rider" in this connection).

Likewise it is impossible for anyone who is completely cramped up or even just rather tense, because he is frightened of a particular horse for example, to be able to sit on this horse in any sort of balanced way.

Suppleness means that the rider, whilst being fully concentrated and perhaps even with a very strong will to perform well, becomes neither physically nor mentally tense, so that his breathing, circulation and entire locomotory system function in a good and economical way (see also "Suppleness of the Horse" in this connection).

How well and how fast the prospective rider can learn to balance and gradually learn to maintain this sense of balance even in the case of unexpected, abrupt movements and changes of direction on the part of the horse, depends on his natural disposition as well as previous train-

itially in one's own ability and subsequently, of course, also in the horse. This is to be done by means of learning correct handling and developing the confidence required to do this properly, e.g. when leading the horse and grooming it. Mistakes made in this phase, perhaps because of too little information or a lack of competent instruction, can very quickly lead to fear. Nevertheless, it must also be considered that carelessness or thoughtlessness in dealings with horses can indeed be dangerous. As a result of their relatively large body mass they have – even when moving slowly – a very considerable energy potential. The considerably weaker human body is thus immediately at a disadvantage if a potentially dangerous situation should arise. From the very beginning onwards it is therefore important to adhere to the principle that the beginner can reduce his overwhelming respect in the fastest and best way if well-trained horses are available. These horses should have an intact sense of trust in humans but at the same time have learned to accept them as higher ranking beings.

In this early phase of training everything can proceed much more easily and more quickly if the prospective rider also acquires theoretical knowledge about the horse, for example

Gymnastic exercises, on the lunge for example, improve the rider's suppleness

Praising the horse by patting it behind the saddle also relaxes the rider

ing and experience e.g. in other forms of sport. Also with regard to motor functions - as implied above - the restricted possibilities available nowadays for youngsters to play and run around mean that, predictably, often not even children have a great spectrum of experience and scope in this context. Specific associated gymnastic exercises can also be very helpful here, in some cases such extra training is absolutely essential.

Also with regard to suppleness and balance the well-schooled, supple and balanced horse is the best schoolmaster.

1.3 The seat and its different forms

In the "Guidelines for Riding and Driving Volume 1" and German riding theory a differentiation is made between three seat forms:

- **Dressage seat**
- **Light seat**
- **Racing seat**

The dressage seat, according to German riding theory, is also the basic seat which should be learnt first. There is a good reason for this because it is the seat in which it is easiest for most riders to find their balance at the beginning. More will follow on this subject later.

The super-ordinate term "forward seat" covers all seat forms in which, as a result of the trunk leaning forward out of the hips, the weight is shifted more onto the thigh, the knee and the feet standing in the stirrups, in other words the horse's back is relieved somewhat of the rider's weight). These include the forward seat and the seat on the young horse. (In German there is a special word for this: the Remontesitz), the cross-country seat as well as the jumping seat (the seat between the jumps and in the various phases of the jump).

The racing seat, as the name just implies, is the form which is ideally suited to riding at high speed on the race course. In some cases special saddles are used here, in any case the stirrups are kept extremely short. The rider's hip and knee joints are bent at a considerable angle so that he has maximum spring electricity in his legs and is in a position to absorb

Balanced forward seat

Correct dressage seat

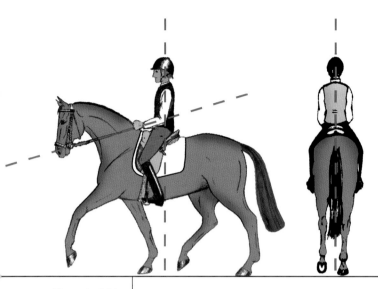

These straight lines can be easily recognised when the dressage seat is correct

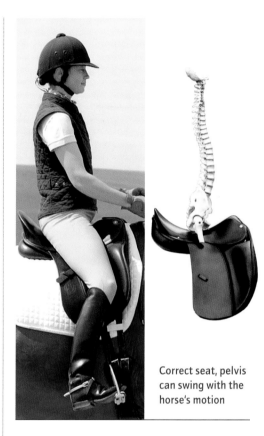

Correct seat, pelvis can swing with the horse's motion

almost completely the movements of the horse at a flat out gallop. Consequently, the horse no longer needs to lift up the rider's weight with every stride. The strongly angled rider's legs may be compared with the longer suspension forks of a cross-country motorbike. As very little direct contact exists between rider and horse in this seat form, outstanding body control and a 100% sense of balance is required on the part of the rider.

Particularly in the context of motoric learning (learning of body motion), it is a great advantage when the learning abilities to develop a command of the body and a sense of balance which prevail in childhood and early teenage years can be used for riding.

According to German riding theory, the dressage seat is to be taught – for good reasons – as the first seat. It is easier to learn than the forward seat on account of the fact that it is relatively easy to sit in a fairly balanced position in the dressage seat. In the case of the forward seat the upper body, including the head, has to be carried and stabilised by the muscles.

The following text describes the dressage seat and, based on examples, explains the functional reasons behind the rules which apply concerning this seat and why they always have to

be seen in relation to the specific circumstances of the individual rider and his horse regarding body conformation and proportions. The important claim in this connection which exists in the theory of movement "function takes precedence over form" always applied for the sensible and competent trainer. Exaggerated formalistic teaching and judging always bore testimony to a lack of understanding.

At this point I should like to refer to an image which gives the riding pupil a good idea of the position in which it is easiest for him to balance:

The rider must take up a position from the head to the feet in which it would be possible for him to stand in well-balanced posture even without the horse, should the horse suddenly disappear from under him!

This image, moreover, also applies for the forward seat.

Fork seat, pelvis
tipped into the
end position

Chair seat, pelvis
tipped bachwards
in the end position

It makes sense to begin the description of the dressage seat at the basis of the seat, the so-called middle posture. Particularly for the beginner, it is important to sit on a horse and in a saddle which suit him and are appropriate to his physical proportions, for example with regard to the width of his pelvis and the agility of his hip joints. Only the supple (see above) rider sits close to his horse thanks to a relaxed seat muscle system as well as from a normal pelvis position, sits into the movement of the horse and lets himself go with it. The thigh length and thickness should also be taken into consideration.

On no account should anyone try to force a leg to be more stretched by using a dressage saddle with thick knee rolls or too long stirrups to fix the legs in position. Such a forced position would impose too much pressure on the thighs and thus prevent sitting deeply into the saddle. Furthermore, and this is the most serious disadvantage of such saddles, the rider would be forced into sitting with an hollow back, a position which quite definitely prevents suppleness and elasticity. The calves slip back too far, the independence of the hand is restricted.

The entire position of thigh, lower leg and foot must be optimised or corrected from the hip, in other words from the top downwards. Only then is it possible to apply the driving aids correctly and to achieve the desired more-or-less parallel foot position. As the rear thigh muscle system is responsible for the driving leg aids with the calf, the knee has to be sufficiently bent. An exaggerated pressing down of the heel or, as when riding without stirrups, raising of the fore-foot only causes a cramping up of the legs and is therefore counter-productive. The same applies for slanting stirrups or stirrup inserts, which bring the foot and ankle joint into an unnatural position.

The angled knee and the foot perpendicularly beneath the rider's point of gravity are a precondition for the rising trot which should also be an easy movement from the point of view of the horse. Only then will the rider be in a position, elastically and supply, without any interference from the hands or reins, to rise and sit again softly.

The rider sits, viewed from the side as well as from the back, with an upright, straight upper body and also head position. If this is not the case, he should think about improving his body posture by pulling himself up by his own hair.

Upright and above all supple shoulders are essential for breathing and head posture, particularly however for the ability which is to be seen almost as a cardinal requirement, to be able to

Standing in the
dressage seat
position

A well-balanced rising trot

apply the rein aids with hands which are independent of the seat. In order to do this, the shoulders have to be brought back; if the rider imagines simply letting his arms dangle and opening his chest whilst doing this, he will avoid pulling his shoulders up in a cramped way.

Sadly today there are people, some of them only young, particularly however people who spend a lot of time at a desk or in front of a computer, who suffer from a contracted pectoral muscle system and therefore are not able to achieve upright upper body posture. This problem is stated here as a typical example of poor posture or posture defects which can make riding more difficult. These are problems, however, which can rarely be solved in the context of normal riding lessons – rather they require specific physiotherapy and gymnastic exercises, perhaps on the lunge.

As the human being is controlled physically as well as mentally by his head, the importance of the position in which the head is held can never be exaggerated, deficiencies in this context

should be considered as more than minor blemishes

A crookedness to the side with the rider bending more than his horse, as is frequently seen riding turns or lateral movements, causes an unwanted sideways bend in the spine, an incorrect shift of weight and thus a dysbalance.

Letting the head hang forwards has an effect as far as the middle posture and reduces its elasticity, in other words the ability to swing with the movement. Sometimes false reminders about looking under the ceiling, in other words exaggerated raising of the head, causes a blockage in the neck, more precisely in the occipital joint between the cranium and atlas.

In her book "Centered Riding" Sally Swift requires the gentle gaze and this really is an important condition for suppleness.[1] It is easiest for the rider to improve in this context if he actually does let his gaze wander somewhat instead of keeping it firmly fixed on the horse's neck or head.

Also as far as arm and hand positions are concerned, the proportions of the rider in question have to be taken into consideration:

The shoulders should be supple, held slightly back, but not raised and the upper arms should fall slightly along the sides of the body. The arms

---

[1] Udo Bürger already described this in a similar way in his book "Vollendete Reitkunst" (The Way to Perfect Horsemanship), First German Edition 1959

Slanting stirrup inserts prevent a natural positioning of the feet

Forward seat

have to remain slightly angled in order to ensure the independence and movability of the hands. The frequently quoted straight line elbow-hand-horse's mouth should virtually always be kept, seen from the side as well as from the point of view of the rider. The hands should only be closed tightly enough for the rider to have control over the length of his reins, but not so tight that the hands are cramped. The slightly roof-formed bent thumb is one of the pre-requisites for an agile wrist, and an agile wrist is essential in order to apply subtle rein aids. The fundamental elasticity of the contact, however, results the movability of the entire arm, in other words, that of the elbow and shoulder joint.

The forward seat, as already mentioned above, requires better control of the body by the rider, but also more strength in certain groups of muscles. The different degree of sitting forward to relieve the horse, but also the length of the stirrups, depends on the ability of the rider, and also on the purpose, i.e. what is to be ridden.

In contrast to the dressage seat, the basis of which is the buttocks and in the case of which a tight closing of the knees is actually undesirable and obstructive, in the case of the forward seat, in order to relieve the horse's back by leaning forward out of the hips, the weight is increasingly shifted to the thigh, the knee and the feet leaning on the stirrups. In this situation a little tighter gripping with the knees is necessary and the rider has to imagine he is kneeling in the saddle (especially over jumps), as a result of which a large proportion of the weight is shifted via the knee rolls on the saddle, to the sides of the horse, the rest of the weight is absorbed by means of an supple ankle in the stirrup. By means of the leaning forward of the trunk ("bending in the hip") and the accompanying shortening of the reins, the rider's point of gravity comes somewhat further forward. From the point of view of the rider's balance it is therefore important, that the lower legs remain securely in position and do not slip backwards.

Naturally it is also possible to sit in a normal dressage saddle in such a way as to relieve the horse of the rider's weight, even with long stirrups. If it is intended, however, to ride for a longer time or in a more extreme form of the forward seat, it makes sense to use a general purpose or jumping saddle which enables the rider to keep the knees in a secure position, even with shortened stirrups.

Standing in the position of the forward seat

Climbing is a good exercise for improving balance, also in the forward seat position

Learning the forward seat should be a challenge and an important aim for every rider. As the balance situation for the rider is somewhat more instable than in the case of the dressage seat, it is essential for the rider to concern himself with this seat and practise it accordingly in order to achieve a confident sense of balance. Particularly the ability to guide with hands which are independent of the seat, also in this seat to have the horse's confidence in the rider's hand[1] through a constant and elastic connection, is a decisive pre-requisite for fruitful work.

Riding in the forward seat is in any case the seat form to choose for working on young horses, particularly in the breaking in phase, for riding cross-country and in jumping training. It is less usual, however no less useful because of this, in the work with dressage horses. In the suppling up phase, in small relaxation or reward interludes during the work phase as well as by way of relaxation at the end of the work or on active relaxation days, it provides a wonderful, refreshing change for horse and rider alike. Anyone who is experienced, will also have a horse confident-

ly on the aids and responsive in the forward seat, and therefore this type of work can be a real therapy for over-strained horses and riders.

1.4 Feeling for the horse and its movements

In the brief form of the rider's training path as presented so far, feeling and its significance has only been discussed in general terms, now it must be thought about and schooled more specifically:

In order to be able to ride with feeling and sensitivity, it is first of all a fundamental requirement to have a good and reliable feeling for one's own body, or to work on improving this. Eckart Meyners apostrophised the term "movement feeling" in the title of the first edition of his book which is so important for this subject as "the rider's inner eye", an image which really expresses everything. Only someone who is able to feel the position and posture of his own body, in particular of his limbs, can have control over them. This is why riding lessons can only be successful if train-

---

[1] The horse accepts contact to the bit and goes forwards willingly. Provided it is supple, it will engage the hind legs without faltering, particularly also in the transitions. Furthermore, it also shows good willingness to stretch when chewing the reins out of the rider's hand. It is possible, however, that the horse will try to lean on the reins if the rider does not apply enough driving aids and yield at the right moment.
➜ Instinctively Correct?; Half halts and full halts; Chewing the reins out of the rider's hands

er and pupil are aware of this significance and work on it consistently. Everyone will have experienced at some time or other that the trainer criticises an incorrect leg position or a leg aid and tries to correct this, without a mirror or video recording, however, the pupil did not really know what was meant because he was not aware of this mistake in the first place. In such a case it is necessary to target the problem in a purposeful way before being able to continue with the lesson which had previously not worked on account of this problem. On this subject the books by Susanne von Dietze "Balance in Movement" (also available in video form) and by Eckart Meyners "Das Bewegungsgefühl des Reiters" are to be highly recommended.

Via the gradually improved feeling for movement, the supple and balanced rider becomes increasingly confident in the control and coordination of his movements.

It is also possible to work on the improvement of the feeling for the movements of one's own body and the control and coordination without a horse. The above-mentioned books also include some ideas for this.

For the rider, and this is the great challenge for everyone who wants to practise this sport, it is important to acquire also feeling for the horse and its movements as soon as possible and to work constantly on improving these.

Thus, for example, the success of any suppling work is very dependant on whether the rider feels and rides the right individual basic speed for the horse, especially in working trot.

An example:
Only if a rider feels exactly when the horse is in what moment of support phase of the walk or canter, is it possible for him to practise fine timing in the application of his aids for cantering on or doing the flying change. With increasing experience and training the good, sensitive rider will even be in a position, not only to feel the movements of his horse, but also to sense them in advance to anticipate how his horse will move in the next moment.

This is why the ability to react is included as a further aim above these two sections on the training of feeling. As already indicated, in the case of a good rider, naturally with appropriate talent, from the **reaction** ability, an improved **action** ability will also ensue.

Although sensitivity in the human being, as also in the horse, is to a great extent a matter of natural disposition, it is also something which can be quite specifically trained. A very helpful and effective method here is to close your eyes for a moment when riding in order to be able to concentrate better on the feeling aspect. The control and, if applicable, confirmation is best to come from the trainer; if this is not possible then a riding school mirror or video recording can help.

Sitting on a horse bareback improves feeling for your own movements as well as for those of your horse.

1. ➤ The Training of the Rider

The aim and therefore also criteria of correct application of the aids is to make the horse sensitive to these so that the rider can gradually apply them in an increasingly fine and subtle way.

It is not our primary aim to absolutely drill our horses. Instead we try to use their natural reactions and reflexes for our aids. Therefore the significance of the rider's sensitivity here can not be valued highly enough. Only someone who feels how the horse reacts to the aids can improve and refine the dosage and the timing of their application.

Although only the combination of several well-coordinated aids together can achieve anything worthwhile, as a single aid alone can never do this, it makes sense to draw up a systematic list of the aids which are available to the rider, in order to make it easier to understand them and to analyse their special features, before going into detail about the interplay or coordination.

1.5.1 The weight aids

The rider can use his weight in the following ways:

- **by increasing the weight on both seat bones**
- **by increasing the weight on one seat bone**
- **by easing the weight on the seat bones**

In order to apply the weight aids better and more correctly, it is necessary to consider the manner in which they work.

In this context it is useful to imagine carrying a "rider" on your own shoulders, and having to move with him (see page 23). You will grasp the principle very quickly: When the person being carried shifts his weight, e.g. to the right, the person carrying is more-or-less forced to move to the right also, in other words under the point of gravity of the "rider", in order to re-establish stability. And this is exactly how it should function

Closing your eyes occasionally when riding improves your feeling for the movement

1.5 The rider's aids and their co-ordination

The rider communicates with the horse via the aids; this is why they are sometimes also described as the mutual language which unites them. In order to understand the horse's answer, however, it is necessary for the rider to have developed enough feeling to be able to sense the interconnections between his own movements and those of his horse, and also to be able to interpret them.

The rider can exercise influence on his horse by means of his weight, his legs and his reins. These forms of influence are known as aids. On account of their nature, the weight and leg aids have more of a driving effect whereas the rein aids have more of a restraining effect.

Correction of the leg position
by the riding instructor

in transitions, the rider must do justice to these dynamics of balance and sit slightly forward or behind (see chapter Instinctively Correct?).

In the case of the **weight aids increasing the weight on both seat bones** the rider's weight should be increased on both seat bones. This follows as a result of the so-called "bracing the back".

For this the rider must have his upper body in a naturally upright position and, by means of momentarily tightening of the muscle systems of the stomach and lower back, the pelvis is tipped slightly backwards ("erect posture") (see illustration page 17). In order for this application of increased weight in conjunction with the leg aids to be able to stimulate the horse to step further forwards with both hind legs towards the centre of gravity, it must be in harmony with the horse's movements and ensue from an interplay of tightening and relaxing the muscles.

This aid must always be applied whenever it is a question of particularly activating the horse's hind legs, in other words in the case of all half halts and halts and – consequently – also in all transitions.

Leaning back with the upper body, raising the thigh and the knee as well as the slipping forward of the lower leg, which is an automatic consequence of the above, hinders the effect of this aid. Above all, the rider should never have the idea that he can push his horse on with his seat. As a result of his upper body leaning backwards, which automatically ensues, he will lose elasticity in the middle position, sit behind the move-

In this way you can get an impression of the effect of the weight aids.

between the rider and a schooled horse. For this purpose it is particularly important for the rider's point of gravity to be as close and vertically perpendicular as possible to that of the horse.

A rider who, during all movements, can keep his own point of gravity in unison with the constantly changing point of gravity of his horse, is able to apply the weight aids in a particularly effective manner. Such a rider is not a load, he is a pleasure for the horse to carry. By contrast however, a rider who is not in balance and, due to a lack of suppleness, is not swinging with the horse's movements, is a disturbing influence on the horse's gait and posture and will restrict its enjoyment in working together with him.

When it is mentioned above that the two points of gravity should be virtually perpendicular to each other, this only applies at halt or in very even forwards movement. Always when it is a question of increasing or decreasing the tempo

ment and probably also have a backward effect with his hands.

In the case of the **weight aids increasing the weight on one seat bone** the rider shifts his weight somewhat more onto one seat bone. Consequently the hip is dropped somewhat and the knee should take up a lower position. The increased pressure on the inside seat bone comes about mainly as a result of the fact that the outside leg is brought back from the hip in a regulating or guarding function, being "made long" in the process. A shifting of the weight of the upper body is not only unnecessary, it has a disturbing effect on the common balance between rider and horse. In order to improve this aid, e.g. in half-passes, it can be helpful to imagine sliding towards the middle of the saddle with the outside seat bone.

Many riders tend to exaggerate the shifting of the weight. They therefore collapse sideways in the inside hip and slip outwards with the seat, the rider's point of gravity consequently even shifts to the wrong side. In order to avoid this, when applying a one-sided weight aid, the rider should think about applying this aid in such a way that it is hardly noticeable for an outsider. In normal turns the horse will "lean into the curve" as much as necessary, thus positioning the rider correctly and the rider simply needs to go with the horse. Only in turns which are ridden very fast it may be correct for the rider to lean more to the inside. In this way he can help the horse not to have to lean too much into the curve, which can be problematic if the ground is somewhat slippery. In order to prevent collapsing in the hip, a mistake

Left: Because the rider is collapsed in the hip, he is sitting to the wrong side
Right: The rider remains sitting straight and the horse takes him quite naturally into the turn

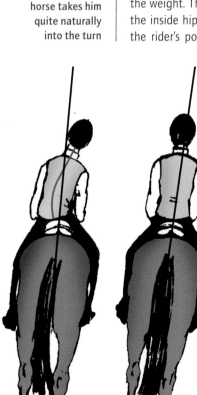

When trotting on from a halt or at the beginning of an extension, slight leaning forward can make it easier for the horse to strike off.

frequently observed in connection with this aid, the rider should try to sit with his inside knee positioned as low as possible, too much stepping in into the inside stirrup usually causes stretching the inside knee and therefore the rider ends up sitting to the wrong side[1].

The increased weight on the inside seat bone supports the effect of the inside leg which is positioned on the girth, when it is a question of driving more onto the outside guarding rein, in other words, when the horse should move in flexion or bend.

In all turns this aid is required to support the rein and leg aids, in the case of a well-trained horse it is indeed the decisive aid.

Particularly in leg-yielding, the forehand turn, and also shoulder-in, it is important to use the increased weight on one seat bone weight aid very subtly, otherwise the horse will be encouraged to move in precisely the wrong direction.

In the case of the **relieving weight aid** the rider shifts his weight more onto the thigh, without

[1] The knee, therefore, has to be bent at a good angle. If, on the contrary, it is "pushed through", the leg will be "extended", but in fact rather more upwards so that the pelvis is actually pushed outwards. This position only has to be corrected by increased outward positioning of the inside stirrup in a situation when the saddle also has slipped outwards.

Sitting in the backward-leaning position prevents elastic swinging with the horse's movements in the middle position, the hand usually also exercises backward influence.

Relieving weight aids, here whilst reining back – the lower legs are positioned slightly too far back.

raising his seat or even taking it out of the saddle. In addition he brings his trunk, moving from the hips, slightly ahead of the vertical, without rounding his back[1] and without altering the position of his seat.

The "easing" weight aid is always used in order to ease the horse's back or hindquarters, -e.g. when breaking in young horses, suppling up and in the first rein back exercises.

It is also useful, in an appropriately fine dosage, when doing transitions into an extension, into a piaffe or passage or if the horse is intended to trot or canter on precisely from the spot. This aid makes it easier for the horse which enjoys working together with the rider and is well on the driving aids, to develop active thrust with the hind legs from a supple back, to step or stride off, but also increasingly close up (with the hindlegs) and take up weight.

Good elasticity of the seat as well as an increasingly more reliable feeling for the horse's rhythm and sequence of movement make the application of weight aids more effective and enable the rider to use leg and rein aids more subtly.

1.5.2 The Leg Aids

The leg aids can be used for

- **forward-driving,**
- **forward-sideways driving and**
- **regulating or guarding purposes.**

The **forward-driving** leg is positioned close behind the girth, so that the heel is perpendicular to the hip, and incites the relevant hind leg to additional stepping off. This effect is particularly good, when it always gives an impulse in accordance with the sequence of movement, when the hind leg on the same side steps off: the leg should always be positioned close to the horse's side without gripping too tightly.

---

[1] In this connection it is sometimes recommended "to think of the back being made hollow" – but not actually to do this, of course!

Renewing the legs

their legs significantly further back, which leads to difficulties in balance, suppleness, but also in the precise positioning of their legs.

The leg should be applied evenly, depending on leg length approximately up to and including the calf. The muscles in the calf tauten and relax alternately due to the slightly raised fore-foot and the ankle elastically springing in the stirrup, the leg "breathes". A leg which is either constantly sliding backwards and forwards or one which is gripping tightly de-sensitises the horse, many riders tend to the latter because they have (been given) a wrong impression of driving aids and believe they have to exert constant pressure in order to push on this "lazy animal" or keep it in motion.

In order possibly to ensure a better or more prompt acceptance of the leg an energetic, precise impulse may be necessary, which is applied with the help of the upper leg muscle system (more on this subject later); in the case of sensitive horses which are finely tuned to the leg aids, it is frequently enough to loosen the leg somewhat from the hip and position it against the horse's side again or to suddenly take away the lower leg (renew), in other words to behave as if a strong impulse is to follow.

The **forwards-sideways-driving** leg is intended to have the effect that, according to the exercise or movement being ridden, the required hind leg, or hind and fore leg together, step over forwards-sideways. For this the leg is brought back approximately one hand's width behind the position of the driving leg, but under no circumstances should it be pulled upwards. This aid also is most successful when the rider applies his influence just at the moment when the horse steps off with the relevant leg(s) .

Moving the legs too far back is usually counter-productive, especially when they touch the horse's flanks because then the horse either tenses up or evades with the hindquarters. It is the "forwards" aspect of this aid which must always be emphasised in order to enable the legs to cross rhythmically and fluently.

In all exercises and movements which require the horse to have a longitudinal bend, the inner forward-driving leg is the decisive aid; the horse should bend around this leg, particularly in the area of the chest (bending of the ribs). The rider must be particularly aware of this on the side on which the horse is stiffer and less flexible. Here the horse tries to evade the longitudinal bend by pushing into the bend or turn with the shoulder; the rider must apply determination in counteracting this with the inside leg close to the girth[1].

On account of the dressage saddles with very thick knee rolls which unfortunately are very popular today (see "Saddles") many riders slide

---

[1] In this connection please refer to the boxes on flexing and bending in the chapter about Straightening

Position of the
forward-driving leg

Position of the
forward-sideways driving leg

Position of the
guarding leg

Exactly how far the leg has to be moved backwards in this context depends on how easily the horse accepts the sideways-driving aids and crosses its legs. If the rider notices e.g. when leg-yielding, in the travers or half-pass, that the horse is stepping sideways too much, and with the forehand perhaps even too little, then he must ensure that the sideways-driving leg is not positioned so far back.

The **regulating or guarding** leg is in about the same position as the forward-sideways driving leg, it does not exercise as much active influence however, only occasionally if it is not being respected enough, it can – and indeed must – be actively applied; however there is no advantage in bringing it further back (see above with the forwards-sideways driving leg).

The rider's task is to restrict the horse's hindquarters and prevent the respective hind hoof evading sideways. Always when the horse should be more clearly bent around the inside leg, the supporting leg is the decisive counterpart to this.

Here the rider must position his leg significantly less far back when he is riding on the rein on which the horse tends to make itself slightly concave (in other words can be stretched less well), in connection with the guarding outside rein would like to prevent the horse from trying to evade outwards with the shoulder or rib area.

> **The regulating or guarding leg also
> is always co-responsible
> for the forwards movement.**

As a matter of principle all leg aids should be applied with a calm apposed leg. A temporarily stronger application may only take place in individual cases, as a sort of admonition, as a kind of impulse; for this purpose the rider may also briefly turn his heel more inwards.

More will be said about the occasionally necessary stronger application of the legs for corrective purposes later on in the section about the coordination of the aids.

Holding the reins correctly

rein, in other words when the hands – with slightly angled arms – are held far enough away from the body that it is possible to ride confidently up to the hand so that the rider has the horse ahead of him. If the reins are too long, however, the rider will automatically "ride backwards".

Yielding and asking rein aids always have to be seen within a complete context. Whether the yielding or asking should be done first depends on the situation and the countenance of the horse. What is important here is the appropriate, fine, sensitive "dosage" applied from the wrist, which is only possible if the reins are held correctly with the fist in an upright position.

These aids can be applied (in conjunction with the relevant weight and leg aids)

1.5.3 The rein aids

With a view to the training aims of our riding theory rein aids may only be applied in connection with weight and leg aids. Only in the case of a through horse going well through the back, the rein aids can have the required effect via mouth, poll, neck and back through to the hindquarters. The rein aids can have the following actions:

- **yield,**
- **ask, (take)**
- **regulate or guard,**
- **non-yield and**
- **sideways-leading**

- **in the case of half halts and full halts, therefore in the case of transitions from one gait to another, in the shortening of the pace (tempo), for the improvement of self-carriage, by way of preparation for every new exercise and when halting,**
- **always when the horse should be flexed or bent and**
- **if necessary in the rein back.**

For the **asking rein aid** riders should be particularly warned against "getting stuck" in the process of doing this. In order to apply this aid, the hand is turned inward from the wrist, with the small finger in the direction of the tummy button (see Video Die Reitschule 2); on no account should it degenerate into a pulling on the reins instead – if necessary – it must be repeated in alternation with yielding aids if the desired effect is not achieved immediately. Frequently it is only necessary in order to be able to yield subsequently.

In connection with the rein aids I should once more like to draw attention to the importance of the correct position of the hands: this is always dependent on the posture of the horse and should always be such that the lower arm and rein form a straight line; also seen from the rider's point of view, elbow, hand (including the back of the hand) and the horse's mouth should be in a straight line. It is only with the correct length of

In the case of the **yielding rein aid**, the rider must be particularly careful not to apply this jerkily. It is important that the contact between the rider's hand and horse's mouth remains intact, and that the rider's hand **becomes light** but it is not opened. As it almost always succeeds an asking or regulating rein aid, which involves a slight tightening of the arm and hand muscles, for the subsequent yielding rein aid it is normally sufficient simply to relax these again. This Is sometimes referred to as "freeze and melt".

The yielding rein aid prepares the asking rein aid or follows immediately afterwards. By way of positive confirmation, indeed praise, it is the most important rein aid.

The extent to which the rein should be given depends on the particular situation. If a lot of rein should be given, e. g. in order to allow the horse to stretch, to open its neck, it is essential for the rider to move his hands forward towards the horse's mouth.

The **guarding rein aid** is, in every bending or flexion movement, the diagonal opposite to the inside leg and to the asking or sideways-acting (determining the flexion) inside rein. With this aid the rider has to yield the right amount with the outside rein so that the horse can flex in the poll and/or bend in the neck, it has to be done within limitations, however, and avoid the neck being turned too much so that the horse even "falls out" onto the outside shoulder or that the bit is pulled through the mouth.

Particularly in this aid the hand has to be held well down. If the horse does not respect this rein aid enough it may be necessary, as a kind of admonishment, to take up the rein and yield it again momentarily, without pressing over the crest of the neck, however.

If the horse needs to be bent somewhat more in the neck by way of correction, it is advantageous to take the guarding rein hand slightly to the side so that the outside rein runs straight from the rider's hand to the horse's mouth and is not bent around the neck. (see graphic page 206!)

The **non-yielding rein aid** consists of keeping the hands firmly closed in their position and enduring the horse's increased pressure on the bit until the horse is pushing off itself from the bit, yields in the poll and becomes light. In order to

This is also a possibility for "framing the horse"

achieve this the rider must sit in good, upright posture with the elbows loosely against the trunk. Essential prerequisites for this non-yielding rein aid are a "bracing of the back" (see above) and effective driving leg aids, in order to make clear to the horse what is expected to do, the hand has to become light by way of reward at the right moment, without relinquishing the contact. The non-yielding rein aid is used in the case of horses which go against or over the rein; with well trained horses – applied in an appropriately fine dosage – it can replace the asking rein aid, e.g. in halts and rein back.

When the horse has learned to step forward to the bit trustingly and to "pull", a well-dosed non-yielding rein aid can be applied in order to convey the message to move forward more actively again. The horse will react accordingly because it has had relevant experience and "knows" that the rider will immediately become lighter in the hand again.

The **sideways acting rein aid** should, as the term states, indicate the direction to the horse when riding turns (in further training also in the case of lateral movements). It is usually in conjunction with the slightly asking rein aid which

Sideways leading rein aid to move sideways

1.5.4 The coordination of the aids

Although the principle of "Learning by Doing" is indeed highly recommendable in many areas, in the interest of the horse it should be treated with considerable caution as far as riding is concerned. This means that the rider may only venture on to a new exercise or movement after acquiring some knowledge about it, having had it explained to him and – ideally – also shown (if necessary on video). The more precise an idea he has of an exercise, the greater is his chance, of succeeding at least in part with it and thus feeling the positive benefits of such an "aha" experience.

This valuable preliminary knowledge includes such fundamental things as the significance of the so-called diagonal application of the aids.

flexes the horse or bends it for the turn and therefore is applied with the inside hand. For this purpose the rider takes the hand, which he has turned slightly inwards from the wrist for flexing or bending (small finger in the direction of the tummy button!), a few centimetres away from the horse's neck as if he wants to turn the horse's nose in the appropriate direction.

Every rider must be constantly aware of the fact that the human being is a manual worker by nature, in other words he relies instinctively on his hands, and in any case of doubt always tries to achieve or prevent everything imaginable with his hands. This is why the rider must always try to manage with increasingly refined rein aids as his training progresses and rely more and more on the improved application of his weight and leg aids.

Two very good exercises for checking whether the rider has worked correctly in this respect are taking the rein forward and down and "Überstreichen" (see sections on these subjects).

> The diagonal application of the aids is one of the constantly recurrent themes throughout our riding theory. By "diagonal application" we mean that the inside leg should drive in the direction of the outside rein, particularly when the horse is intended to be flexed and/or bent, especially on any curved line and in the lateral movements. Accepting this aid is a prerequisite for any successful straightening and progressive work, because for this purpose it is necessary for the rider to become soft on the inside rein and to have the horse on the outside rein. It is essential to achieve this first before the horse can swing through in an optimum way and take up weight with the inside hind leg.

It is only when weight, leg and rein aids are well coordinated and inter-act correctly that it is possible to guarantee reliable influence. In order to have the horse "well in front", the influence of the driving aids must always predominate slightly.

This applies particularly in the case of a very eager horse. The rider will only be able to handle this (over-)enthusiasm effectively, if he works with the idea of occupying the horse so well particularly with the driving aids, through correct half-halts (brought about by the application of all aids), that it is "working to full capacity" so to speak and becomes content as a result. The restraining rein aids, which are doubtlessly also necessary in this context, should however never give the horse the feeling that it is being held in or restricted. It is better to apply these rein aids rather more strongly and decisively but then to follow on quickly with the yielding rein aids.

In the case of a horse which is behaving sluggishly and obviously not enjoying its work with the rider, it is important to find out first of all what the cause of this is. Because in the first instance we can assume that, by their very nature, all horses enjoy movement and that the rider only has to take measures to maintain this pleasure in movement, to arouse it again or to regulate it. This is why the rider constantly has to try to sit and exert influence in such a way that the horse feels well under, or rather, with him, indeed has pleasure in moving together.

In the case of a lack of activity in the hindquarters or lack of pleasure in work with the rider, it is worth considering whether the hand is yielding enough and whether the horse has enough confidence in the hand; if there is disorder or confusion here, no amount of driving will achieve anything – indeed this is even counter-productive.

In order to use driving and restraining aids in the right proportions, it is helpful when the rider thinks as often as possible to want to convey positively to the horse what he expects it to do but not what it should not do. For example, in a transition from canter to trot, the rider will want to demand the new gait of the horse and ride increasingly towards the hand as well as using the driving aids, instead of wanting to terminate the canter and thus have a backward, pulling effect.

Generally speaking, it makes good sense if the rider imagines framing the horse in between the

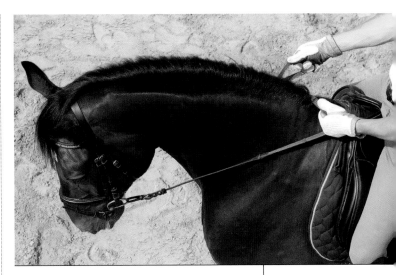

Holding the reins when the horse is flexed; the direction in which the reins go to the horse's mouth remains unchanged due to the slight shift in the hand position (cf. page 206)

driving aids on the one hand and the restraining aids on the other hand and sets himself the aim of being able to apply the individual aids in an increasingly subtle way as time progresses. Frequently it is then sufficient to apply the aids, so to speak, solely as a signal e.g. after an extension to slightly take and give the rein for the half halt whilst sitting well with the leg against the horse's side. The horse comes back almost automatically in yielding and can thus engage the hind legs in an ideal way.

For this purpose, as already mentioned above, the improvement of the rider's feeling is of great significance.

A training aim for the horse has to be a constantly improving sensitivity to the rider's aids. This means that when in doubt a resolute, through-going, but short and precise aid is preferable to one which is cautious and therefore usually imprecise.

If the horse reacts too little or with delay to a leg aid, an energetic impulse must be given, possibly in connection with spurs and/or whip, to urge the required action. This impulse must come immediately, it must, be very precise and well-considered, however. If more diligence and forward movement are required, both legs should be applied close to the girth. If more pressure should be applied through the sideways-driving or guarding aid, pressure should be applied by one leg only whilst the other leg remains in the same position. Many riders find it difficult to apply this unilateral impulse.

In any case the horse must be allowed to respond appropriately to such a hearty call to go forwards. For this purpose the rider must give well with the rein and go along well with his weight, ensuring he never sits behind the movement and hangs on the horse's mouth.

The training and schooling of a horse will proceed in an optimum way when the aids are always applied in an understandable and completely consistent way. That means the rider always has to try to show clearly exactly what he wants and always act or react in the same way in identical situations.

The best way to so-called conditioning[1] is – and always will be positive confirmation by means of yielding, allowing pauses for stretching and/or praise.

As only exceptionally few people are born riders or are so ingenious that they are really in a position to exercise correct influence on a horse without having to think about it, even the experienced rider will constantly have to apply his mind and be quite consciously aware of why, when and to what degree he applies which aids. He has to examine himself, or have examined, whether, perhaps unconsciously, mistakes have crept in and use his powers of critical thinking in order to control his – sometimes misleading – instinct (see Instinctively correct?).

Only if he is willing and able to completely concentrate on the demands being posed on him as a rider at the particular moment in question, will the rider be able to keep his error rate to a minimum. As far as the sensitivity of his horse to the aids is concerned, and the horse's willingness to accept these without hesitation, it is frequently a kind of ridge walk in training: on the one hand we are striving for obedience and optimum throughness, on the other hand however, no anticipation, in other words a pre-emption of the horse. Therefore it is a question in the re-

peated practising of movements, and quite particularly in the case of complete tests, of adapting immediately and riding differently to what the horse expects. After practising the salute position several times, it is recommendable for example to ride down the centre line again a few times without halting, or perhaps incorporating a volte at X.

The most important prerequisites for confident and effective influence in all seat forms are

- always the correct, balanced and supple seat, which makes it possible for the rider, thanks to his agility and litheness in the his middle posture,
- to apply leg and rein aids which are independent of the seat,
- the ability and willingness to feel himself into the horse, in order, with sensitivity, to be able to coordinate all aids individually in accordance with the situation in question,
- the rider's willingness and ability to concentrate completely on riding,
- as much consistency as possible as well as
- thorough knowledge of riding theory with the resulting
- correct idea of the exercise or movement to be ridden and
- the appropriate awareness for the correct application of the aids.

Naturally no rider will ever be able to exclude mistakes with his horse completely; however the better he fills these prerequisites and the more experience he has with different horses, the more frequently he will be able to react correctly – for his own benefit as well as that of his four-legged partner.

One point should not be neglected under any circumstances, it is the most decisive aspect when it is a question of achieving success:

The right mental attitude.

➢ The best way to so-called conditioning[1] is and always will be positive confirmation by means of yielding, allowing pauses for stretching and/or praise.

[1] In this context to condition a horse or a human being positively means, very consistently, to give positive confirmation in response to desired reactions or appropriate behaviour, psychologists also refer to this as reinforcement. By means of yielding or becoming light in the hand, as well possibly as taking up a light seat, the rider has to show the horse that moving in a stretch posture is a pleasant experience. The term conditioning is not to be confused with "improving the horse's physical condition".

The significance of the mental attitude features in almost every report when it is a question of victory or defeat, regardless of what sport is concerned. However, the fact that this plays a decisive role long before the competition takes place, in other words in daily training at home, is especially true in the case of equestrian sport. Horses have a very finely tuned antenna; they are very quick to sense whether the rider is approaching the task on hand with determination and self-confidence, whether he is confident that he and his horse will be able to complete the exercise of movement successfully. In a similar way to humans, horses tend to react as it is expected.

Two quite simple examples:
• **Transition walk – canter:** Only when the rider himself is convinced and believes that the transition is well prepared for him and is easy for his horse to execute, is it sure to succeed.

Otherwise the horse will probably, if at all, react hesitantly, cantering on "stiffly" rather than actively because the rider is clamping with his legs, trying to push and consequently sitting behind the movement, or is not soft enough with the inner rein.

• **When jumping:** when an over-cautious or nervous rider approaches a fence wondering whether his horse will jump, or perhaps even hoping that it will stop before the fence, the horse will not "disappoint" the rider – it will indeed stop!

Particularly because the rider is quite clearly subordinate to the horse in terms of physical strength, he can and should always show that he is the dominant partner in terms of psychological strength and willpower.

As a reward for following these rules and recommendations the rider will increasingly experience that wonderful sensation that he only needs to think of something and his horse "automatically" implements it.

1.6 Riding technique

Riding technique means the abilities which make it possible to execute certain equestrian tasks skilfully, with as minimal an investment of strength as possible, and in accordance with the rules of our riding theory. In the context of basic training this can mean very simple things, for example riding in and out between cones, jumping a sequence of fences or a full standard course or in dressage training in particular the so-called technical movements, such as a walk pirouette or flying changes, for example.

In order to do this everything is necessary which has so far been acquired, refined and consolidated in the course of training. Additionally, however, good theoretical knowledge is increasingly important. The more demanding and comprehensive the task in question, the more important it is for the rider to have as precise a conception as possible about the correct sequences of movement, the criteria and also the typical mistakes which are to be expected. Only then it will be possible for him to arrive at his target exercise and complete this successfully and in correspondingly systematically increasing steps, without too many big detours or meanders.

This knowledge and these perceptions can be acquired in a wide variety of different ways. By observing demonstrations by experienced riders live or per video – preferably with accompanying explanations –, by reading good equestrian books or by means of theory lessons. Ideally a combination of all these.

The best medium in the further training of technically correct riding is a correctly trained schoolmaster, which ideally should be suited to the rider's current ability as far as sensitivity is concerned.
An example:
In the first attempts at riding a flying change, it would be ideal to have a schoolmaster with a firm

This is not really what we mean by "riding technique"!

child or adolescent has the best prerequisites. Sports scientists indeed believe that it is only possible to learn completely new schemes of movement easily and effectively until puberty.

- Thus anyone of a more advanced age who would like to start to learn to ride will certainly find it easier if he had the opportunity to develop his locomotory abilities well as a child or adolescent. A high degree of body balance, feeling for movement and coordination ability, to mention but a few of the important points, make the rider's training path easier as well as shorter.

- As our classical riding system is, as a whole, very logically structured and has also been recorded by generations of extremely experienced horsemen, the genuinely interested pupil can also further his own progress as a rider by reading and consulting the relevant books. On account of the fact that in riding two living creatures come together whose existential state can change constantly, however these different states have to be brought onto the same wavelength as a prerequisite for good riding, the consequence is that riding by its very nature can not simply be learned in a more-or-less casual way. In particular this applies for those riders who would like to use the wonderful riding possibilities offered by our modern, usually thoroughbred coined, and therefore also particularly sensitive warmblood horses.

2.2 Selection of a suitable horse

Anyone who has hopefully learned to ride well enough on suitable schoolmaster horses and has caught the riding bug to such an extent that he would like to buy a horse for himself, should take care not to make the frequently committed fault of overestimating his own equestrian abilities. In the process of looking for and choosing a future horse he should always heed the following principle:

> The young, inexperienced rider needs an experienced horse, the young horse can only be brought on and trained well by an experienced rider.

This principle even appears in the preface to the FN Principles of Riding. Therefore anyone who looks for a horse in accordance with this and is lucky enough to find one which corresponds well to his own equestrian skills, has the right prerequisites to experience many enjoyable hours in the saddle, riding in a relaxed and supple way. This suppleness can, for example, easily be recognised by the fact that the rider is breathing rhythmically and does not start gasping for breath too quickly or even suffer from unpleasant side pains caused by tension.

2.3 Attitude and approach

As already mentioned, riding should be done with sense, sensitivity and – above all – complete commitment from the heart. Then it will not be difficult, even at the end of a hard day at work, to concentrate fully on riding and get rid of all the stress which has built up. It is worth taking enough time to at least give the horse a quick brush or tack it up yourself. Proper grooming and getting the horse ready, including caring for the hooves, bandaging etc., are very good ways of achieving the first phase of mental and physical suppleness.

Naturally there are also many gymnastic exercises which are good ways of preparing and stretching your own body, either in the stable or the riding arena.[1]

When the horse and rider are both ready, the rider should not have any inhibitions about using some form of assistance to mount the horse. If a mounting block is not available, a stool can be used or a helper can give you a leg-up onto the horse.

---

[1] Bibliography: Balance in Movement by S. von Dietze (also available as a video or DVD); Das Bewegungsgefühl des Reiters von E. Meyners; Fit fürs Pferd von Frau Dr. C. Heipertz-Hengst

2.4 General information concerning equipment

As the saddle is the connecting piece, we could almost say represents a kind of adapter between the rider and horse, it is naturally of decisive importance for both parties concerned. Please consider the following comments (more on this subject in the chapter on "How the saddle influences the way you ride"):

- It is essential that the saddle is carefully fitted to suit the horse's back, pressure must be well and evenly distributed and the saddle must be positioned in such a way as to avoid any problems in the shoulder area and in the back. The saddle must lie well almost without the influence of the girth which should only be used to keep the saddle in the correct position – rather than to try and achieve this. Fastening the girth too abruptly and/or pulling it too tightly can have a negative effect on the horse's suppleness.

- Depending on what kind of riding is planned, the saddle must allow the rider to sit correctly with stirrups of the appropriate length. Although today almost all riders believe they have to have at least two different saddles, I should like to emphasise that the rider who does not have very strong ambitions regarding riding in specific disciplines can indulge well in his hobby with one good multi-purpose saddle.

The following crunch points should be avoided. Unfortunately they occur quite frequently and are disturbing for the rider, particularly with regard to his suppleness:

- Too small a saddle, particularly in the case of riders with a large seat, long thighs and legs.
- Too large a saddle with too long saddle flaps and – particularly unpleasant – with a seat area which is too wide and not shaped enough.[1]
- A saddle, the deepest point of which is positioned too far back, and which is possibly too high in the area of the pommel. This could possibly cause a chair-seat.
- A saddle, the deepest point of which is positioned too far forward and which is too high in

the rear area so that the rider is almost forced into a fork-seat.

- Similarly, there are problems with many of the present-day dressage saddles. The current emphasis on knee rolls and thigh blocks means the rider gets too much pressure on the thigh. This consequently forces the rider into an overstretched leg position which may not even by realistically be possible for him from a muscular point of view. These saddles are often recommended and preferred because they put the rider into a very firm position and give him a feeling of security. It is important, however, to consider that a rider firmly fixed into the saddle is not really in a position to sit supply, particularly not if his pelvis is tipped forward with his back becoming hollow as a result.

- In this connection it should be emphasised that the best dressage saddle, which brings the rider into a very stretched position, is only suitable for him if the necessary physical conditions for this are created through appropriate training (possibly also gymnastics).

- Similarly as regards the stirrup length: starting with a normal medium length, the rider must then gradually learn and train his body accordingly to use slightly longer stirrups for dressage and shorter ones for jumping.

The rider can imagine the saddle is an electric socket into which he positions his two seat bones – rather like inserting a two-point plug

[1] As the the male and femal pelvis differ significantly with regard to shape and moveability, the design and construction of an ideal saddle should take these sex-specific differences into account, this applies particularly with regard to dressage saddles.

2. ➤ Suppleness of the Rider

These exercises make it is easier for the rider "to find the centre".

- Stirrups and stirrup inserts which cause a bend position of the ankle restrict the natural and supple position of the leg and foot. (see illustration page 18, right)

It is also possible that the rider's equipment may have a restricting effect on the suppleness:

- unsuitable underwear which might even rub raw patches on the skin,
- jackets or breeches which are too tight will restrict the rider's freedom of movement,
- too wide breeches which might form creases and be uncomfortable around the seat or knee
- too long boots or chaps which rub in the hollow of the knee,
- too stiff or too tight boots which restrict the movement of the calf and the foot,
- too soft or too wide boots which make it more difficult to keep the calf of the leg in a good position, particularly when riding dressage,
- Boots made of a material e.g. rubber or with a coating which make the calf stick etc.

2.5 The rider's influence on the horse in the suppling up phase

If, after all these preparations, the rider is hopefully in the right frame of mind and mounts the horse in a fairly good state of concentration, he can then use the time of riding at walk in the suppling up phase in an optimum way to supple up himself. (If the weather is very cold, he should also start off wearing some appropriate extra layers of clothing.) Whilst riding a horse at walk the rider has an ideal opportunity to concentrate on his seat. He is now able to sit in the way, which hopefully he has learned correctly, and which is suitable for him and now close his eyes briefly to go in on himself, thus training his feeling for movement and perhaps even checking this for himself by taking an occasional glance at the mirror. He should certainly not focus rigidly on his horse and simply stare at it. He must also try to feel the carriage of the horse as well as the nodding movements which can and should be felt well at walk, instead of merely absorbing these via his eyes. In order to gain the posture which is so important particularly also for the balance, he can imagine sitting in such a way that – even if his horse disappeared from under him – he would be able to stand on his own feet in a sure and balanced way. This, furthermore, applies for all different types of seat.

As already mentioned above, movability is an important pre-requisite for suppleness and indeed there is a whole series of exercises which are very good for doing on a horse at walk.[2]

Initiating the action from the hip, take each leg away from the saddle or side of the horse separately and re-position them.

---

[2] Bibliography: cf. Centered Riding by Sally Swift Volume 1; Balance in Movement by S. Dietze (also available as video or DVD); Guidelines for Riding and Driving Volume 6 Lunging

Taking the reins in one hand and praising the horse.

Here are a few especially easy exercises worthy of mention at this particular point:

- Bend the upper body alternatively as far as possible sideways to the right and left in order subsequently to be able to find the middle better,
- try with one hand to bend down and touch the opposite foot,
- activating them from the hips, move each leg individually away from the saddle or the horse's side and re-position them again,
- make circular movements with the shoulders in both directions,
- make circular movements with the head etc.

For the independence of the hand from the seat, which is so extremely important in riding, the overall suppleness, particularly also in the middle posture, is very important. On the other hand, the rider also has to learn and practise, how to keep an elastic and even contact to the horse's mouth from his own shoulder and elbow joint. Riding at walk on a long rein is an ideal way of practising this. The rider can do this particularly well if, as he is riding, he imagines that he has reins with an integrated spring balance in his hands and wants to accompany the horse's mouth so evenly that this spring balance remains constantly with the desired amount of extension.

During riding at walk, which should be done for at least ten minutes at the beginning of every riding session, the rider has an ideal opportunity to feel what it really means to sit in the horse. In doing this he must try, in the pelvis and hip area, to feel himself very supple into the three-dimensional movement of the horse's back.[1] He can imagine that the saddle is an electric socket into which he "inserts" his seat with the two seat bones rather like a continental electric plug. He should never on any account try to drive or activate the horse by active and extensive pushing. If he should have the feeling that the horse is not diligent enough, or is slacking somewhat, he must apply one decisive driving aid with the leg (as an impulse). If the horse is reacting as desired well forward as desired it is very important that the rider responds positively by relieving hand his hands and his weight, sitting forward (light seat).

Before starting to do trotting work, the rider can change the horse's frame by shortening the reins slightly ("close the horse") and letting the horse chew the reins out of his hands again a few times.

Another exercise to do whilst riding at walk and which is very beneficial for the suppleness of rider and horse, is to ride for short phases with the "reins in one hand", whereby the rider must continue to ensure he maintains elastic but constant contact with the hand in which he is holding the reins whilst using the other hand to praise the horse. This praising by way of patting

---

[1] The horse's back moves up and down in the direction of movement (particularly at a canter but also at walk), at the same time (in all three gaits) its trunk swings slightly from side to side and from this a lateral up and down movement ensues on the respective side of the horse's back; additionally, the pelvis also has to be able to move around the vertical axis in order to be able to give correct weight aids.

Only hands which are independent of the seat will avoid any spills.

up very smoothly and without any assistance from the reins, the rider's calf and foot must be positioned in such a way from the knee that the foot is positioned as precisely as possible below the rider's point of gravity. Sitting slightly forward from the hip in order to relieve the horse, naturally without holding in the stomach and/ or rounding the back, makes this considerably easier. The reins should be shortened slightly so that the hands and lower arms are clearly enough in front of the rider's body, as a result of which the centre of gravity is shifted slightly forward. At the rising trot more than the sitting trot, it is the case that you can ride forward to the bit better if the rider's hands are held significantly in front of his body, whereas with somewhat long reins more backwards influence is automatically exerted. As it is more difficult to be in optimum balance at a rising trot, it is also more difficult to hold the hands independently. Therefore it requires careful practice in order to avoid the movements of the rising trot automatically being passed on to the horse's mouth. This can be practised very well on the lunge by doing the rising trot without reins; the rider can also always practise this alone, however, by really concentrating on it, possibly even closing his eyes in the process, in order to go in on himself and to check on the situation with his hands. More over the rider can imagine carrying a glass of water in each hand without spilling anything. Also at a rising trot it is highly recommendable to check your balance and improve supleness by taking the reins into one hand from time to time and putting the other hand over the crest of the mane and patting the horse on the other side of its neck.

can either be done on the horse's flank, behind the rider's thigh or further forward in front of the shoulder, ideally on the opposite side.

In this connection it must already be emphasised that a good rider has to be able to sit calmly, sitting calmly is certainly not synonymous with sitting still, however. The more movement there is on the part of the horse, in other words particularly at trot, at canter, in all possible movements and of course very obviously when hacking out or jumping, the more aware the rider must be that this balance between rider and horse which is so decisive for good riding, is something very dynamic.

After the supling up work at walk, the trotting work begins. Normally work is done at a rising trot first of all as this is slightly easier for both rider and horse and in this phase the aim is to do what is beneficial for the supleness of the centres of movement, in other words the horse's back and the rider's back. The close connection between supleness and balance have already been mentioned several times so it is now easy to understand that particularly in the case of the rising trot, during which the rider's balance is less stable due to the rising and sitting down again, very great attention must be accorded to the rider's balance. In order to be able to stand

It can frequently be observed that – just as the rider takes the reins into one hand – the horse brings its nose forward better, "swings through" in a more supple way and snorts contentedly. One advantage of holding the reins in one hand is the consequently calm position of the bit in the horse's mouth – with one hand it is not possible even for there to be slight moving about from side to side (fiddling) – the second advantage is that one hand cannot exert as much strength as two hands. For this reason it makes good sense – also in the further course of a work session – to come back to this exercise if any tension should become obvious.

Also in the further suppling exercises the close interlinking and simultaneous independence of the suppleness of the horse and of the rider can be very clearly observed and also made use of. Therefore it is appropriate to repeat at this point that a rider who has problems with his own suppleness indeed does not have much of a chance of improving this situation on a horse with a tendency to tense up, to say nothing of actually making the horse supple.

The simple transitions done in the further course of the suppling up work – walk-trot-walk and trot-canter-trot promote suppleness, simply through the change in the sequence of movement, the tempos and therefore also the balance. In order in a supple way to maintain or re-establish the mutual balance immediately in the transition and in the new gait, the rider must try to use the driving aids to bring the new gait forward from behind rather than to terminate the previous gait and simply concentrate on the transition. This of course particularly also is valid for the transitions from the higher to the lower gait.

Some examples:

If the horse is to canter out of trot, the horse is first of all made alert by means of correctly executed half halts, therefore particularly also with the driving aids and closed from behind, before applying the cantering aid, precisely and decisively, particularly with the inside leg. If the rider has prepared this well and is also convinced himself that his aids are correct and the transition will succeed, he will also come along well with the movement when cantering on and immediately feel the rhythm of the sequence of movement and therefore the balance in the canter.

In the transition from canter to trot he has to communicate to his horse with all aids, par-

Rising trot on the lunge: The lower leg is slightly too far back here.

ticularly however with the driving aid, that he should now trot. If he approaches the matter with this notion of having enough self-confidence and conviction, he will avoid any faltering in the transition and therefore maintain balance and suppleness.

The more demanding the exercises become for the rider with regard to his stamina and his concentration, the greater the danger will become of the necessary positive tension becoming a negative bracing. This must be prevented by a correspondingly frequent change of strain. Whatever the degree of concentration, the rider should think about this connection between inner and outer suppleness which is always wonderfully reflected in the rider's face. In her book "Centred Riding" Sally Swift talks about the gentle and the fixed gaze. That means, and every rider can feel for himself that – even in phases of greater concentration – it is a big advantage to let his gaze wander, for example to look around to see where the other riders are. By contrast, anyone who concentrates so intensely that he only stares or gazes into his horse, will automatically tense up.

When you should find yourself doing this, it is important to change down a gear, possibly do a transition to walk and not continue working again until you are rather more relaxed and in a position to breath calmly and deeply again.

Stiff standing up in rising trot

A smooth rising trot

It is well worth thinking rather more careful-ly about the validity and significance of relaxed breathing:

One point is that it is a pre-requisite in or-der to work reasonably economically, for exam-ple in order not to get tired too quickly because the body and brain are not receiving enough ox-ygen. Another point is that it is a very good indi-cation of whether the positive tension is begin-ning to change into negative bracing. If the rider should start to feel short, sharp pains (stitches) in his side then this should be a very clear signal to interrupt work for a lengthy relaxation and re-generation phase.

2.6 Summary

Only a rider who, with all the mental and phys-ical tension required, is in a position to sit on a horse in a sufficiently supple way, in other words in a healthy alternation between tensing and re-laxing, can prepare the way for his horse also to become supple and thus have pleasure as well as success with his horse. The following points are worthy of consideration in this respect:

- Correct and sound basic training under appro-priate supervision, on a suitable "schoolmas-

ter" horse and with enough time.
- A permanently sufficiently critical estimation of one's own ability, possibly also with the help of a competent and honest trainer.
- A consistently conscious inter-linking of feel-ing and understanding.
- The not always easy selection of the right horse, which should be chosen to suit your own riding ability.
- Demands imposed on your riding which are also selected to suit your current level so that encouraging "aha" experiences are possible and lessons may also be concluded on a satis-factory note.
- The awareness and willingness always to keep yourself fit and healthy for riding.
- Focussing on the essential thought that the greatest satisfaction in riding ensues from the feeling that you are able to pursue sport in harmony with the horse, irrespective of the level concerned.

Note: In the case of physical problems on the part of the rider it is necessary and also very helpful to seek qualified advice and possibly fol-low-up treatment from a physiotherapist who has equestrian experience himself.

3. Horse and Rider in Balance

After initial confidence-building encounters in the stable and grooming and caring for the horse, a prime aim for anyone starting to learn to ride is to be able to balance on the horse. Naturally people with a good sense of balance due to experience in other forms of sport as well as feeling acquired through specific exercises for this purpose, are at a considerable advantage here. The first balance exercises for the rider are always done on a horse which is standing still, indeed sometimes a wooden horse is used at this stage. This gives the riding pupil the opportunity to take some time to feel the basic form of the riding seat and find out for himself the individual form which is correct for him because the finer details always vary from person to person, depending on physical build and proportions. It is of immense value here if the pupil is able to use a horse which is of a calm temperament as well as the right size and conformation to suit the rider's build and dimensions.

Without wanting to go in further details concerning the form of the seat at this stage, it is nevertheless useful to call to mind a frequently used image which can usually help the pupil to acquire a good concept of the balanced basic seat:

The rider should take up a position – from head to foot – in which it would be possible for him to stand in a well-balanced way without the horse, should the horse– hypothetically speaking – disappear from underneath him.

All this is relatively simple at a halt and the same principle also applies when the horse, al-

Correct, balanced forward seat in the turn

though this is only theoretically possible, moves forward in an absolutely straight line and at a completely even speed. This more or less static balance between the rider and horse immediately starts to falter when the horse changes its speed or its direction. Then the static balance has to be converted into dynamic balance.

This can be more easily appreciated if you try to imagine carrying a rider on your own shoulders (see page 23). It is very easy to understand that, depending on the degree of acceleration, you will not only lean forward to a greater or less degree yourself, but also the "rider" on your shoulders will only avoid causing balance problems to his "carrier" and make it easier for him to increase speed, if he also leans forward accordingly. Conversely, when hesitating, in other words reducing the tempo, slight leaning backwards is the correct reaction in order to achieve optimum balance.

The same also applies in the case of lateral acceleration as it occurs in turns, which again is dependent on the tempo in the "curve". Neverthe-

> The rider should take up a position – from head to foot – in which it would be possible for him to stand in a well-balanced way without the horse, should the horse–hypothetically speaking – disappear from underneath him.

A rider sitting straight will also automatically be brought into the right position by the horse in the turn.

Centaur – Unity of human and horse

A speedy turn

This is the correct way to sit on a bent horse.

less, with a view to riding turns, we must not forget that the horse then, depending on the speed, actually lies into the "curve" to a certain extent, so that the rider does not yet have to lean sideways in addition – at least as long as it is a question of normal cantering speed and the horse is moving on ground with a good grip which also permits the necessary inclined position.

In jumping training these connections seem completely natural during taking off and landing at a fence. In dressage riding however, they are unfortunately rarely accorded the consideration they deserve.

Thus when trotting off from the spot, in other words from a halt, as is so frequently required, or in the case of resolute and willing transition into an extension, the rider should always try to make it easier for his horse by going well with the movement, also with his hands, and at all costs avoiding sitting behind the movement. Then there will also not be any problem with the horse expanding its frame (lengthening its outline) – which is indeed desired – and also so important for the horse to step forward in an optimum way, particularly also with the hind legs. It is almost even more important to acknowledge and confirm the desired positive reaction of a horse to an energetic driving impulse from the leg, instead of actually punishing the horse's obedient reaction to this impulse by hanging in the reins and in the back.

In this connection I should like to mention another situation which also occurs not infrequently: If a young horse starts to rush, possibly also after jumping a fence during the course of which the rider has remained behind the movement, the rider must then try to maintain particularly good balance when halting so as to avoid the horse cramping up as a reaction to the balance problem, trying to flee from him and really bolting. This is particularly important when, for reasons of space, i.e. in an indoor school, a turn follows immediately. The rider has to sit close to the saddle, try to make himself small, but on no account he should stand into the stirrups and pull

on the reins. This will only succeed well for a rider who has an established well-balanced forward seat with well-closed knees and a stable lower leg position, from which it is possible for him – even in such a situation – to exert influence with his hands independently of his seat.

➔ **Application of the Aids;**
   Instinctively – Correct?

3.1 The rising trot – an easy movement for horse and rider?

The rising trot is a particular form of the light seat. In this context the rider uses the swinging movement of the horse's back in order, alternately, to stand up lightly in the stirrups with slightly closed knees before sitting down smoothly for the next trot stride. If the rising trot is to be pleasant and of a relieving nature for the horse too, it has to be done well, i.e. it has to be executed in good balance and smoothly by the rider – and this is not really so easy.

The rising trot relieves the horse's back on the one hand and also makes trotting work more pleasant and less strenuous for the rider.

A rising trot is appropriate in the following situations:

- **during suppling up at the beginning of work, in relaxation phases during training and in the recuperation phase at the end of a work session,**
- **always in the case of young horses which have not yet had much training and whose**

muscle systems are not yet strong enough,
- in the case of all horses which have suppleness and back problems,
- under normal hacking out circumstances,
- frequently in dressage-type work with jumping horses.
- furthermore some riders do a rising trot in order to relieve their own backs, a very experienced rider who is able to do a rising trot in perfect balance whilst keeping his horse in front of him and reliably on the driving aids, can indeed do everything as far as the collected movements, including the lateral movements, at a rising trot.

The riding pupil should be made familiar with the rising trot as soon as possible, already at the stage of the first seat exercises.

3.1.1 What are the decisive points to consider in the rising trot?

When rising the rider should only come up as far from the saddle with his middle position as ensues naturally from the horse's sequence of movement. He should only rise so far that his knees can remain slightly angled. Otherwise the knee-grip which is important for the rising trot gets lost completely, the rider just stands in the stirrups and his whole sequence of movement becomes disharmonious and jerky.

In order to avoid this mistake, the rider should try to keep thinking when he rises that he wants to go slightly into a kneeling position. He must try to rise and sit again in one fluent movement rather than as two separate ones. This will only be possible when the foot is correctly in position in the stirrup iron directly under the rider's centre of gravity. And to achieve this, the knee joint must always be well angled; too long stirrup leathers are a disturbance because the heel cannot remain low enough which makes the elastic absorbing of the movement in the ankle joint impossible.

If, however, the lower leg is so insecurely positioned that the foot constantly moves forwards

and backwards, the rider will have to use the reins as support in pulling himself up, and when sitting down will more or less let himself fall with the pull of gravity into the saddle (he bumps).

Also when doing the rising trot the rider should sit with a fundamentally upright upper body and ensure he sits down in the middle of the saddle. If the back is to be somewhat more relieved, it is possible to do the rising trot with the upper body leaning slightly forwards. Particularly when done with shorter stirrups, this can be advantageous for a smooth, harmonious sequence of movement. The rider must ensure, however, that he does not lean too far forwards and push his buttocks out behind him. He must always sit down in the middle of the saddle and keep the horse ahead of him.

Also disturbing in the rising trot are reins which are even slightly too long because this has a negative effect on the balance and makes it considerably more difficult to carry the hands independently of the seat and the sequence of movement; it also applies here that: "A long rein pulls".[1]

The rider as well as the trainer must take care to ensure that the hands are carried completely independently and do not constantly move up and down with the body.

Left a stiff rising trot, centre and right a smooth, supple rising trot

> A very ◄ experienced rider who is able to do a rising trot in perfect balance whilst keeping his horse in front of him and reliably on the driving aids, can indeed do everything at a rising trot.

---

[1] In this connection please refer to the chapter on hand faults of the rider for more information

3. ➤ Horse and Rider in Balance

3.1.2 Rising trot on the "right diagonal"

In dressage riding the rider usually rises on the inner hind foot, i.e. so that the rider always sits in the movement phase when this foot is on the ground and rises when this foot is brought forward. The correct way to recognize this phase is to pay attention to the horse's outside shoulder which, on account of the diagonal sequence of movement, goes forward at the same time as the inside hind leg.

In this way more weight will be imposed on the inside hind foot and it will be encouraged to step forward more.

In the case of young horses or, quite generally, horses which are not yet able to take up more load with the inside hind leg, it is also possible to sit down on the other hind foot and then to rise. This avoids the horse evading with the hindquarters in turns and moving outwards.

Also when hacking out in the countryside it is important to change the diagonal from time to time in order to avoid too much pressure being imposed on one side. Here the rider must quite consciously pay attention to the diagonal on which he rises because otherwise there is a realistic danger that he will always sit on the one on which his horse "puts" him as a result of its natural crookedness.

➜ **Inside – Outside; Basic paces (trot); Suppleness**

3.2 "The twisted seat" (German: Drehsitz): shoulder-hip – rider-horse

In order to be able to improve the seat, the rider always has to follow the objective of sitting correctly on the horse, i.e. supply and well-balanced enough. Only thus he will be able to apply his aids independently and consciously. This applies particularly to the leg and rein aids.

In some cases, even in specialized equestrian literature, the rider is recommended to sit on a horse in such a way that the rider's shoulders are parallel to the horse's shoulders and his hips are also parallel to the horse's hips; this is sometimes described as the "twisted seat".

It is something which is certainly worth thinking about, nevertheless the rider would become irritated and restricted in his suppleness if he allowed himself to become too much absorbed in these considerations whilst riding.

As even a very well gymnasticised horse is only able to move very little in the area of the ribs and not at all in the small of the back and pelvis area of the trunk, it is only on very strongly curved lines that the shoulder and hips of the horse form a sharp angle to each other. In this connection we should not have any illusions about the fact that today in many cases in the relevant movements (e.g. on the circle, in voltes, but especially also in lateral movements) horses are unfortunately presented with a too strongly bent neck, but frequently with too little bending in the ribs.

When the rider sits completely evenly and well-balanced he will probably find himself with his shoulders and hips on exactly half of this angle (see illustration page 47). A conscious increased taking back of the inside shoulder would involve the danger of the rider collapsing in the inside hip and/or restricts with the inside rein aid, consequently preventing a swinging through of the inside hind leg, indeed it can even cause problems in rhythm. This is why it is considered an essential pre-requisite for riding such movements well that the horse is well on the inside leg and outside rein (diagonal application of the aids) and the rider can therefore allow the inside rein to become light.

A rider with a correct basic seat who is also supple and well balanced on his horse and always makes an effort to apply his aids on the one hand consciously, but on the other hand always more sensitively and to exercise influence with more feeling, automatically sits well and will not have any problems in this respect. (You can say: The rider has to look to where to and think what he wants to ride then his horse will follow his gaze and respond to his body-language.)

With reference to the application of the aids, e.g. when riding a volte, this means:

When the rider takes back his outside leg somewhat, moving it from the hip joint and stretching it well at the same time, in order to guard, a little more weight will automatically be imposed on the inner part of the seat. If additionally he tries to keep his inside knee well deep (see page 24), he will succeed in applying the weight aid on one side even without the almost common disturbing collapsing in the hip. His hips are correctly placed and he will be brought to sit in the middle of the horse. The inside leg remains reliably in the driving position against the girth so that the horse can be bent around it.

In order to give the horse the necessary flexion and bending in the neck, he has to shorten the inside rein slightly before turning, at the same time applying the asking and sideways-leading rein aids from the wrist and, most important of all, become light again with the inside hand at the moment of turning. The guarding outside leg has already been mentioned.

When the rider has learned to use his leg and, above all his rein aids, completely independently of his seat, he does not need to turn deliberately in his trunk.

In order to prevent this hanging behind with the inside hip, it is helpful if the rider constantly reminds himself of the significance of the driving on to the outside rein. Of similar significance is to avoid hanging back of the inside shoulder in connection with pulling on the inside rein. In this connection the rider should constantly check through becoming light or "sounding out"[1] on the inside rein, whether his horse is stepping up well to the outside rein. Here he should take care to ensure that his inside hand is not closer to his body than the outside hand.

A twisted seat with collapsed inside hip can be seen particularly frequently in cantering work and here in the riding of extensions. Usu-

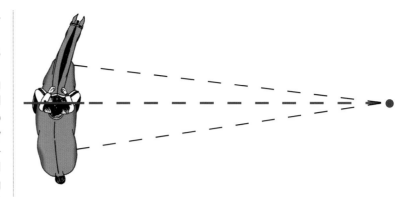

ally this is caused by the fact that the rider has an incorrect conception of how he should keep his horse straight also at a medium or extended canter. Instead of using the driving inside leg to drive forward more to the outside rein and thinking of shoulder-fore, riders frequently attempt to position this leg further back in order to push out the hindquarters. The principle here is wrong, however, because as a consequence the horse is encouraged to press increasingly against this leg, and therefore becomes even more crooked. This type of correction is the famous treating of symptoms instead of looking hard to find the cause and working to eliminate it.

Another very typical example in this direction is riding shoulder-in:

Here a lack of knowledge also means that many riders try to push the hindquarters out with the inside leg, instead of bending the horse around the inside leg (on the girth) and riding each step as if about to begin a volte.

---

[1] The rider feels and checks whether the horse - despite stepping forward willingly to the appropriate rein (usually the inside rein but occasionally the outside one) - is yielding at the poll and in self-carriage. At the same time the rider relaxes the relevant muscles in order to become light in the relevant hand, whilst still maintaining gentle contact.

The high hand is making the horse over-flexed at the poll and bringing it behind the vertical line.

The downwards pressing hand is provoking the horse into resistance and raising its head higher.

4. Instinctively – correct?

The average modern human being does not normally accord prime consideration to his instincts. Sometimes, however, it would certainly be beneficial if certain instincts which were so well developed in former times had been preserved better until today.

In the following section we shall be taking a look at instinctive reactions when riding which actually have a disturbing effect and where it is imperative for the rider to consciously apply his knowledge to control his actions.

4.1 Position of the hands

In this connection let us start by dealing with the position of the hands and their influence because the problems in this connection are easiest to understand.

With our modern riding horses, indeed particularly on account of the fact that they usually have wonderful neck formations and very well formed polls, the problem frequently occurs of not allowing them to come too deep and too narrow. During a riding lesson, how often do you hear the instructor calling: "Keep him up!" Unfortunately, however, riders far too rarely receive a proper explanation of how this is to be done. Without giving any further thought to the matter, the rider's instinct frequently dominates and, with a hand working upwards, sometimes even held higher, he tries to remedy the situation. This is absolutely incorrect, however, and indeed rather achieves the opposite; the more upwards the effect of the hand, and also the higher it is carried, the more longitudinally bent the horse will be at the poll. Consequently – particularly if the horse is very sensitive in the mouth – the less it will want to step up confidently to the bit and swing through.

If the horse comes too deep, it has to be driven on impulsively to the deep hand by means of the weight and leg aids, whereby a simultaneous decisive but short asking and, in particular becoming lighter with the reins, reminds the horse and actually achieves improved self-carriage. If, in addition to coming too deep, the horse is also not stepping up to the bit enough, or indeed even going behind the bit, these forms of corrections of the symptoms will not be sufficient, but

The hand must always be held in such a way that the lower arm and rein form a straight line.

Turning the lower arms: ulna around the radius

confidence in the rider's hand must be improved in the long term.

When riding a horse in a double bridle, the hand being brought up or held too high is of course completely counter-productive because on account of the lever effect, the curb bit will be automatically accepted more strongly through the higher position of the hand and consequently it will have the effect of the horse being even more flexed at the poll and shorter in the neck. In order to avoid this, the curb reins have to lengthened slightly at such moments.

Completely the opposite applies when the horse raises itself, goes against the hand or even just stiffens in the poll. Frequently, without giving too much thought to the matter, riders try to position the horse better again with a lower, pressing down hand. This pressing down influence of the hand, however, will incite completely the opposite reaction from the horse; it is really being provoked to rebel to go against the hand.

Instead the rider has to follow the horse's mouth with his hand completely consistently and to position his hand carefully so that his elbow-hand and the horse's mouth form a straight line again. In the moments in which the horse

presses upwards, does not yield in the poll or even goes against the hand, reliable application of the driving aids must be pursued with non-yielding rein and any yielding of the horse has to be positively rewarded by becoming light or going correspondingly lower with the hand. The hand actually does have to be held slightly higher at the beginning. Here, however, people unfortunately tend to tense the arm up more, possibly even to cramp it. This has to be avoided at all costs. Only if the connection between the rider's hand and horse's mouth out of the shoulder and elbow joint remains particularly elastic, the hand is able to have a positive effect. In order to remain supple in the arm, the rider should keep turning his lower arms around the radius with the ulna so that the elbows come close to the body again better and the thumbs are directed briefly outwards.

It is also very important to pay attention to this when riding jumping horses in the light seat. If a horse – as occurs particularly frequently with thoroughbreds, canters with a slightly higher nose, the hand also has to be carried high enough so as not to interrupt the straight line mentioned and described above; otherwise the horse will react by holding its nose even higher, thus also restricting its supple back activity.

As far as the position of the hand is concerned, this straight line formed by the lower arm and

Whip contact on the outside shoulder

Even if the horse canters with its nose held slightly higher – as is the case here – the straight line elbow-hand-horse's mouth should be maintained.

rein, should be observed in every situation. There is an old German saying which is very valid here:

> "Hoher Zügel zäumt, tiefer Zügel bäumt!" – that means: High rein brings the horse low, low rein brings it up!

Another mistake in connection with the rein aids, which is also caused by intuitive but false reactions, is pressing one hand over the crest of the mane in some cases.

This begins by such simple things as evading via the shoulder on the open side of the circle and continues with demanding collected dressage movements such as walk pirouettes, lateral movements and also canter pirouettes. This mistake is unfortunately made very frequently with the inside as well as the outside hand.

If the horse does not turn around willingly enough with the forehand in a walk pirouette, or if it does not have enough angle in shoulder-in,

because the horse, usually with too much neck bending, pushes towards the wall with its shoulder, pressing over with the outside hand is completely counter-productive, because this means the outside rein has a very serious backwards effect which is then bound to hinder specifically the movement which is desired. It is also very similar in the case of half passes, if the horse does not show enough parallelism on one rein, seems to lead with the hindquarters, but in reality it is not prepared to cross enough with the forehand and to move sideways in the appropriate direction.

In these cases the horse usually accepts the outside rein too much and leans on it. The rider has to react to this with clear asking and yielding with the outside rein, it may be useful here to get the horse straight or put it into counter position for a short interlude. However this correction can only function if the driving aids are applied for the horse to go forward keenly. Touching the horse on its outside shoulder with the whip can support the whole process.

The pushing over with the inside hand usually happens on the stiffer (compulsory) side because the horse does not want to flex and bend enough here. It is essential for the rider to prevent the pushing over of the forehand into the direction of movement with his inside leg, the inside hand has to indicate decisively the flexion by means of the sideways leading rein aid, whereby the outside rein has to prevent the bit being pulled through the horse's mouth.

4.2 How does a horse learn "this little positive pull"?

This subject is of significance from an early stage onwards and already occupies an important place in the training of a young horse (Remonte). As early as possible, the riding horse must become accustomed to stepping forward trustingly and willingly to the bit, to step and to stride well. Only then it will engage with the hindquarters when being closed from behind, in other words allow itself to be collected and also, for example, when hacking out, allow itself to be brought more firmly onto the aids in potentially dangerous places and continue moving obediently. This is why the rider must always drive the horse on consistently and decisively, possibly even with the use of the whip whenever the horse becomes hesitant. It is, however, very important to maintain the connection to the horse's mouth, indeed even to get this slightly firmer, in order to become immediately lighter with the hand when the horse goes forward again, in other words "pulls positively". Frequently less experienced riders react incorrectly here by yielding with the hand to their hesitant horse. This false reaction only needs to be repeated a few times and a clever horse will already have learned that it can easily evade or escape a slightly more non-yielding rein hand when it hesitates. Consequently it will become very difficult to ride such a spoiled horse well on the aids and going through the poll to any reliable degree.

Anyone who adheres to this principle when riding will not only be able to have their horse responding with "this little positive pull", such riders will also be able to react correctly with overkeen or, as people say today, "hot" horses. The decisive thing here is for the horse not to feel in any way compelled or restrained. When the rid-

In trying to push the horse forward with his seat, the rider takes up a tense and blocked middle posture and usually exerts backward influence with his hands.

er is able to sense just the right moment to yield, such horses will become more relaxed and calm relatively quickly. Naturally correct halts, in other words applied with all the aids, are necessary here. With regard to the rein aids, the rider must use his mind to force himself to apply these preferably slightly more decisively, as well as possibly rather more strongly, in order to be able to yield again as quickly as possible. On no account should he hold the horse in and pull.

This also applies in the case of jumping training: Anyone who exerts backward influence with the reins until shortly before the fence and tries to hold the horse in, will make it increasingly "excited", and train it increasingly to pull.

Conversely a horse which tends to be rather sluggish when jumping can hardly learn to canter more diligently towards the fence and to pull in a positive way if the rider does not offer an elastic, but above all reliable, indeed even rather firmer contact in combination with the driving aids. Here also the driving aids have to be applied decisively and rather shortly and sharply as an impulse. Permanent pressure and constant use of the whip and spurs only serve to deaden the horse's sensitivity with the possible result that it may even start to resist the driving aids.[1]

4.3 Can weight aids "push"?

Another instruction – as the "Keep him up!" quoted above – which is frequently heard in riding lessons is: "Push him forwards!" This is the reason why

---

[1] When a horse resists the driving aids, it holds back even more in response to the rider's driving aids - in other words, it has a contradictory reaction. A similar situation occurs with some mares when they are in season: the more pressure the rider applies with his legs or even with spurs, the less the mare accepts the driving aids, the rider has the feeling she is becoming increasingly fat.

4. ➤ Instinctively – correct?

➤ In the case of all half and full halts it is important to position the hands very carefully so that the straight line elbow-hand-horse's mouth is always maintained.

The correctly trained rider, when he hears the cue "do a halt!" always has the conception of working from behind forwards to the hand, with which of course he collects something, but above all with which he allows something.

Also when practising half halts, positive confirmation is the best method of conditioning, in other words the horse will learn to respond to the aids most quickly and most reliably when it is rewarded in some form every time it accepts the aids willingly.

An example: in the case of all transitions from one gait to another, particularly in the case of transitions from a higher to a lower gait, i.e. from a canter to trot, the rider should close the horse from behind somewhat by way of preparation. He should take the reins slightly more whilst applying good driving aids and think about having the horse generally better framed in between the forward-driving and the restraining aids, to shorten it somewhat in order then to yield in the transition and be able to give rather more frame again.

Important for the success of such a half halt is also the attitude of the rider: When doing the transition he should think in terms of requesting the new gait, in this case the trot, rather than wanting to terminate the canter. This will make him automatically apply the aids more correctly and not exercise too much backward influence. As horses are very sensitive to the rider's general mental state, it is important for the rider also to apply the aids with conviction and confidence and to believe in their success.

Frequently half halts are badly accepted by the horse if it is short in the neck and not supple enough in the back. If the horse is then ridden with too much hand influence, the rein aids tend to disappear to a certain extent in the neck, which becomes even more contracted without the half halt getting through to the horse as far as the hindquarters.

It would be completely wrong to try and remedy a horse's poor accepting of halts with a severe bit or more tightly fastened noseband. The horse has to be supple, also in the mouth and at the poll, this is why it is essential to ensure that a horse has a well-fitting bridle and is comfortable around the mouth, also with regard to the teeth (see also "Nosebands" in this respect).

Again and again riders who have problems with half halts and therefore cannot regulate their horses enough, are requested to, "drive more with your seat, sit down more heavily". This is an incorrect description in terms of terminology and only partially correct in terms of content. Naturally the riders have to sit deep and supply in the saddle, he should not sit on his thighs, and certainly not stand in the stirrups. On the other hand, in the case of horses which have great pleasure in movement under the rider, and are sensitive in the back, heavier, more intense sitting into the horse would encourage more tension in its back and cause it to get stiffer and hurry more. In such a case it may actually be necessary and correct for purposes of correction to sit slightly forward in the transition, by leaning slightly forwards out of the hips, to transfer some weight from the seat to the thigh. This way the horse will feel more comfortable in its back and it will accept the aids better.[1]

In the case of all half and full halts it is important to position the hands very carefully so that the straight line elbow-hand-horse's mouth is always maintained. **Also in this context it would be ideal if the rider could act prophylactically to potential mistakes on the part of the horse and not simply wait to react after they have happened.** If, for example, he expects or even knows that his horse will try to raise its head in the transition, he can even carry his hands somewhat above the straight line, however he must bring them back into the correct position again immediately afterwards if the horse is still yielding at the poll. If, on the contrary, it is to be expected that the horse will become too light in the halt, come deeper or even behind the bit (duck), the rider has to drive forward to the hand which is held well down low. (see "Instinctively Correct?" for more on this subject)

[1] It only makes sense to influence more with the seat when the horse is well trained, particularly regarding the muscles, and also already has good experience regarding the weight aids (seat).)

4.4.2 Full halts

The full halt to stop the horse is always prepared by a series of half halts and, technically speaking, is in no way different from the half-halts. Therefore virtually everything which has been said about the half-halts applies equally with regard to full halts. Above all, the rider must ensure that his horse gets to know a full halt in terms of a pleasant experience and in no way feels "wedged in" as a result.

This is why the rider must have the aim of gradually managing with very slight aids (particularly rein aids) as training progresses and the coordination between rider and horse becomes more subtle. As the horse should stand evenly on all four legs and in good self-carriage at a halt, it is important that the yielding rein aid follows immediately and not just when the horse has stopped moving. If there is hesitation in becoming lighter, the hindquarters will either not close up completely, possibly even step backwards, however the horse will at least start to lean on the bit and step forward at the salute when the rider takes the reins into one hand.

If the full halt is not accepted in a submissive way, the application of the aids has to be repeated completely. If it is accepted well the horse will only position itself correctly and stand in self-carriage if it is used to standing with gentle contact at a halt, but not with very tight reins.

If the full halt is not accepted in a supple, through way, the entire application of the aids must be repeated. Only if the horse is used to being held with a gentle contact – but not too tightly held reins during the halt, it will position itself correctly and stand in self carriage.

Also in the full halt, the rider should have the perception of having his horse in front of him – he must remain sitting comfortably and keep his legs in the basic forward-driving position. A correction of the rider's seat can have a disturbing effect on the horse's composure. The more calm and even the connection between the rider's hand and horse's mouth remains, the

better the horse will chew calmly. Unfortunately it is often recommended to give the horse something to do with the hand when standing still; this is incorrect and diminishes its confidence in the rider's hand, it even makes the mouth dead. If the horse stiffens in the poll and at the mouth when halting, the connection can be made tighter by raising the hand a little in order, however, to reward any yielding in a positive way by immediately becoming lighter.

In the case of horses which find it difficult to do a full halt, this should be practised initially at the rails and possibly with the assistance of a second person who stands at the horse's shoulder, talking quietly to it and patting it appropriately. Once the horse has learned to stand calmly, you may progress to the next stage, standing closed, straight and in a square – which is the ultimate aim to be achieved here. In the case of a sensitive horse which has pleasure in working together with the rider, it is important to ensure that the horse is sufficiently supple and has had the opportunity to work off its superfluous energy before attempting such exercises. The duration of the halt is to be extended only gradually. The horse should learn from the very beginning that it is the rider who decides when it is time to move off. A calm halt at the rails must be possible before any attempt is made to improve the quality of the halt and also execute the halt at another place.

Once the horse has learned to do a straight and calm halt at any place, it will normally also stand closed in accordance with its degree of collection, in other words with all four legs standing square and with the hind legs closed up. If however, any correction should be required, this should always be done in a forwards direction. This is why a horse should always be allowed to go half a step forward if it has come in too close with one or even both hind legs. At novice and elementary levels it should not be judged too

Help from the ground helps a horse to remain calm and composed at a halt

4. ➤ Instinctively – correct?

| Hands held too closely together cannot yield properly and therefore prevent any friendly contact. The right wrist here is bent and tense. | The inside hand is pressing over the crest of the neck | The outside hand is pressing over the crest of the neck |

well-gymnastizised horse which is a pleasure to ride. Only a very good rider is capable of maintaining this sensitivity or even improving it further. For this purpose, however, he must want to, and also be able to offer his horse gentle but constant contact, he must be in a position to hold his hand as calmly as possible in relation to the horse's mouth. This means, for example, even when the horse is not yet fully supple, it is not yet allowing the rider to sit so well or even at the rising trot, the hand holding the reins must not move together with the rest of the rider's body. From the shoulder and elbow joints, rather like a shock absorber, the arm must intercept all bumps and unevenness in such a way that the rider could even carry the proverbial glass filled with water in front of him (see illustration page 40).

This idea of the glass of water in the hand can indeed be very helpful, also because it promotes the upright position of the hands.

The uncramped movability, also of the wrist, together with this upright position, is a further pre-requisite for subtle rein aids applied from the wrist. A wrist joint which is bent in some way cannot be relaxed, this is why the lower arm and back of the hand should form a fairly straight line.

• **The position of the hand**

A frequently posed question in many different situations, also in the context of tests riding badge, relates to the correct position of the hand. **This always has to be seen in relation to the horse's posture and, with regard to the height, has to be chosen so that elbow, wrist and horse's mouth form a straight line, and the same applies in the light seat or when jumping.** Particularly concerning this point, most riders have to work on eliminating mistakes and trying to apply the aids more consciously and therefore correctly. Frequently the attempt is made – more on the basis of instinct than careful consideration – to raise a horse which is coming too low by bringing the hand higher or conversely to press down a horse which is raising its head or not going through the poll by means of bringing the hand very low. These reactions do not remedy the fault, in fact they tend to further provoke or reinforce it.

The reasons for this are as follows: the higher hand or even the hand exerting upwards influence exercises more influence on the corner of the mouth, this means more severely and therefore with more direct longitudinal flexion,

Tilted in the poll, here in shoulder-fore with too tight an outside rein

Protruding elbows and hands facing downwards ("piano hands") fists prevent sensitive rein aids

Reins held too long

so that the horse gradually not only comes too low but also becomes short in the neck, possibly even hides behind the bit.

The rein held particularly low or pressing downwards[1], rather like the (German) standing martingale, causes the horse to resist and, done on a permanent basis, can even cause strengthening of the muscle system of the lower neck. In order to avoid this downward-pressing effect, the not inconsiderable weight of the lower arm and hand have to be actively carried. For most riders this is obviously very difficult to do, particularly with the left hand, which is frequently simply left hanging and thus presses downwards. This is especially striking when the horse is being ridden on the left rein, and has an obviously negative effect because it is precisely the inside hand which should be reliably positioned on the straight line elbow-hand-horse's mouth. Therefore one should not only take note of, but also actively heed the old German saying: **"Hoher Zügel zäumt, tiefer Zügel bäumt!"** – that means: **High rein brings the horse low, low rein brings it up!**

• Length of the reins

There is also one other phrase which my trainers often used and I still have clearly in mind, and which says something about the position of the hands holding the reins: **"Long reins pull"** – **Why?**

The longer the reins, the less direct the influence on the horse's mouth. If the constancy of the contact then also gets lost (slacking rein), this provokes contact faults like going above or behind the bit. Furthermore, riding with a longer rein means that more strength comes from the shoulder and upper arm and the elbow joint is kept at a tighter angle which means the rider's biceps are tense.

The fact that some top-class riders, particularly in the discipline of show jumping, are also successful with too long reins, only proves that – despite of this fault – their exceptionally good feeling for the horse means they are nevertheless in a position to influence it.

Naturally reins held too short also have a negative effect because this position means the arm is almost completely stretched and therefore not elastic which makes gentle contact impossible.

A slightly obtusely angled elbow should therefore be the aim and, particularly in the case of riders with short arms, this indeed requires fairly long reins.

[1] Pressing downwards: As mentioned in the chapter "Instinctively - correct?", in the case of a horse going against the bit or raising its head, riders are often mislead by their instinct to use the reins to try and prevent this and push the head down.

Reins being held well with trusting contact

It is also worth thinking about the distance in which the hands are kept apart from each other:

The frequently mentioned distance of one hand's width is only correct when riding in a double bridle and here with "holding the reins 3:1, three reins in the left, one in the right hand", because then the left hand has to be above the crest of the mane. Otherwise it depends on the thickness of the horse's neck because – also seen from above – in other words from the rider's viewpoint, the line from the elbow via the hand to the mouth should be straight.

If the fists are held more closely together, the horse's neck tends to interrupt the line so that they can no longer exercise direct influence.

This is similar to the effect of the hand pressing over the crest of the mane.

• **The upright fists with elbows against the body**
Also in this point, as in the case of too long reins, top-level competition riders are not always the best examples. And the same also applies here: these riders can be successful not on account of, but rather despite of the "piano hands" (hands facing downwards). Because only upright fists, with the little fingers actually being slightly closer together than the thumbs in the basic position, make possible subtle taking and yielding from the wrist possible, whereas in the case of flat, in other words almost horizontal positioning, this is only possible with the entire upper body out of the shoulder. A further aspect to be considered is that in the case of holding the reins with virtually horizontal fists, riders tend to hold their stomachs in. Tightening the stomach muscles in order, for example, to give a short and resolute non-yielding rein aid, is almost impossible, instead the rider will tend to pull backward. In this respect every rider should always think carefully about this in a self-critical way, particularly as many believe that these kind of corrections are of optical value only.

• **Rein aids with little strength but more feeling**
As human beings by their very nature are usually most skilled with their hands, when riding they tend to try to eliminate problems mainly by using the reins. This is why there are unfortunately also so many other individual hand faults:

For example many people, in an effort to establish gentle contact, ride with a constantly open fist, which rarely enables controlled, constant contact. The contact actually becomes gentle through the elasticity in the shoulder and elbow joint as well as in the wrist.

Also the attempt, particularly when halting, to want to ensure better mouth activity by slight vibrating with the hand on the medium term achieves the opposite; the horse will learn best with a calm hand and a bit kept still in its mouth, to push itself off the bit, to yield in the poll and to chew contentedly with a closed mouth.

Generally speaking, it always becomes clear that only the rider with a "good hand" and who is thus in a position to keep his horses in gentle contact and active in the mouth, or even to improve them in this respect, who rides with correct rein aids and does not allow himself to be misguided into making mistakes or even so-called tricks.

Horses which are trained and ridden in such a way are easy to ride afterwards and also maintain their natural pleasure in working together with the rider and willingness to perform for the rest of their lives.

4.6 What is the meaning of "inside" and "outside"?

Good knowledge and correct application of equestrian terminology facilitates communication between trainer and pupil. In addition this often improves the correct concept of equestrian connections and an appreciation of this. A good example is the correct use of the terms "inside" and "outside":

Quite fundamentally it applies that in the case of doubt, the description inside or outside leg depends not on where the rails or fencing of the arena are, but rather the side described as "inside" is always the side towards which the horse should be flexed and/or bent – and hopefully also is.

> **Two examples on this subject:**
> - **When the rider stops on the left rein on the track (in the indoor school on the second or third), in order to ride a forehand turn, the horse has to be flexed to the right (no longitudinal bend). Thus here also the former outside leg and rein become the inside leg and rein.**
> - **And a further example: When the rider cantering on the right leg changes from the right rein to the left rein, in other words to the counter canter, the horse must remain flexed to the right (here also no longitudinal bend), thus the right leg and right rein remain the inside leg and rein.**

In order to avoid any confusion, the term "outside flexion" should also only be used, if the horse – on the right rein, for example, goes incorrectly and unintentionally with left flexion.

If, however, the horse is consciously flexed and sometimes also bent to the left, for example in the counter canter, counter shoulder-fore or counter shoulder-in on the right rein, we always have to talk of counter flexion.

→ **Application of the aids; turn on the forehand; cantering work; lateral movements**

4.7 Auxiliary aids: voice, whip, spurs

Sometimes it can be useful to use the rider's voice, the riding whip and spurs in order to improve communication with the horse and support the application of the aids.

The voice is indispensable as an aid in the initial training and breaking in phase with a young horse. In case of older horses it should gradually be used more sparingly in order to avoid the horse becoming deafened to it and, above all, in order not to disturb other riders when riding in company. In dressage tests the audible use of the voice is considered to be incorrect.

When using the voice, the intonation is the decisive element. A calm, deep voice has a calming effect on the horse, whilst a short clicking of the tongue at precisely the right moment or in the right rhythm has a very good encouraging effect. Sibilants, by contrast, tend to get the horse excited. Riders frequently try to calm their horses down by using sibilants, applied in the same way as is sometimes done to warn children to be quiet. This is not quite correct and, initially at any rate, does not work. Nevertheless, it is quite surprising how horses can get used to all kinds of things with time.

If, when the rider is doing certain exercises or movements, he selects the same words and the same intonation as the horse perhaps knows already from preliminary exercises on the lunge or in hand, then the horse will also understand what the rider wants from it under the saddle: if occasionally you try to rein back for a few steps at the rails with a very young horse in

Correctly carried dressage whip

Correctly held jumping whip

Correctly positioned spurs

hand or on the lunge – touching it with the hand or with the lunging whip in front of the shoulder helps – at the same time saying quietly "back, back, back", this can then be very helpful later on if said in the same intonation from the saddle. The same applies particularly also when practising the full halt.

Due to its large, movable ears the horse has a much better sense of hearing than the human being, so that very loud words are not only unnecessary, they are indeed disturbing.

When riding very young horses and in jumping training the jumping whip can be used. According to the German Rule Book it may be a maximum of 75 cm long, it should have a strong grip which fits the hand well and a leather swatter at the end. It is used on the horse's shoulder, if possible in rhythm with the movement. The sound of the swatter has an encouraging effect on the horse, it can indeed have a much greater effect on young horses during the first jumping exercises than the use of spurs. Occasionally it can be used very well in order to support the outside guarding rein, so as to avoid the horse breaking out over the shoulder.

The only problem here is that, unless used skilfully, the hand – via the reins – can very easily have a disturbing effect on the mouth. The rider therefore simply has to practise just using a wrist movement to bring it onto the shoulder.

The dressage whip should be approx. 110 cm - max. 120 cm long and certainly not so elastic that the end of the whip bends up and down and could touch the horse unintentionally. It is held not completely at the end but rather somewhere nearer its point of gravity, because the rider can then use it more subtly and purposefully. The end of the whip should normally be directed diagonally, pointing downwards across the rider's thigh.

It can be used to support the leg aid or rather, if the horse does not respect the leg enough, it can be used by way of admonishment. This is why it is so important to touch the horse close behind the rider's calf, which means the rider has to move the hand with the whip slightly to the side in order to take the whip past his thigh and touch the horse better. On the one hand this may seem a bit awkward, however on the other hand it prevents constant unintentional touching which would dull the horse's sensitivity. This movement with the hand and lower arm also has to be done so skilfully as to avoid disturbing the horse in its mouth.

Touching in the area of the flank or under the belly is normally incorrect because on the one hand it very easily causes weals, on the other hand many horses tend to react with a high croup, but not with improved activity of the hind leg. In this connection it is important to differentiate between the use of the whip by the rider and the use of the whip during work in hand, in other words from the ground.

Naturally the dressage whip, just as the jumping whip, can be used beneficially on the shoulder.

When riding in an indoor school the whip is usually carried by the inside hand so as to avoid it scraping along the wall and causing irritating noises.

If the whip is to be changed from one hand to the other, both reins are taken into the hand holding the whip. The hand taking over the whip slowly draws the whip out from the top of the other hand, then goes on to the other side at the height of the reins again and before taking over the reins there. (In England however the whip is usually changed in a different way)

The same applies with the whip as with the other aids: better short, precise and decisive than constant, half-hearted and dulling to the horse's sensitivity! The horse should always react to the whip aid with respect, but never with fear. The dressage whip should also be used in careful coordination with the rhythm of the sequence of movement as otherwise it can cause irregularities in the gaits.

The spurs are intended to reinforce the leg aids; and they should also be used with the purpose of further sensitizing the horse for the leg, and not dulling it. A pre-requisite for this is therefore that the rider knows how to apply his leg aids consciously and independently of the seat, and that the spurs have been selected and attached to the boots in accordance with the purpose for which they are intended: For normal use a 2-3 cm long blunt spur should be used. Longer spurs are only appropriate if the rider has very long legs in relation to the horse's trunk. In any case the spurs should be fastened very firmly and positioned high at the top of the heel, so they can be applied very specifically. Every rider should be well aware of the fact that even a very blunt spur, if used constantly and incorrectly, can cause bare, raw patches, in the case of unreasonably harsh use on the horse they can even cause invisible bruising which can involve considerable long-term pain.

There is no advantage in using rowel spurs. Blunt discs, with which it is intended for the spur to roll on the horse's skin, can also not compensate for the faulty use; sharper, serrated discs can, if at all, only be used beneficially by a very accomplished rider.

If it should ever be necessary, on account of a lack of pleasure in working together with the rider and lack of respect for the driving aids, to command a horse to go forwards energetically, it is essential to ensure that when the horse wants to go clearly forwards, in other words reacts as required to the command, it does not experience any unpleasant jerking through the snaffle bit in mouth. Rather it should consistently notice that a clear forwards movement is allowed subsequently to such an energetic command. This means that at such moments the rider should not only react clearly with the hand, he should also sit in the light seat so he can react accordingly if the horse moves forward suddenly.

The same, furthermore, applies when a horse is intended to be admonished with a harsher rein aid on account of a lack of throughness in halts; in such a case the rider must keep his weight and legs on the horse at the same time, but on no account he should also include simultaneous use of the spurs.

Spooky horse

As a criterion for the correct use of all auxiliary aids it always applies: The less frequently they continue to be necessary, the more they become superfluous and the more correctly they are used.

When using auxiliary aids, the same applies as with the entire application of the aids: Any application which does not result in an immediate reaction by the horse, is not only a waste of time and energy, it also sends a clear signal to the horse that it does not need to take the rider seriously.

4.8 How to ride and handle timid and spooky horses

As is the case with humans, amongst horses also there are brave and inquisitive characters as well as cautious and timid characters and, of course, a whole spectrum of individuals in between; these different natures can already be noticed in foals, but also in adult horses, when observing them out at grass.

The more timid ones, for example when they move to a different grazing place in the group or in the herd, prefer to remain behind their mother or another member of the herd, they tend almost to hide rather than go out ahead and play a kind of reconnoitring role. This situation can be very well observed on particularly expansive spaces

Any application which does not result in an immediate reaction by the horse, is not only a waste of time and energy, it also sends a clear signal to the horse that it does not need to take the rider seriously.

e.g. in the case of the Dülmen horses in the Merfelder Bruch, (Westfalia, Germany). This is why you find real paths there, which the animals follow when they change their location.

These individual characteristics, of course, also make themselves noticeable under the saddle. For example such more cautious horses will be spooky or even jumpy in a strange environment but also in response to significant changes in their own familiar surroundings. If a rider wants to get on well with such horses, or indeed work successfully with them, he has to learn to cope with these characteristics and to deal with them correctly. The effort is well worthwhile because such horses are frequently very sensitive animals which are very willing to perform and also learn particularly well. A pre-requisite here is that the horse recognizes and respects the rider as its superior ("alpha-animal"), because it feels safe and secure with him and comfortably framed in by his aids (in particular by the driving aids). Then, increasingly, it will also be prepared to go forward even in unfamiliar and sometimes even frightening situations. This is similar to a child which, thanks to unshakeable confidence in his parents – because it has never known disappointment – continues to move forwards because they are holding the child firmly by the hand beside them.

In the case of a nervous, timid horse, the nervous reactions – and related problems – are very quickly increased if the rider tries to prevent the horse taking fright each time by exerting harsh influence or even punishing it. As it is not possible to prevent such perception in the horse, this situation very quickly leads to the horse not only shying but reacting even more seriously on account of its fear of the rider's reactions. The good trainer, on the contrary will try, as often as possible, to recognize such situations in advance or at least to sense them, he will then frame the horse in well between the aids and thus encourage its concentration on itself, e.g. by means of more bending and flexing for a short time. The rider should try to control the horse better by riding travers-style, in other words use the inside leg to keep the shoulder on the line to be ridden and use the outside leg to bring the hindquarters in somewhat. On no account the horse should have the possibility of evading by means of becoming faster, getting out or turning. Instead the rider should collect in good time before getting too near the "suspicious" point, in cases of doubt even do a transition to a walk, and make it clear to the horse that there is only one way forward, in other words the way where the rider is telling him to go. In such situations the horse has to realize that the rider's will is stronger, but also that it will come to no harm by responding to the rider. Even in the case of very cautious horses, you can always rely on the fact that very soon their curiosity will get the better of them and, with a little patience, they will actually soon want to take a look at the "suspicious" point and smell it.

It is then also decisive for me that the rider then applies his aids more subtly, yields and praises the horse once the horse has passed this point, if rather tensely at least obediently.

Usually it is recommended to ride shoulder-in style in such situations. In my opinion, however, travers-style offers even better possibilities for exercising influence and assertiveness.

In very difficult cases it is necessary to take a lead horse by way of assistance; this horse, however, must be really reliable and confident and also be ridden in this way. The possibility of the lead horse becoming infected by the timid horse and being encouraged to shy or snort by this horse must be avoided at all costs.

It is important with such horses to differentiate very carefully between decisive and resolute, in other words commanding riding, and on the other hand, exerting annoyed or even punishing influence, done with the sole purpose of preventing something.

The correct handling of these timid and spooky horses in such situations makes the situation less stressful for both parties and is the only possible way of using and promoting the qualities of the horse despite these inherent character problems.

Naturally situations also occur when horses which are otherwise self-confident and inquisitive shy unexpectedly at some object or incident. Normally with such horses, however, the rider only needs to bring them into a position from which they can see properly from their normal perspective and also use their sense of smell. Sometimes it is merely a case of unfavourable lighting conditions. On account of the horse's range of vision, it is not a good idea to try to ride them straight at such a point and confront it head on, it is much better to approach from an angle. If there are animals or people who cause such spookiness, they simply have to be asked or encouraged to move in order for the horse to realise that indeed they are not dangerous.[1] If, particularly for use in sport, we would like to have sensitive horses, we have to learn how to handle them, because it is a natural consequence that they are also very receptive to all outside influences. If we wanted to completely forbid this perceiving and looking at everything, this would be equal to a kind of psychological castration and would also deprive them of some positive qualities. Therefore from an early age onwards, we have to show them that, although they may perceive and take in everything, they can also carry on working at the same time and should increasingly devote most of their attention to the rider.

4.9 How to ride and handle sluggish horses

Horses by their very nature are creatures of movement and normally take pleasure in this. Of course differences also exist here. These depend, on the one hand, on the breed and, on the other hand, on the nature and temperament of the individual horse. Therefore in each individual case consideration should first of all be given

to possible causes for the sluggishness, for the laziness of the horse.

In this context it can be very useful to find out whether this lack of pleasure in movement only manifests itself under the saddle or also at the lunge, when the horse is let run loose, or even out at grass. It is essential right at the beginning to exclude problems relating to health, equipment, feeding or how the horse is kept, for example:

- any lameness – possibly also relating to how the horse is shod – however slight, indeed almost unperceivable this may be;
- possible diseases of the inner organs, not forgetting the heart
- pain in the mouth (teeth problems) which are reflected in how the horse eats as well as possible contact problems;
- an unsuitable, badly fitting or even damaged bridle, as well as bits;
- a poor quality, unsuitable and/or simply incorrectly fitted saddle;
- poor quality, incorrect or even overabundant feeding leading to deficits, under-nutrition or over-nutrition;

No horse will ever become more diligent and active when the rider is leaning backwards.

[1] It can happen that a horse shies more at a particular object when it approaches from one side than the other - the very same object makes a different impression on him depending on the perspective; this is due to the fact that the two halves of the equine brain are not as intricately linked as those of the human brain.

4. ➤ Instinctively – correct?

4.9.1 What must the rider avoid or do differently?

Important first of all is the rider's attitude to or idea about the horse:

> He must have the concept of making the horse's work under the rider as pleasant as possible so that the horse maintains its natural pleasure in movement under the rider or, if necessary, finds it again. For this purpose he has to sit in as supple and balanced a way as possible (see "Horse and rider in balance"). This is particularly important when riding younger horses or horses which are not so far on in training. The less capable he is of doing this, the more important it is for him only to ride horses which have already been brought on well and are fairly settled.

The aids will only be understandable for the horse if they are well coordinated and applied consistently – and this is essential if the horse is to remain co-operative and willing to perform.

For the sake of simplicity, I shall list some very typical examples here of mistakes made by riders which, on the medium to long-term, will make the horse unwilling and lazy. On the basis of this list everyone can do a kind of self-check to find out if there is anything they need to change. (Most of these are also points which are mentioned additionally in other chapters.):

Even at a walk many riders incorrectly believe that they have to expulse each individual step. They usually try to do this by pushing with their seat and actively driving with their legs, applied either together or alternately. This constant, laborious driving only has the effect, however, of making the horse increasingly dull, particularly when spurs or the whip are also used incessantly. The horse tends to make itself oblivious to the rider's commands to a certain extent.

Rather every horse should actually go forwards keenly enough of its own accord at a walk,

In the „pushing seat" (Schiebesitz)" the rider is locked in the middle position and hanging on to the reins thus bringing the horse's noseline behind the vertical.

- deficiencies or serious mistakes in the way the horse is kept which have a negative effect on the horse's mental well-being, making it feel "unhappy" (e.g. being kept alone, being kept permanently in the box without any variety or outside stimulus etc.).

Not infrequently a careful check through this list may reveal several elements, each one of them seemingly minor in itself, but the total sum of which have a serious negative effect and indeed restrict the horse.

Unfortunately, however, very frequently mistakes or deficiencies on the part of the rider are responsible for excessive sluggishness of a horse. If these go unheeded over a period of time with nothing being done to eradicate them, the situation can lead to serious health problems.

Much better than any kind of remedying of mistakes and deficiencies is naturally prevention in the form of correct, good riding.

provided the rider does not try to exceed the horse's natural basic speed. The rider only needs to sit in a supple and elastic way with his legs positioned calmly against the horse's body and go with its movements. If the horse's keenness should then really slacken, the rider should give a decisive driving impulse with both legs applied close to the girth, possibly also further supported by the whip. Nevertheless, and this is something the rider often fails to do, he has to allow and accept the – hopefully clear – forward reaction by the horse when this follows, with a yielding hand and slightly forward seat, he has to ensure that the horse does not get a jerk in the mouth or, through his seat an unpleasant thrust in the back. Basically this principle of a resolute impulse is valid in cases of particular requirement with allowing the subsequent forwards reaction in all three basic gaits.

4.9.2 The wrong conception of "driving"

Such a precise driving aid used not too often maintains or improves the horse's sensitivity for the rider's leg aids. In the case of most horses it is enough, after repeating such an impulse a few times, if the rider briefly stretches his legs once and takes them away from the horse's side as if he is going to renew the impulse, in order to remind the horse and request it.

Unfortunately many riders try, perhaps encouraged to do so through the constantly repeated request to drive more, to ensure an active forwards movement by exerting stronger leg pressure and, above all, by applying it for longer. This, however, causes the horse to tighten the relative muscles so that it is then even more sluggish.

The mistake of applying the weight aids to try to push the horse further forward and thus leaning further backwards is equally widespread. Naturally a deeper, more elastic seat is more comfortable for the horse and thus encourages its willingness to move forwards well. When the rider, however tries to drive with a constant-

ly tense back and also leaning a little backwards, he consequently reduces his elasticity in the middle position and, at least with his hands, exercises backwards influence. This way of sitting causes an unpleasant feeling in the horse's back, on the medium to long term it can even cause real pain, the horse will therefore keep itself increasingly stiff and consequently not be able to step off forwards-upwards so actively with its hind legs (more on this subject in Chapter 4.3 about weight aids).

In order to correct these horses first of all have to be ridden more over the back in a stretch position, preferably at the rising trot. They have to learn to relax again physically and mentally, which in more difficult cases will only be possible under an experienced and sensitive rider.

4.9.3 Finding the right basic tempo

A very typical mistake particularly in the case of quieter, perhaps more placid horses is to exceed the basic tempo, particularly at the medium walk and working trot. Unfortunately in the case of such horses, the rider is often mislead by his instinct, in an effort to encourage more keenness, to demand a fresh, indeed hurried basic speed. If, when he mounts the horse, his mind is already occupied with the idea of rolling his sleeves up for some good, hard work doing hard work in order "to ride the horse forwards properly", he will influence his horse with this incorrect, constantly exaggerated driving, thus provoking resistance from the horse right from the very beginning. **Particularly in the case of horses with a calmer sequence of movement, attention has to be paid to encouraging increased activity but under no circumstances demanding even slightly excessive speed.** The driving aids have to be applied more resolutely and more precisely but not more quickly, they must be exactly coordinated to suit the rhythm of the sequence of movement in question (more on this subject in Chapter 3. concerning suppling up work).

4. ➤ Instinctively – correct?

Another frequent mistake in this connection, which is sometimes even further promoted by the rider's instinct, is the idea that a loose rein connection will permit the horse to go forwards better. Only if the horse has learned, preferably already in the basic training, to step forward confidently to the bit and to „pull positively" (more on this subject in Chapter 5, concerning impulsion), it will be willing to go forwards with a swinging back. However, the better it swings in the back, the better the rider can sit, and this conveys a more pleasant feeling to the horse which then responds gratefully by conveying pleasure in working with the rider.

4.9.4 What can be done to promote a horse's enjoyment in working with the rider?

In English-speaking countries people talk a lot about the "happy horse". Naturally this refers in the first place to the horse's mental condition which is reflected directly in its willingness to perform.

Concerning appropriate ways of keeping horses, luckily today riders and owners give more thought to this than was ever the case previously. As far as equestrian training is concerned, however, it is not merely a question of correct and well-founded work. Rather in daily training great emphasis must be placed on varied and interesting arrangements which also provide mental stimulus for the horse:

- **The sequence of the daily training unit must be varied on a daily basis.**
- **A riding arena outdoors if possible, with different kinds of extraneous stimuli, promotes the liveliness in a horse's nature and also its ability to cope with unusual situations – also at horse shows, for example.**
- **Frequent work together with other horses has a stimulating as well as a calming effect.**

- **Regular hacking out, also in different types of countryside, has a positively stimulating effect on all its sensual organs.**
- **Hacking out in a group, possibly also taking part in a well-organized hunt gives every horse a sense of pleasure in going freshly forwards and thus also promotes its pleasure in working together with the rider. In Trakehnen, the famous Principal and State Stud located in former East Prussia, young stallions used to be hunted in their first year of training.**

In the case of most sluggish horses it is indeed relatively easy to improve their keenness and pleasure in working together with the rider. The less experienced rider, however, should not hesitate to ask for competent advice, possibly also for some practical support to avoid his horse developing incorrect automatic reactions and getting the impression that riding involves boredom and stolidity. Also in this connection, therefore, we have to remind ourselves about how important it is for young horses to be broken in and given initial schooling under the saddle (familiarization phase) by experienced and appropriate riders. In this phase every horse has to experience that it is also possible with the rider – indeed it is actually very enjoyable, to move in a supple and balanced way, and in this way to satisfy its quest for movement.

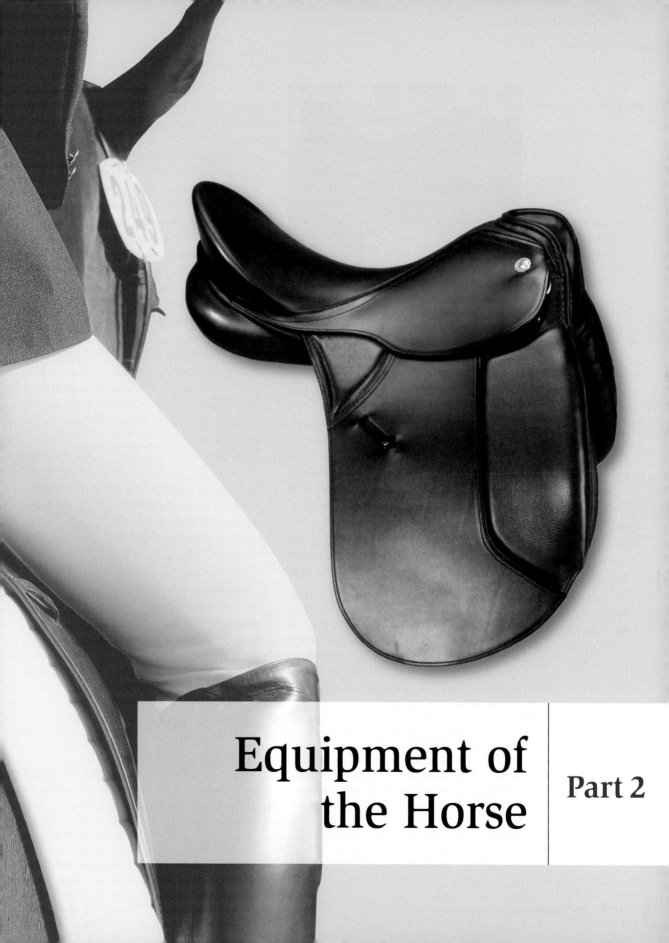

Equipment of
the Horse

Part 2

1. ➢ The Saddle

Conventional dressage saddle with normal depth seat and knee rolls which do not fix the rider.

1. How the saddle influences the way you ride

It is very surprising to observe how much money a lot of riders, particularly female riders, are prepared to spend on saddles. If they then purchase such an „object" – sometimes at a cost of several thousand euros – , they expect on the one hand to have a better seat and consequently better influence on their horse, but they also expect their horse to feel more comfortable. Naturally both are very much inter-dependent and therefore it is not possible to stipulate clearly which is to be aimed for as the first priority.

Unfortunately some of these investments are not only unnecessary, they can indeed even be damaging. Anyone who believes they will always be correctly advised and served in an equestrian sports shop may frequently discover this to be an illusion. I shall therefore list a few critical points here and explain their significance:

1.1 How does the rider acquire the right seat in the saddle?

Only a rider who is able to sit in a supple and well-balanced way can feel at ease on a horse himself and also be a fairly pleasant, easy-to-car-

> ➢ Only a rider who is able to sit in a supple and well-balanced way can feel at ease on a horse himself and also be a fairly pleasant, easy-to-carry load on its back.

ry load on its back. Together with his horse, he will be able to enjoy our sport. As riding always involves movement on the part of both partners and this movement involves constant changes in relation to gait, speed and balance, the common balance between rider and horse has to be seen as something very dynamic. Consequently there can be little point in a good saddle which serves the objective of keeping a rider as firmly as possible more-or-less fixed to the horse's back. In many cases, however, this idea seems to prevail in the heads or, to be more precise in the "seats" of many riders. All that is still needed is large pieces of Velcro to keep the breeches "fastened" to the saddle, boots and saddle flap are frequently stuck together anyway. A good saddle has to be designed in such a way as to put the rider into a good basic position but at the same time permit enough freedom of movement to be able to adapt in an optimum way to every movement of the horse and every situation; and this also concerns the legs.

The easiest part is certainly to find the right size and shape for the rider. The seat as well as the shape and length of the saddle flaps have to suit the rider's seat and leg length, in particular the length of the thighs. Particularly in the case of smaller riders and riders who are slimly built in the pelvis area, the seat must be correctly shaped to enable the rider to position his legs correctly.

Another criterion which is very important for the right position of the rider's seat is the location of the deepest point of the saddles seat (people frequently talk incorrectly about the point of gravity of the saddle). This should be more or less exactly in the middle when the rider is sitting in the saddle.

1.1.1 Criticism of saddles currently available

If the deepest point is located further back, e.g. because the gullet is too narrow and/or too high for the withers of the horse in question, the rider will be induced into taking up the chair seat. That might indeed seem quite comfortable for

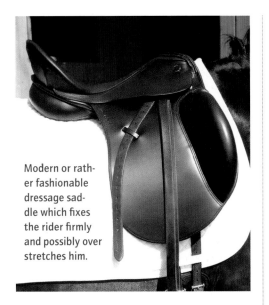

Modern or rather fashionable dressage saddle which fixes the rider firmly and possibly over stretches him.

The rider gets too much pressure on the thigh; consequently the pelvis is pushed into a hollow-back position and his lower legs slip too far back.

him; however since this position automatically brings his lower legs too far forward, he will be disturbed in his balance and restricted in the influence of his forward-driving leg aid, particularly at the rising trot. This disturbance in the balance leads to the fact that the rider tends to find himself in a backward-leaning position and usually, holding the reins fairly long, exercises backward influence on the horse's mouth.

A lot of the dressage saddles currently available on the market, however, have their deepest point located significantly further forward, perhaps because people are in the habit of positioning the saddle fairly far back, sometimes in fact significantly too far back, and then try to provide compensation for the horse's back by sitting further forward. This, however, has very negative consequences for the rider's seat: He constantly gets a slight thrust to his seat, which conveys the feeling that he is leaning forwards and then automatically tries to compensate for this by leaning backwards somewhat. If, in addition, the saddle is equipped with these excessively large thigh blocks which force the rider's thighs into a very straight position, the rider's pelvis will be brought into a hollow-back position, thus almost literally forcing the rider into a fork seat. Here

also the rider gets balance problems and feels as if he is sitting in front of the vertical. In an effort to counteract this, he usually brings his upper body further back and exerts a strain by hollowing his back even more.

This tendency to the fork seat is also further promoted by the usually very steeply cut saddle flaps because these sometimes encourage the rider to use excessively long stirrups.

A well-stretched seat is doubtlessly important as well as beneficial for dressage-style riding. When, however, the degree of stretch – which is prescribed by the proportions of rider and horse (and limited particularly in the case of very tubby and broad horses) is exceeded – even by as little as one hole of the stirrup leathers , this is extremely detrimental to the seat. It reduces the elasticity in the middle position, too much pressure is exerted on the thighs, the lower legs with limp calf muscles slip increasingly backwards and the very important independence of hand and seat is restricted considerably.

The secure and correct position of the lower leg, however, is of fundamental importance. Unfortunately many riders (and unfortunately also many trainers) believe that having the leg positioned further back makes it more easily possi-

Saddle with billet (foregirth) strap: Consequently a lot of pressure is exerted on the withers. The horse will be constricted behind the shoulder.

ble to have the horse on the driving aids, in other words in front of the rider. This is not correct, however, because then the so-important (rib-) bending around the forward-driving inside leg is made much more difficult and also the differentiation from the sideways driving and guarding aid is only possible by means of shifting the leg back almost into the flank area.

Generally speaking, people nowadays prefer dressage saddles with a very deep seat because this, in combination with the sizeable thigh and knee blocks mentioned above, give the rider the feeling of sitting particularly firmly in the saddle. Naturally then it is easier to ride sitting trot on horses which – for whatever reason – throw the rider off more (horses which are uncomfortable to sit).

Nevertheless this does not happen on account of better suppleness on the part of the rider (better swinging in the pelvis area in keeping with the horse's movements) and horse (swinging more supply with the back), but rather solely on account of the rider being more firmly fixed in the saddle – preferably also with the "glue", as mentioned, on the inside of the boots.

Furthermore, it is also completely misleading to believe that with such a saddle the rider has closer contact to the horse; indeed the opposite is the case.

Being fixed into the saddle in such a way as to prevent almost every movement of the seat and the thigh, is extremely detrimental to the suppleness of the rider. Consequently there is no realistic chance of the horse achieving optimum suppleness.

A further aspect worth paying heed to with such saddles, is the fact that it is hardly possible to ride with slightly shorter stirrups, as, for example, is recommendable with very young horses (Remonte) or even out hacking or over cavaletti. A rider who is even just slightly taller and/ or broader than intended for the saddle, has no chance whatsoever of being able to sit properly in it. Particularly in the case of adolescents and young riders, consideration should be given to the question of having to buy a new, larger saddle every six months. Moreover in a general purpose saddle particularly for dressage (GPD) it is indeed possible to rider dressage very well, better even than in a saddle which forced the rider into an overstretched seat.

1.1.3 The position of the saddle

And here now some information about the position of the saddle on the horse's back:

The panels of the saddles should be fairly softly flocked and adjust quite flexibly to fit the horse's back, even if minor changes occur here. The distance between the panels should be wide enough to provide sufficient space for the horse's spine.

In the area of the gullet and front blocks it is important that the movement of the shoulder blades is not restricted, because otherwise this can cause serious problems with the horse's muscle system and nerves which can have an effect extending along the cervical spine as far as the head. Nevertheless the conclusion should not be drawn here that the saddle flap has to be almost

vertical or even cut back because otherwise jumping saddles would not be used at all.

Nowadays it is more frequently the case that dressage saddles, as mentioned above, are positioned too far back on the horse. But if a strain is imposed on the horse's back behind the 15th dorsal vertebra this will cause an interference and the back can hardly be raised up anymore which, however, is of considerable significance for its carrying ability.

Often saddles which are too large, and therefore also go too far back on the horse, are used on relatively small horses (particularly also saddles with extended panels).

Another somewhat controversial subject, which can only be outlined here, is that of the **short girth** or dressage girth, because meanwhile it is used on dressage saddles almost exclusively:

Many riders use it for the simple reason that very few saddles are offered with a long girth. But why is this the case? The common argument that the knee can be positioned better and closer to the horse, does not hold water, particularly when we consider what thick numnahs and saddle cloths are quite often used. If a long girth is used in exactly the right length, it does not disturb the knee position in the slightest.

The disadvantages of the dressage girth, however, not only affect the rider – indeed they are even more serious for the horse:

- **As a result of the fore girth (billet) straps, usually positioned directly at the gullet plate increased pressure is imposed on the withers, in other words very far forwards.**
- **Measurements have been conducted which have proved that when a short girth is used excessive pressure is exerted in the area of the buckles. Tightening the girth after mounting is awkward and requires a lot of effort therefore many riders make the mistake of tightening the girth too much beforehand.**

- **This also increases the tendency for the saddle to rise upwards at the back.**
- **In the case of horses with conformation which is not optimum for the girth, e.g. very young horses or horses with a particularly round belly, the rubbing action of the girth can easily cause bare or even raw patches.**
- **The buckles of such girths are usually too thick and this is visually disturbing in the girth position directly in front of the rider's legs.**

Luckily the short girth has not become established in show jumping sport.

1.1.4 Summary

Anyone who wants to do something good for himself and his horse, anyone who wants to practise harmonious and perhaps also successful sport together with his horse, always has to keep working at his seat. Only a rider who has learned to sit in a supple and well-balanced way, even in difficult, unforeseen situations, will feel comfortable and well on his horse and be able to convey this sense of wellbeing to his horse. For this purpose the saddle not only has to fit the horse well, it also has to suit the rider's build as well as the condition of his muscles and his equestrian abilities. Faults in the rider's seat, particularly with regard to suppleness and balance, can certainly not be compensated by some kind of "special saddles" or "seat prosthesis", as some people call them.

The same applies with regard to selection of the bridle and/or bits: Suitable and well-fitting equipment is indeed essential to have, however specially selected it may be or perhaps even newly invented, it will never be able to compensate for a lack of ability on the part of the rider.

➔ Suppleness of the rider; horse and rider in balance

Suitable and ◅ well-fitting equipment is indeed essential to have, however specially selected it may be or perhaps even newly invented, it will never be able to compensate for a lack of ability on the part of the rider.

Correctly fitted
snaffle bridle

2. The Snaffle Bridle

According to our riding theory the saddle and bridle are part of the riding horse's basic equipment.

Something about the history of the different forms of bridles for horses is included in the section about double bridles.

The snaffle is the most suitable bridle for basic training. This also applies at the beginning of special training in the disciplines of jumping and cross-country, and, of course, it is particularly applicable in the area of leisure riding.

> The snaffle bridle is composed of
> - the headpiece,
> - the cheek pieces,
> - the throat lash and
> - the browband.

Additionally a noseband is usually also worn (and is obligatory in competitions).

Snaffle bits exert influence on the bars of the horse's mouth as well as its tongue, which is also what we require in accordance with our riding theory. The more trustingly the horse steps into the bit with a yielding poll, the better it will swing through in a forward direction with its hind legs

(→ Chapters 4 and 5 Contact and Impulsion). Occasionally nowadays it is argued, particularly by trainers in the discipline of western riding, that a bit which exerts influence on the tongue prevents the horse from swallowing and relaxing properly in the poll. This argument is not correct – as can be experienced by anyone who has learned to ride according to the riding theory themselves or who watches a good rider at work.

The thinner the bit is, the sharper its influence on particular points. Nevertheless the thickness of the bit is subjected to the restrictions imposed by the size and shape of the horse's mouth (→Part 2, Chapter 3 on double bridles); which is why no-one should dwell on the erroneous idea that there can be nothing wrong with a thick, 22 mm bit. In a small mouth it can indeed be an extremely disturbing factor! For a warmblood horse with a normal sized head 18 mm thick bits are normally correct.

The size of the bit has to be exactly suited to the width of the mouth and, in particular, to the distance between the two mandibular branches. Too large mouthpieces are frequently chosen due to fear of smaller models pinching the lips and corner of the mouth.

This is wrong, however, because too large a bit
- slips about in the horse's mouth, in other words it cannot settle calmly,
- easily comes into too high a position and presses against the roof of the mouth,
- pinches the lower jaw ("nutcracker effect", particularly in the case of the single broken bit) and possibly
- animates the horse to pull its tongue up.
- in the case of a double-jointed model, involves the risk that the joint will lie on the bars of the mouth.

The better the bit fits the mouth, the more comfortable the horse will be and therefore willing to chew and yield in the poll.

Bits have to be checked regularly to see if they are worn, damaged or if there is a problem with the material; otherwise the horse can suffer injuries in the mouth area.

2.1 The bits

• The **loose ring snaffle**, is the most common bit and can be used for all different purposes. Normally solid, heavy mouthpieces are preferable because they remain more still in the horse's mouth whereas the hollow versions induce the horse to play around with them.
Loose ring snaffles are available in simple and double jointed form. As the double jointed mouthpieces adjust better to suit the mouth, they are chosen more frequently nowadays.

• In the case of the **egg butt snaffle** the rings are connected to the mouth piece by a joint. This makes the position of the bit in the mouth slightly more stable, it is, however, also made to move when the rings are moved by use of the reins. The horse does not have so much of a chance to position the mouthpiece appropriately in its mouth.

• The **cheek snaffle**, formerly known as the French creek bit, has side pieces, which keep the bit in the right position in difficult situations and are intended to prevent the bit being pulled through the mouth. It can be used in competitions, on jumping course or cross-country course, if the horse is not supple and through enough and does not accept the aids for turns.
A similar effect can be achieved by rubber discs on a loose ring snaffle or through a so-called D-ring snaffle bit. (A large proportion of the bits which come from America, and which are currently very popular, not only have a very thin, sharp mouthpiece but also D-shaped side pieces.) In the case of these variations it has to be considered that such a bit can very easily press the inside of the lips too strongly against or even between the molar teeth and it can lead to injuries of the mucous membrane.
These auxiliary aids should not be used for daily dressage-style work.

• As everybody knows there are dozens of different kinds of **special bits**, often described in good faith as particularly effective by sales persons, although sometimes this is done for purely

From above:

Double broken loose-ring snaffle bit with round centre piece

French link snaffle bit

Egg butt snaffle bit

Very thin bit as used in Western riding

commercial reasons. **Therefore it is always well worth remembering that a lack of throughness cannot be compensated for by a sharp bit.** What may seem like initial success usually very quickly transpires to be the opposite. Hand faults on the part of the rider have a particularly serious effect when very thin, sharp bits are used.
Anyone who believes they have to try something new, or even unusual, should ask himself very self-critically if he is in a position to exercise fine enough influence with his hands and to sense the reactions of his horse and interpret them correctly. In case of doubt he should ask a serious and experienced expert for advise and also practical help, e.g. by means of lessons.

• I should like, however, to mention two special forms of bits because they are very commonly used:
The **double-jointed snaffle** is also available in a version in which the middle piece is not shaped like an "olive", but rather like a little plate, it is referred to as the French Link snaffle. It is very commonly used particularly as a bridoon for the double bridle. It also, however, makes good sense to

2. ➤ The Snaffle Bridle

➤ Deficiencies in training cannot normally be compensated for by means of special bridles!

use it in a slightly thicker form as a snaffle bit e.g. in the case of horses with a very flat roof of the mouth and horses which tend to play with their tongue.

The **three-ring snaffle bit** is frequently used for show jumping horses. Providing the reins are attached to the middle large ring, it functions in almost the same way as a normal loose ring snaffle. If, however, the reins are attached to the lower ring, particularly when taking the reins, the bit exerts an upward influence towards the corner of the mouth and is thus much sharper.

Some words of warning must be spoken about bits which – apparently – should encourage the horse to chew more. It is only possible to talk about good chewing activity if it is obviously an indication of the horse's wellbeing and its ensuing relaxation; when it takes place with the horse's mouth barely opened and the tongue only moving very little.

Some of these bits are made up of parts consisting of various metal alloys or have different insertions. This causes unpleasant feelings for the horse and makes it chew so much, sometimes to an extent which is so exaggerated that we cannot consider this to be our genuine aim. We can perhaps understand better how the horse feels if we imagine chewing with a metal tooth filling on metal foil.

In this connection, I should also like to say a word about the very thin special bits originating from western sport and which are very fashionable at the present time: it is indeed correct, as mentioned above, that too thick a bit in a rather small, narrow mouth can be very disturbing, even if the size is right. This is why the horse's well-being should be a very decisive criteria in the selection of the bridle and especially of the bit; the well-informed observer can recognize this very easily by means of

- good chewing activity (see above), with closed mouth and slight frothing,
- relaxed lips,
- concentrated but relaxed facial expression,
- alert but calm eye and
- alert but calm activity of the ears,

simply to mention the indications in the head area; the good, experienced rider will feel it quite naturally. There is little point in taking measurements. Experience proves that it is also not correct that any contact with the roof of the mouth is disturbing.

Furthermore, it has to be considered that in western-sport contact, in other words the constant connection between the rider's hand and the horse's mouth, is by no means desired, rather the horse is quite consciously ridden, with very different and, in my opinion, for the major part very dubious means, away from the hand, indeed in our terms behind the bit. Concerning the side pieces of these bits, which are usually D-shaped or in bar-form, some comments have already been made above.

2.2 The reins

The reins are attached by buckle to the snaffle bit.

Occasionally hooks are used for this purpose in order to be able to undo them more easily, when changing the bit for example. This has the disadvantage that it can easily involve a "jingling", if the rider is not able to keep absolutely ideal contact; sensitive horses are easily disturbed by this and sometimes tend to go behind the bit.

There are very different types of reins. The width is normally 2 cm, however for riders with small hands it is better to choose narrower ones because otherwise it will be almost impossible to close the hands enough. The combined length of both halves should be approximately 2.75 m.

Reins have to lie flat in the hand and have a good grip in order to be able to maintain reliable contact. At advanced level dressage-style training it is not particularly recommendable to use reins with sewn-on stoppers, smooth, continuously variable follow-up shortening is virtually impossible and it is therefore difficult always to ride with a precisely adjusted rein length with these reins. More suitable would be rubber-coated reins, fine webbed reins with an appropriately smooth finish or, best of all, simple leather reins. In the grip area, however, these should only be cleaned with saddle soap, no form of grease or oil should ever be applied.

As in the case of all items of equipment which play a role in connection with safety, the saying applies quite particularly with reins: cheap is not always good value for money!

2.3 Fitting the snaffle bridle

The snaffle bridle can only contribute to good communication between horse and rider if all parts fit perfectly and are fastened correctly:

- **The bit has to be positioned so high that, even when the reins are taken, the cheek pieces are not too lose, there should be one or two creases at the corner of the mouth.**
- **The throat lash is fastened so loosely that at least one upright hand's width can be inserted at the throat.**
- **The browband has to be large enough to avoid any tautness across the brow, which automatically pulls the headpiece towards the ears. Even just a little tautness causes pinching at the base of the ears which leads to serious irritations, on the long term it can even cause the horse to become head shy.**
- **As there are several different kinds of nosebands, which all have very different advantages and disadvantages, these will be dealt with in a separate section.**

Finally, I should like to repeat the warning: Deficiencies in training cannot normally be compensated by means of special bridles!

→   Contact

2.4 Nosebands

In accordance with a very decisive principle of our riding theory the training of riders and horses should take place in a way which is as suited and friendly to horses as possible. Now in the German Rules and Regulations for Competitions (LPO) it is stipulated that the horse's equipment must include a noseband, which many people, who consider themselves to be particularly dedicated to the well-being of horses, see as a means of coercion and therefore reject.

How can this contradiction be resolved?

The fact that the LPO regulation is to be assessed as completely horse-friendly can indeed be quite easily explained:

During riding pressure is exerted with the bit via the reins on the mouth, i.e. on the bars of the mouth, tongue and corner of the mouth, the horse will quite automatically react by yielding in the lower jaw. How much strength the rider uses in doing this on the one hand depends on his ability as a rider, particularly the feeling he has in this capacity and, on the other hand, on the riding qualities of his horse. In any case this strength is exerted initially exclusively on the horse's mouth. If the horse is wearing a noseband, however, the pressure is transmitted further by the yielding lower jaw to the ridge of the nose. The fact that the influence on the nose functions very well can be clearly felt when using some bitless bridles, the cavesson and also when quite simply leading the horse in a headcollar.

Naturally the use of a noseband can only be described as horse-friendly if it is correctly designed, carefully fitted and correctly fastened. This will be dealt with later on in specific connection to the different types of nosebands.

In the case of all nosebands the leather must be wide enough not to cut into the skin. This is why, according to the German Rules and Regulations, only leather is allowed (with the exception of top-level competitions). Nosebands made out of any kind of cord, for example, are not permitted. The other point is that they should not, of course, be fastened too tightly; fastening the noseband too tightly restricts the chewing activity or even prevents it completely. Consequently in turn the willingness to become supple and yield in the poll is restricted and the well-being of the horse is quite certainly also restricted.

Whether or not a horse feels at ease under a rider, can be detected fairly easily by the rid-

A drop noseband, correctly buckled

er himself on the basis of a wide variety of different criteria, provided he can already ride reasonably well and is thus also able to concentrate on the horse. Also the observer, however, i.e. the judge or trainer for example, can recognize very well from the overall facial expression, and quite particularly from the way the horse chews and the position of the lips, whether the horse is in good contact and stepping up confidently to the bit.

Now let us discuss the different types of nosebands

2.4.1 The drop noseband

Previously in Germany the drop noseband used to be the version which was commonly used with the snaffle bit. In recent years, however, it has been used much less. This is certainly partly due to the fact that riders and owners are not so keen on the optical impression it makes. The main disadvantage of this noseband, however, is the very deep position of its nose strap on the lower, particularly sensitive end of the nasal bone, which is why it is really no bad thing if it is hardly used any more. An additional aspect is that most drop nosebands are designed in sizes which are no longer a proper fit for the average, rather small size of horses' heads with the quite short mouth nowadays. Usually the nose strap is too long so that the small rings at the side, to which both parts of the chin strap are sewn on, are positioned too far back. This in turn leads to the fact that pressure is exerted on the bit in this area when the nose strap is positioned as high as it actually ought to be, in other words 4 to 5 fingers' width over the edge of the nostrils.

There are, however, sometimes horses which do actually go best with this noseband in a snaffle – although a precise reason for this cannot always be given. Then it is important to ensure that the nose piece is short enough, something which can be dealt with by any saddler. When

the nose strap is closed it should still be possible to insert one to two fingers underneath.

2.4.2 The ordinary noseband and the flash noseband

The ordinary noseband is obligatory with a double bridle and can, of course, also be used with a snaffle bridle. In order to be able to fasten it really high enough, the left cheek piece to be short enough to prevent the buckle being positioned virtually on the browband and exerting pressure. The nose strap should be positioned slightly below the zygomatic bone, in other words as high as possible so that the lips do not become pinched between the nose strap and the bit. Frequently the two cheek pieces are attached to the nose strap at too short a distance from each other so that they go directly over the zygomatic bone. A saddler's help is required here, to move them slightly further back.

Not infrequently the buckle piece on the nose strap is too short itself. It should normally be long enough, coming from the right, to extend over both mandibular branches, the buckle thus being positioned slightly to the left. If it is shorter, the end of the strap can finish precisely on the left mandibular branch which can sometimes even cause pressure points where horny skin can develop. In this case the problem can quite easily be solved by putting a piece of foam rubber or felt underneath.

Very frequently the ordinary noseband is used with an additional nose strap as a so-called flash noseband. This second nose strap is indeed not of any great significance. It can only contribute to a better and more stable position of the bit in the horse's mouth.

Also in the case of the ordinary and flash noseband it is important for one to two fingers to fit beneath the nose strap to ensure that the horse is not restricted in the very important chewing activity. Under no circumstances the lower nose strap should be buckled more tightly than the

Flash noseband, the noseband could even be buckled one hole higher.

2.4.3 The grakle noseband

With the grakle noseband the intention is to transfer the point on which the pressure on the nose is exerted further up and, as far as possible, to keep the respiratory tract free better.

If a rider decides to use this form of noseband and is of the opinion that it suits the horse concerned best, then it should be used in the way in which it is frequently used today in show jumping and eventing. In this design at the end at the end of the two cheek pieces there are small rings to which the nose strap and chin strap are attached. These small rings are then in fact positioned above the lower end of the zygomatic bone, which is why this form of noseband may really only be fastened relatively loosely.

With the older form of grakle nosebands the two front-crossing nose straps at the side were positioned slightly below the zygomatic bone, as in the case of the flash noseband. As these two nose straps are not firmly connected with each other in the rosette area, it is not possible to fasten the top one slightly more tightly than the lower one, so that this cross piece always slips relatively far down on the ridge of the nose, which is indeed precisely what should be avoided.

Well positioned grakle noseband, possibly too tightly fastened

upper one, because otherwise this would pull the entire nosepiece down and this would have a negative effect on the function as well as the optical appearance. This is why the top nose strap must always be closed first. As the lower nose strap usually gets dirty and sticky with the horse's saliva (mixed with titbit remains), it is important for it to be carefully cleaned after every time you have been riding in order to avoid any rubbing or sore patches around the horse's mouth.

A special form of the flash noseband is often referred to as the Swedish noseband. In this model a double buckle piece runs down around both mandibular branches, by means of which - with a type of reinforcer - the nose can be buckled closed. This is why extreme care is required to avoid tightening too much around the mouth. Otherwise, these nosebands function very well, they lie nice and evenly on both mandibular branches providing the relevant underlay is long enough. Otherwise it can cause pressure points on the lower jaw bones.

A well-fitting and correctly fastened ordinary noseband or flash noseband is suitable for all purposes and, due to its high position, does not restrict the horse's breathing in any way.

2.4.4 The combination level noseband

In the case of the combination level noseband, the nose strap is positioned slightly higher than it is the case with the drop noseband and slightly lower than the ordinary noseband. In order to ensure that the horse's lips do not get pinched by the side pieces, this noseband has to be put on and fastened with extreme care. It should be positioned so high that the lower chin strap is positioned just slightly below the bit because otherwise this strap will not lie properly in the chin groove. Also with this noseband, as with the

Combination level noseband

drop noseband, it is very important that the nose-piece is not in any way too long because otherwise the side pieces will be positioned too far back and probably collide with the bit. With regard to how tight the noseband is to be fastened, the same applies as with the other nosebands.

Occasionally it helps in the case of minor tongue faults, e.g. to restrict a horse in sticking its tongue out to the side. Here, however, the same also applies: it is only possible to apply a proper remedy if the genuine cause is discovered and dealt with. In the case of horses which tend to push their upper and lower jaws against each other at the sides, this can also be restricted somewhat by the two side pieces. Very important here, however, is also to check the horse's teeth.

Finally, once again the reminder that although the bridle has to be carefully selected and fitted to suit each individual horse, **even the best and most expensive equipment cannot compensate for a lack of ability on the part of the rider, particularly with regard to a good hand which is independent of the seat.**

3. Riding with a Double Bridle

3.1 The significance and use in the past

It is not possible to determine precisely when which bits came into being. What is certain, however, is that the double bridle was not invented as an auxiliary aid to permit particularly subtle guidance of the horse.

What and how much can be inserted into the horse's mouth in the form of a curb bit is demonstrated impressively in books about bits of the 16th and 17th centuries.

In view of its long lower cheeks, as well as other features, curb bits of early Modern Times are sometimes described as tools of torture. In making such an evaluation, however, it should not be forgotten that these double bridles used to be fitted sometimes with and sometimes without a fairly long curb chain.

The relatively sharp curb bits and the relatively long, pointed spurs used in the Western world during the Middle Ages and early Modern Times reflect the fundamental conception of the horse in terms of a resource, as well as of the brutal subordination of the animal to the will of the human being. This attitude towards the animal was determined in particular by the demands imposed by riding during war time. The use of the double bridle was also dictated by these purposes, as the mouthpiece made it possible for the rider to dominate the horse rigorously and direct it in an optimum way. Thus not only perfect riders were able to be in complete control of their horses, the double bridle also made this possible for those who were less talented. Furthermore, only one hand, the left one, was required to guide and control the horse – thus leaving the right hand free to hold the weapon.

The double bridle in the form described above continued to be used to and including the final phase of military riding in the 2nd World War. Not gentle guidance but rather optimum manoeuvrability – with only one hand being needed to guide the horse by good riders as well as by unable ones – was the decisive reason for using this mouthpiece. Even in the final completion of the bridle with a thin bridoon, the action-determining aspect – an extra rein and an extra bit in case of damage or malfunctioning – originally remained the moment of security.

As riding gradually became disengaged from the demands imposed by war and in the course of the "humanisation" of the use of the horse to

Such colossal and violent bits had a
severe effect on horses in the Baroque period.

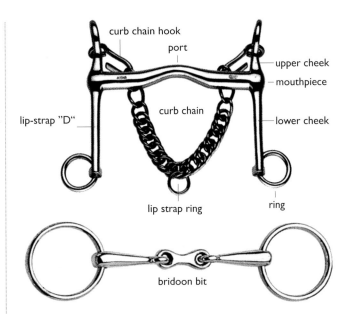

A modern curb bit with a description of the individual parts (the upper and lower cheeks.)

which this process was intricately linked, the application of the double bridle was ideologically adopted and asserted to be for "more subtle guidance". Naturally however, it is only more subtle is so far as its sharper effect permits the rider to exert influence by a finer application of the aids.

3.2 The use of the double bridle today

In the basic training as well as in more advanced training of dressage horses the double bridle plays a relatively subordinate role today. In a competition context it is demanded in some cases in dressage tests at elementary, medium and advanced level exclusively. It is worth mentioning here, however, that even at higher level, there are horses which perform just as well, occasionally even better, when ridden in a snaffle.

In the interests of the correct training of horses and in accordance with the philosophy of our riding theory, great emphasis must be placed on the significance of the horse feeling comfortable in its bridle. Only then it can step into the bit trustingly and experience pleasure in working together with the rider, swing through with the hind

legs, in other words develop genuine "impulsion" (Schwung).

Therefore any rider who wishes to work with the double bridle should always try to acquire extensive knowledge about everything which is important in this connection.

3.2.1 What conditions must a young rider fulfil before becoming familiarised with the double bridle?

What conditions must a young rider fulfil before he is really qualified to start learning to use a double bridle? The most important, as applies generally for good riding, is a fairly perfected, correct dressage seat in good balance, which makes it possible for him from an elastic middle position, to sit into the horse in such a supple and balanced way that the horse becomes supple underneath him and feels comfortable. This is essential in order for the rider to be able to guide the horse with hands which are independent of the seat and apply coordinated rein aids, consciously and sensitively.

It is also beneficial for the young rider to be able to undertake his first attempts with the

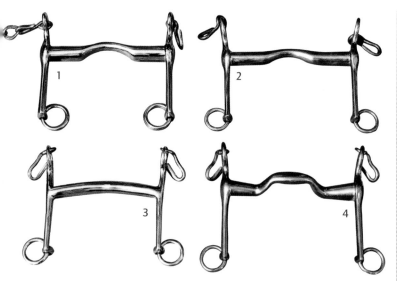

Four modern and very common curb bits, all with medium-length lower cheeks (7 cm) – 1 + 2: Bits with slight port, medium strength (18 or 19 mm), which the author likes to use; 3: Bit with which a slight port is created as a result of the even curve in the mouthpiece (14.5 mm); 4: Bit with a more pronounced, somewhat square port and somewhat thicker bars

other words the horse very quickly becomes short in the neck.

• If a horse is to be positioned slightly deeper, in order to chew the reins out of the rider's hand, for example, the rider has to give more with the curb rein than the snaffle rein, because otherwise the horse would come behind the vertical, it may even become overbent and behind the bit.

• As the curb bit is a bar, it is important – even more so than with the snaffle – not to exercise influence on one side with one rein because otherwise the horse will immediately become tilted in the poll. For the same reason it is particularly important when riding in a double bridle never to press across the crest of the mane with the hand.

• In turns the outside hand must be held somewhat lower so that when yielding with the guarding outside hand the flexing and/or bending is also permitted enough with the curb rein.

Right from the beginning the young rider should try also to allow the curb rein to have a little contact. It is only when both bits exercise some influence that pressure in the mouth is distributed in an optimal way and finer riding actually becomes possible.[1]

Practice in handling the four reins can be done very well initially on a learning appliance for carriage driving. With a certain amount of technical talent, it is relatively easy to construct one of these yourself.

Under no circumstances the young rider should try to learn to ride collected exercises and movements or exercises and movements with which he is less familiar at the same time as gaining fundamental experience with the double bridle. Rather, on the hopefully suitable schoolmaster as mentioned above, in calm work initially at walk and then also at trot, he should take up sensitive contact to the horse's mouth, practise adjusting the reins on large curved lines and once more concentrate intensely on his hand always taking up a position which guarantees the straight line elbow-rider's hand-horse's mouth.

double bridle on a horse which is familiar with this type of bridle and feels content with it. In order to exclude unpleasant influences for the horse right from the beginning, the double bridle should only be used under the auspices of an experienced trainer in the initial stages.

Prior to these first practical attempts the rider should try, if possible, to become informed about some of the technical problems which occur in connection with this bridle:

• On account of the lever action, the curb bit exerts considerably stronger influence on the mouth than the snaffle bit. Therefore a horse which steps reliably into the bit will always pull the snaffle rein slightly more out of the rider's hand than the curb rein.

This, in turn, is the reason why the rider must always shorten the **snaffle rein** more.

• On account of the lever action it is also particularly important to avoid holding the hands too high, because this automatically causes an overbending effect (increased longitudinal flexing), in

[1] Unfortunately it is often recommended just to take up the snaffle reins initially and not to touch the curb reins at all. Here it is forgotten, however, that the bridoon alone is a relatively sharp bit and also that this method induces the horses to play and jingle with the bits. In most cases this is not a good recommendation. The same applies when familiarising the young horse with the double bridle.

3.2.2 At what stage can a horse be introduced to a double bridle?

First of all, it is essential to ensure that this task is taken on by a very experienced rider, who not only is aware of the above-mentioned problems, but also is very experienced and competent in using this bridle with the four reins. Normally the horse should be about 5 years old and be quite confident at Elementary level at least. Above all, it should move in reliable contact and have learned to step confidently into the bit, due to a supple back with the hind legs well swinging through and engaging with the hind legs to take up more load at least to a certain extent .

In this phase of training it is particularly important to familiarize the horse with the new bridle gradually, for example after warming up in a snaffle, when it is already going in contented style, to ride it for another 10-15 minutes in a double bridle. During this period the horse should only be required to do exercises of which it already has quite a good command. It goes without saying that the right double bridle for this horse has to be accurately fitted beforehand, whilst the horse is still in the stable.

How often and for how long the horse is ridden in a double bridle in the follow-up period has to be decided on the merits of the individual case. Under no circumstances anyone should ever attempt to solve contact problems with the help of a double bridle.

3.2.3 What manner of holding the rein is to be recommended?

It is usual nowadays to ride with the reins held separately, in other words 2:2. The easiest form to learn here is to have the snaffle rein in the usual way around the ring finger, with the curb rein held between the ring and middle finger. (1)

The same principle is also possible one stage lower, i.e. with the snaffle rein held around the little finger, the curb rein between the little finger and the ring finger. (2)

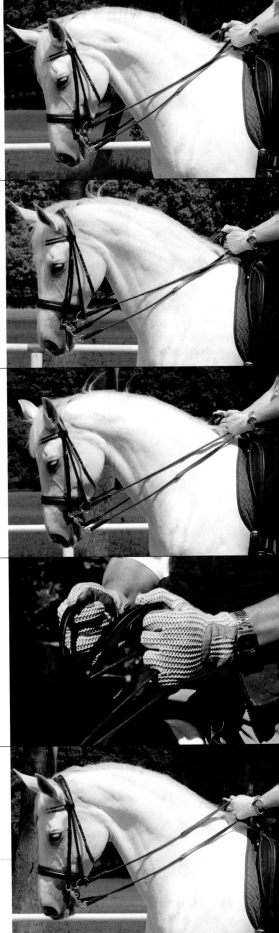

(1) A very common way of holding the reins nowadays

(2) Another quite common way

(3) This way of holding the reins requires greater experience on the part of the rider

(4) Holding the reins 3:1, three reins in the left, one in the right hand

(5) Holding the reins according to the Fillis (or French) method

4. ➢ Use of Auxiliary Reins

"Lauffer" (running) side-reins on the lunging girth

there and, providing the hindquarters are engaging well, also to push itself off the bit, yielding in the poll and becoming light in the mouth. In this way it also gets the necessary limitation – as mentioned above – on the outside shoulder.

The positive effect of this is confirmed by the fact that horses which have been lunged or ridden with correctly attached side reins can also be ridden well without auxiliary reins.

In the case of young riders it is possible, after a certain period of training, to use the side reins during the warming up phase only and afterwards to be able to have the horse on the aids without the side reins.

As a horse only has limited possibilities to stretch and completely relax its muscles when working in side reins, it should not be lunged or ridden in them for too long a period. Particularly when the side reins are buckled too tightly, this can lead to pain and resistance on the part of the horse. This naturally also applies with regard to all other types of auxiliary reins.

Whilst lunging as well as riding, it is important to ensure the horse is working diligently enough and doing enough pace and gait changes. Other-

wise there is a danger of the horse getting used to "hanging on the reins" (and leaning on the bit).

Some trainers criticise the fact that side reins do not permit enough flexing and lateral bending when riding. As riders who are still dependent on such auxiliary aids normally cannot – and in fact should not – ride turns which are any tighter than a large circle (so the horse needs only a little bend), correctly attached side reins are indeed very suitable for them.

This is the reason why it is occasionally recommended to cross the side reins over. I advice strongly against this practice, however, because less experienced riders have difficulty in guarding and limiting with the outside rein on a curved line, particularly when riding on the horse's "hollow" side. This problem is by no means diminished by attaching the side reins in this way, however. Furthermore, horses rather tend to contract more with the side reins attached in this way, the fundamentally essential coming away from the inside rein is virtually impossible. In a similar way to the use of a German standing martingale with a connecting piece, the bit has the well-known nutcracker effect on the lower jaw.

If horses frequently work with crossed over side reins, particularly during moulting, they will get raw patches on the shoulders.

4.2 The "Lauffer" (running) side reins

The "Lauffer" (running) side-reins basically have exactly the same effect as the simple side reins, they offer good contact and thus encourage the horse to stretch forward to the bit. Contrary to the frequently held opinion, however, they do not offer the horse any more scope for movement than the side reins. From a purely technical point of view, the "Lauffer" (running) side-reins are rather more complicated because long enough reins with buckles at both ends are required.

The advantages and disadvantages are exactly the same as those of the normal side reins

4.3 The running side reins

The running side reins are particularly suitable as an auxiliary aid for riders who cannot yet ride their horses so reliably on the aids and through

Running side-reins

the poll. These auxiliary reins are very beneficial in assisting the horse to lower the neck out of the shoulder and yield in the poll. On account of its construction it is unlikely to tempt the horse to lean on the bit. When attaching these running side reins, the same applies as with the simple side reins, that the brow-nose line should remain slightly ahead of the vertical, and that the inner rein should hang a little loose when riding a curve. Here also, the ends of the two sides have to be attached in such a way that they cannot slip downwards, as this could otherwise cause sore rubbing behind the elbows.

As far as work on the lunge is concerned, these side reins have the disadvantage compared with simple side reins that, although the horse comes into a stretch position very well, subsequently it cannot find contact. Stepping into the bit with a yielding poll (and pushing itself off the bit) is not really encouraged. Only by this stretching forward into contact, however, the upper neck and back muscles become correctly relaxed and improved. This does not play such an important role for beginners because they are – hopefully – riding experienced schoolmaster horses.

Also with these auxiliary reins it will become possible in the course of the rider's training, to take the side reins off following warming and

suppling up, and to allow the rider to learn without this support. As this usually functions very well, it is also a wonderful success experience for the rider.

Even if the more experienced rider is very surprised about this, the running side reins can also be very valuable for him if he is working with a problem horse or one which requires correction. With this auxiliary aid, he will be much less induced to exercise too much influence with the hands and can therefore concentrate more on his weight and leg aids.

Strangely enough, some riders consider it almost defamatory to ride with running side reins, whereas they find it perfectly normal to use draw reins.

Also with these auxiliary reins, care must be taken to ensure that they remain attached long enough at the beginning and end of the riding lesson for the horse to be able to stretch completely.

4.4 The German standing martingale

The German standing martingale which is attached to the snaffle bit by means of a connecting piece (from one ring of the snaffle to the other), is intended to help the horse push itself off the bit, lower the neck and yield in the poll. When buckled, however, it must allow enough length for the brow-nose-line to be slightly ahead of the vertical, whereby this is naturally dependent on how high or low the horse is carrying its head and neck.

This martingale indeed helps horses to take up the desired carriage relatively quickly, however they do not find any real contact here and, above all, no limitation forwards-downwards. The stretching

Standing martingale

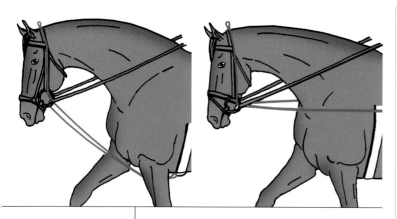

Two different ways of attaching the "neck extender"

forward to the bit or to the hand as mentioned above, and thus the training of the muscle system of the upper neck and back, does not really take place. If horses are ridden or lunged with the German standing martingale over a long period of time, experience shows that they develop stronger lower neck muscles so that even a more experienced rider usually has difficulty in getting these horses on the aids without the support of auxiliary reins.

Occasionally it is concerned as an advantage that it is possible for the horse to bend well on both reins with a German standing martingale. For beginners, however, this does not constitute the main problem because no turns tighter than a circle can be ridden. As riders at this level of training, however, almost always have difficulty in preventing the horse falling out via the outside shoulder, the German standing martingale is not the best choice here.

Formerly people used to lunge young horses which did not have such ideally formed necks and gullets, with normal side reins as well as a German standing martingale. When done under the auspices of an expert, this can indeed have a very positive effect – it is rarely necessary, however, with the kind of riding horses we have nowadays.

When used incorrectly, when the horse resists it, the German standing martingale together with the necessary connecting piece, will strongly pinch the lower jaw (nutcracker effect).

4.5 The "neck extender"

The term "neck extender" is actually completely misleading. At best these auxiliary reins prevent the horse from bringing its head up too high, however they function in such a way that the horse also develops unwanted lower neck muscles; **a more accurate description would therefore be "lower neck strengthener".**

Although – thank goodness! – this device is not permitted in competitions, in many places beginners are allowed to ride with it.

Contrary to some other auxiliary reins, the neck extender only has a negative effect on the horse's contact; instead of improving and consolidating its trust in the rider's hand, making this stretch posture seem attractive, it teaches the horse the exact opposite, in other words that with more forwards-downwards stretch the pressure in the mouth constantly increases. Therefore it is even less possible than with some other auxiliary reins to put a horse in the correct position on the circle line and to bend it, frequently horses with neck extenders actually do this in counter position.

Even the material in itself – very firm rubber – is unsuitable for improving contact: pushing off the bit is not promoted, in fact the horse is rather provoked into going against it. Therefore horses which frequently wear this device are difficult, even for a more experienced rider, to ride in good contact without auxiliary reins. The possibility mentioned above of allowing the pupil to ride without auxiliary reins after the warming up phase, is then excluded.

The correct attachment and adjustment for the normal rider, or not always so expert helper, is even more difficult than with any other auxiliary reins.

4.6 The draw reins

The draw reins can be attached in two different ways:

- They are put over the neck, the ends are threaded through the snaffle ring from the outside to the inside and then attached between the forelegs to the bottom of the girth, or
- they are put over the neck, the ends are threaded through the snaffle ring from the inside to the outside and then attached to side of the girth beneath the saddle flaps.

In the first, more usual form the intensification of strength is slightly less (see illustration), against this, however, the effect is more in a backwards-downwards direction.

The draw reins can be seen particularly frequently being used in work with jumping horses. At horse shows (in Germany) these auxiliary reins are forbidden in dressage and eventing competitions, even in the practice arena.

These reins, if at all, should only be used by riders who have a very good hand which is independent of the seat, also ride with enough knowledge and good sense and are aware of the technical problems associated with using these auxiliary reins:

- Through the transmission, similar to the use of a block (in the context of block and tackle), the rider can exert an effect on the mouth with considerably more strength; in other words, the rider only feels part of the strength which is actually applied to the horse's mouth.
- This increase in strength is at the expense of the way, i.e. the draw reins have to be shortened almost twice as much as the normal snaffle reins. This increased shortening, however, is not as much of a problem as the necessity to yield (lengthening) more accordingly at the right moment.
- In addition, as it is the case with holding the reins of a double bridle, there is the problem that the snaffle rein is pulled more easily, and therefore to a greater extent, through the

rider's hand by the horse, than the draw reins, which means that this can very quickly dominate if the rider does not pay enough attention.
- The force with the backwards-downwards effect, which is particularly the case with the form of attachment mentioned first, is not really suitable for promoting the forwards-downwards stretching of the horse and thus the development of the muscle system of its upper neck.
- For all these reasons horses in draw reins can usually be observed indeed to be going very low, but are almost always significantly behind the vertical and frequently behind the bit.

The draw reins can really only be of positive use when applied for a specific purpose and only for

Two different ways of attaching the draw reins: attention is to be drawn to the fact that the reins are to be attached differently through the snaffle ring! – and to the fact that each variation has a different effect.

Correctly attached chambon

a short time. Here is just one example of this:

In the case of a very large horse with "go" which enjoys working under the rider, it may be necessary, particularly when being ridden by a rider who is not so physically strong, to show it, when slowing down from an extended canter for example, that the rider's aids are to be taken seriously and followed promptly. The draw reins may be considered useful in such a situation, in order to convey a clear signal.

For the sake of completion, I should also like to mention another variation in the attachment of these reins which is to be seen occasionally: it involves taking the draw rein additionally through the throat lash, before being buckled into the girth. This system changes the direction of the effect which is criticized above, so that it is no longer backwards-downwards, there is no doubt about that. Nevertheless the strength is consequently further increased as a result with even more transmission and the sliding of the reins will not function quite as easily, which also increases the danger of becoming tightened up.

4.7 The chambon

With the aid of a correctly fastened chambon horses very quickly lower their neck and take up the stretch position. Its effect is based on the fact that the horse consistently notices that the pressure in the mouth diminishes immediately when it lowers its neck. The same also applies for the pressure which is exerted on the poll via the headpiece.

As in the case of all auxiliary reins, the horse has to be familiarized with the chambon very

carefully and gradually, this applies particularly to the length at which it is attached. For lunging purposes the chambon should always be used in combination with normal side reins because otherwise the horse does not find any contact and side limitation through the outside rein.

In individual cases the experienced rider can also ride with the chambon.

The use of these auxiliary reins actually only makes sense in the case of horses which have developed stronger muscles in the lower neck through incorrect training, e.g. with the neck extender or the German standing martingale. Most horses react immediately in the desired way, a visible improvement in the muscles takes weeks and months, however, depending on how long the incorrect training lasted and/or how great the deficit is.

4.8 The "Dipo" trainer[1]

The Dipo trainer is a form of auxiliary rein which, in contrast to most others, does not have an effect on the mouth and poll, which therefore means it can also not force the horse into short carriage.

With it the horse is actually caused to stretch so that it can become relaxed. As a result of the fact that it yields immediately when the horse takes up the stretch posture, it rewards and conditions correctly.

This function is carried out by the front neck strap. This exerts a stimulus on the respiratory tract when the horse tries to raise its head and neck. A reflex is consequently triggered off which causes the horse to lower its head and neck. This causes a slight curving of the thoracic spine in the withers and saddle area, the shoulder-neck muscles can be moved freely and the entire chest has optimum freedom of movement for breathing.

At the same time the belly muscles, which extend from the sternum to the pelvis, are trained; it helps to curve the entire back and to activate the hindquarters forwards more.

[1] Dipo stands for Deutsches Institut für Pferde-Osteopathie (German Institute for Horse Osteopathy), where it was developed.

The "Dipo" trainer works without touching the mouth of the horse

Correctly attached martingale

Particularly in the case of horses requiring correction, which are not used to going over the back, training with this device, particularly in the first 3-4 days, has to be done in fine doses (approx. 20 min.), so as to avoid stiff muscles; initially work with it should only be done at walk and trot.

Its inventors recommend the Dipo Trainer for lunging only; it can, however, also be used for riding provided this is done under expert guidance.

It is definitely a type of auxiliary rein requiring appropriate instruction for the user beforehand and also a good eye for the horse. If you purchase it directly from Dipo in Dülmen, you will also receive detailed instructions for use.

4.9 The Thiedemann reins

The Thiedemann reins are a kind of milder form of draw reins. As a result of the fact that the rider does not hold them directly in his hands, but rather they are attached to the normal snaffle rein by means of appropriate loops, the degree of influence can be limited. Nevertheless, even the most sensitive rider barely has a chance of feeling when he is having an influence on the horse's mouth without any reinforcement or when indeed the Thiedemann reins are involved. Differentiated use, as in the case of the draw reins, is impossible. Constant use will neither increase the sensitivity of the horse nor the rider.

4.10 The martingale

The martingale is quite different from other auxiliary reins in so far as it can only exert indirect influence on the horse's mouth. In our form of riding it is usually only used as a so-called sliding martingale, with which (see illustration) the reins can slide freely through the rings. When correctly buckled it is long enough, when the horse is in normal carriage and the rider has his hands positioned correctly, to run in a straight, unbroken line from the horse's mouth via the rider's hand to the elbow, also in the area of the reins. Its effect therefore only starts when the horse raises its head too much or the rider brings his hands too high; then it ensures that the bit continues to have an effect more on the bars of the mouth rather than in the direction of the corner of the mouth.

Formerly the reason frequently given for its use was that it can prevent the horse from tossing its head. This, however, is only actually possible with a so-called "standing martingale", which is attached firmly to the bit.

The martingale has proved to be very useful in jumping and cross-country work. It prevents, or at least reduces the danger of the rider unwill-

4. ➤ Use of Auxiliary Reins

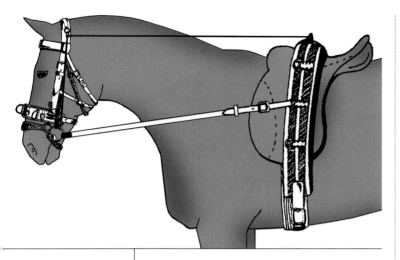

Check reins

ingly applying too sharp influence on the horse's mouth in problematic situations which can always occur, when the horse and rider are not completely in agreement.

Furthermore, it can be used very well by young riders who already ride quite well but are not always able to keep their hands independent of their seat in a reliable manner. The martingale is able to absorb and diminish the movement of the hands somewhat, so that the horse develops more trust in the rider's hand and yields in the poll. Here the martingale facilitates the transition from riding with side reins to riding without auxiliary reins.

From a purely technical point of view, it is also worth mentioning how important it is to ensure that the rings cannot become entangled with the rein buckles and that, particularly when jumping, the strap running down to the girth should never hang loose (especially over the jump when the horse angles its forelegs there is a risk that it may catch one of the legs in this strap so that it can only land on one leg).

4.11 The check reins

The check reins are normally used in collecting work in hand or on the long rein only. They run from the pommel of the saddle or from a ring attached high in the withers area of the lunging girth through a headpiece to the snaffle rings or to the nose strap of a good, stable cavesson. These reins are intended to help to prevent the horse from giving up its self carriage becoming too low and behind the bit.

They should, however, only be used by an expert who has also learnt how to apply them correctly, because otherwise they can cause incorrect reactions by the horse which may go as far as rearing and overturning cannot be excluded. When used and attached correctly these reins usually also hang slightly loose.

4.12 Summary

The use of auxiliary reins can only be valuable and beneficial when the trainer, rider or lunger familiarizes the horse with new auxiliary aids gradually, does not confront it with them suddenly, when he observes and scrutinizes the horse's reactions carefully and with great concentration and, should circumstances require, reacts to them. He must always pay attention to the great significance of the forward-driving aids and make an effort, by means of frequent transitions, regular rein changes and correct assessment of the duration and intensity of work to maintain or revive the horse's willingness and enjoyment in working together with the rider.

As a matter of principle, in the interests of accident prevention, all kinds of auxiliary reins should not be attached until the horse has been taken from the stable and into the indoor or outdoor arena where it is to work. When the reins are attached the horse is not able to balance so well if it should happen to slip going along the stable passageway or through doors. Semi-fastened auxiliary reins which are just attached to the saddle or lunging girth, however, can easily become entangled in door handles.

Please refer to the illustrations for more details about how to fasten the different auxiliary reins.

The Training of the Horse

Part 3

1. ➢ The Scale of Training

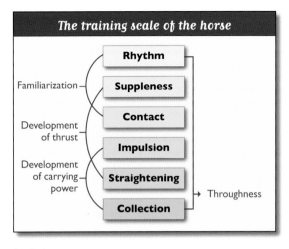

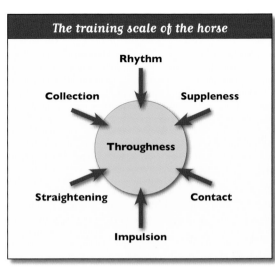

The training scale, presented slightly differently

Rhythm
(Takt)
Suppleness
(Losgelassenheit)
Contact
(Anlehnung)
Impulsion
(Schwung)
Straightening
(Geraderichten)
Collection
(Versammlung)
Throughness
(Durchlässigkeit)

1. The Scale of Training and its Importance for Every Riding Horse

In Germany approximately one and a half million people are interested in horses, which of course usually means they are also interested in riding, and this figure is increasing constantly. Nevertheless, over half of them – and all of them are hopefully horse-lovers – have little or no concept of our "classical" training method. Most of them are so-called "happy hackers" who usually try to ride and look after their horses in their own personal way.

Another group of riders, and the figure here is increasing constantly, too, try their luck in one of the many variations and disciplines of western riding or riding gait horses (e.g. Icelandic or Pasos) or baroque horses (e.g. Lippizaner, Andalusians or Lusitanos).

In the course of my work at the Westfälische Reit- und Fahrschule and to a certain extent also for the German Equestrian Federation, I have been increasingly required to concern myself with these other forms of riding and explore them further over recent years. In this context I have had the opportunity of observing various representatives of these forms of riding and conducting discussions, indeed sometimes even disputes, with them.

And this takes me to the subject I really want to talk about – the principles of the famous scale of training which we have in Germany:

The more I concern myself with these other methods of riding and training, the more I become aware of how fantastic our so-called classical training system is:

- Firstly: there really is a riding theory which is more or less standard and binding!
- Secondly: this theory has been developed over centuries and further refined by outstanding horsemen, logically compiled and recorded.
- Thirdly, and as far as I am concerned this is the really decisive point: this entire riding theory and doctrine is absolutely horse-friendly and makes it possible – thanks to this training – for a horse, despite its application under the rider, to have a longer life expectancy than a horse which lives freely in natural surroundings or simply spends its life out at grass.

Throughout the course of training the classically schooled horse gains in beauty, its muscle system improves and it can move with greater elasticity and elegance. Such horses' willingness to perform improves and their gaits become more expressive. The rider sits closer to the horse and sinks more deeply into it; he feels larger and more competent in the saddle because the horse swings through better with its hind legs and bends better with its haunches, therefore its elevation and, quite particularly, its self-carriage are improved.

A horse which has been trained in such a way can also easily be ridden by different riders.

Naturally there are many books on this subject. Some of them are already very old, some of them are very long and detailed and not always easy to read. Highly recommendable as very useful and compact basic reading in this context is the publication by the German Equestrian Federation „The Principles of Riding".

The basis of our riding theory is the famous scale of training with the following objectives:

- Rhythm and regularity (Takt)
- Suppleness (Losgelassenheit)
- Contact (Anlehnung)
- Impulsion (Schwung)
- Straightening (Geraderichten)
- Collection (Versammlung) / Elevation (Aufrichtung)

Throughness (Durchlässigkeit)

These six points or, more correctly, training aims, are usually listed in this established order, sometimes also in the form of a pyramid, the lowest level of which stands for rhythm (Takt). Nevertheless it would be fundamentally incorrect always to want to progress from one aim to the next in the training of a young horse. For example, a horse will only be in a position to move really regularly and rhythmically when it has been carefully and correctly suppled up. Vice versa, suppleness is also only possible when the rider offers the horse reliable and constant contact. For this reason the attempt has also already been made not to present this scale in terms of a ladder or pyramid, but rather in the form of a circle with corresponding sections. One thing, however, must be clear: a requirement for genuine collection is a command of the other training aims, at least to a certain extent and also at an advanced level of training, all training aims, quite particularly suppleness, have to be accorded reasonable attention every day anew.

In the following I shall attempt to give a brief description of these six training aims:

Under "rhythm" (Takt) we understand the spatial and temporal regularity in the three basic gaits, i.e. walk, trot, and canter. That means, for example, that in the working trot each step has to be of equal length and that the timing also has to be regular and consistent, as if according to a metronome. This is why, particularly also for the trainer, an important requirement is to have good theoretical knowledge of the basic gaits and to train the eye to be increasingly perceptive to them. The trainer has to have a good eye for the individually different sequences of movement, e.g. for the most appropriate basic tempo in each case, this is particularly important in suppling up at working trot. Equally, he must recognize what work at what gait and pace is easier or more difficult for the horse in question otherwise he will not be able to work successfully without this awareness.

Important: observance of the rhythm (regularity) is not only of prime importance in work on straight lines, but also in all turns, lateral movements and in transitions. No exercise or movement is of value if faults in rhythm occur in it. No step in training is correct if it restricts the regular sequence.

As rhythm is therefore the prime criterion for any training work and a horse's reliability in rhythm is certainly easier for the observer to judge than its suppleness, the order of our scale of training is perfectly justified.

"Suppleness" (Losgelassenheit) as mentioned above, is however equally important and very much to be respected in daily work. Only a supple horse can perform to an optimum standard – that is the physical aspect, and can achieve optimum willingness – that is the psychological or mental aspect of suppleness. Anyone who takes enough time for this on a daily basis will keep his horse healthy and in a condition to enjoy performance.

In a horse as in human being, the back is the centre of movement, which is why we should dedicate particular attention and consideration to this part of the body. One of the main

➢ The more trustingly the horse steps forward to the rider's hand, the better it will begin to "pull" (in the positive sense!) and indeed to develop impulsion.

aims, particularly in the training of young horses, is the improvement of the carrying ability of the back. This is why the entire muscle system of the upper neck in connection with the lamina nuchae is of particular significance. Via the nuchal ligament which leads from the occipital bone via the neck to the spinous processes of the withers and the back (lat.: ligamentum supraspinale), it helps to raise the back somewhat. Indeed equally important is the work of the trunk-flexing muscles of the belly; because well-coordinated inter-action of these two large groups of muscles and tendons is an essential prerequisite for strengthening the carrying power of the horse's back (see illustration in Part 3, Section 3.5). Working the horse in stretch posture is most suitable for strengthening these systems, provided it is ridden energetically enough forwards to the hand and to the bit; particularly effective here is correct cantering work e.g. in the forward seat. We shall come back to this when dealing with the connection between contact and impulsion.

Naturally each training session commences with such work. It should also always be repeated at the end by way of review, reward and relaxation. Furthermore, the rider must always go back to this during the training session whenever problems occur which restrict the suppleness and lead to tension.

Concerning the psychological side of suppleness, occasionally we talk in terms of "inner suppleness" here, it should just be said that this is entirely dependent on the trust which a horse has in its rider. The better, in other words the more balanced and supple the rider can sit and the more correctly and sensitively he can exert influence, the more trustingly and contentedly the horse will move under him in good suppleness and freedom from constraint. (These connections are also extremely worthy of note in the case of four-legged patients e.g. in convalescence or rehabilitation.)

And this brings us to the third point, the "contact" (Anlehnung):

In equestrian terms this means the even, constant and at the same time soft, elastic connection between the rider's hand and horse's mouth. This has to be established in the first place by the rider, by his aids driving forward onto the bit. No amount of driving will achieve anything, however, if the horse does not have any confidence in the rider's hand. Only when it steps – strides or jumps – forward trustingly to the hand or the bit, it will push off of the bit itself as desired and yield in the poll. Sometimes it is indeed something of a tight-rope walk, finding exactly the right measure here: On the one hand the reliable accepting of the contact, without leaning on the rein, on the other hand the pushing off itself without becoming overbent and hiding behind the bit.

For me this cross-connection between contact and the following point impulsion represents a kind of key element in our training scale and it can be no mere coincidence that these two terms are placed precisely in the middle.

"Impulsion" (Schwung) in my experience, is the point which is most frequently misunderstood. A horse has impulsion when it has learnt, thanks to good suppleness, particularly with regard to the back, to step off actively forwards-upwards and to swing through far forward with its hind legs. This makes it possible for the horse to develop thrust so that the rider can sit well in to the horse and feels as if he is being taken along by the horse.

And this is the decisive connection which every good rider should have understood and consciously experienced: The more trustingly the horse steps forward to the rider's hand, the better it will begin to "pull" (in the positive sense!) and indeed to develop impulsion.

Here it always has to be remembered that the muscles responsible for the forwards movement, which also bend the spine, or to be more correct curve it slightly, the so-called trunk flexors can only work effectively when the entire system of the trunk extensors is sufficiently supple and capable of stretching (see above).

A horse's impulsion can best be observed and assessed in all extensions and related transitions, particularly well in transitions back to a lower pace following extensions. Particularly in the case of horses with special talent for impulsion it is important to pay attention to the fact that without good suppleness it is not possible to develop genuine impulsion. If such horses start at trot to produce tense steps ("passage trot"), this is – and always will be – incorrect and should on no account be confused with impulsion

This indeed gives rise to some discussion about the order of the training scale, in the context of which it is pointed out that in fact impulsion is not possible without prior straightening. This objection is certainly justified; vice-versa however the straightening work which remains necessary throughout a horse's life can only be done successfully if, due to the work in the prior training aims, the horse goes forward enough and "pulls" (positively). This, moreover, is also expressed in the famous statement by Gustav Steinbrecht "Ride your horse forward and straighten it!"

As a result of **"straightening" (Geraderichten)** the intention is, in the gymnasticizing of the horse, to achieve a state whereby the strains of daily work are evenly distributed over the entire body and all four limbs. A straightened horse steps up to the bit more evenly on both reins and is more receptive to the rider's aids. The rider always has to have the idea of guiding the forehand in front of the hindquarters, not of pushing the evading hindquarters sideways, however. Only then it will be possible, in later stages of training, to ride turns and lateral movements correctly and without any evading of the hindquarters. **Only a rider or trainer who has properly understood the problem of crookedness and has also learned to deal correctly with the hollow (concave) and with the stiff (convex) side of a horse will be in a position to work with it at a walk, trot and canter straightened on both reins, in other words covering the track (tracking up), this naturally applies all the more with regard to the training** of more demanding exercises and movements, e.g. of lateral movements and pirouettes.

The sixth training aim, **"collection"** (Versammlung) as it were includes, as a kind of by-product, the **"elevation"** (Aufrichtung). The objective of the collecting work is to encourage the horse to step more under its point of gravity with its hind legs and thus to take up somewhat more load. A certain amount of collection is advantageous for every horse because this can strengthen the hindquarters with its large muscle parts, which consequently can be trained (in contrast to the forehand which carries the weight mainly with bones and joints). A horse which has learned to accept at least some collection is more content under the rider, is more sure-footed, can be ridden and turned more precisely and becomes more submissive (better throughness).

The further training aim which has already been mentioned, the elevation, is not listed as such in the training scale, however it is directly connected to collection, indeed it is virtually a result of correct collection. When a horse accepts the collecting work and closes up with its hind legs, it will bend increasingly in the haunches (the joints of the hip, stifle and hock) and its croup will be lowered. As the forehand with the shoulder remains unchanged, however, the horse appears to move somewhat uphill and it will really come somewhat higher with its neck and head, it actually seems to be taller.

We refer to this form of elevation as "relative". In contrast to this, in the so-called "absolute" elevation, only the head and neck are pulled upwards; consequently the back becomes hollow and the hind legs are not able to close up, they will work "backward-outward", there is a German saying: it shows the shoes of the hindlegs. Such a form of elevation is undesirable and extremely damaging.

And this takes us to the superordinate training aim **"throughness"** (Durchlässigkeit), which accompanies the entire training of a horse. As the term already implies, "throughness" describes the horse's ability and willingness to accept all

"Ride your horse forward and straighten it!"

2. ➢ Rhythm

➢ A horse acquires the highest degree of throughness of which it is capable when it accepts collecting work.

the rider's aids and to respond to them without hesitation. It accepts the driving aids right through to the mouth, the rein aids through to the hind legs and the diagonal aids, for example, from one leg to the diagonally opposite rein.

A horse acquires the highest degree of throughness of which it is capable when it accepts collecting work.

Because in the course of this work it has learned to move with its hooves on a small area, as a result of which it becomes less stable in its balance. This consequently makes it more receptive to all influences of the rider.

Dressage-style exercises and movements serve as beneficial work specifically relating to individual training aims and, in particular, for effectively reviewing the training. Movements should never be an aim in themselves and not be taught to the horse as circus tricks. With a trot extension, for example, the collecting work can be reviewed, it is only of value if the transitions at the beginning and end can be executed rhythmically and without tension.

To ride or even to train a horse in this so-called classical way requires ability coupled with feeling and understanding, it costs reflection, concentration and consequently time. Anyone who wishes to experience genuine pleasure in riding must be prepared to make this investment and to embrace wholeheartedly this wonderful and ambitious challenge. Thanks to his experiences of harmony between horse and rider which ensue, quite irrespective of the level, he will become a convinced friend and advocate of this form of riding.

To work according to these principles means being able to enjoy pleasure together with horses in our sport for a long time!

➔ Basic paces; suppleness, contact; impulsion; straightening; collection; throughness

2. Rhythm (Takt)

2.1. A matter for experts: The basic gaits[1]

Every rider and – it goes without saying – every trainer can only do justice to his horse if he is able to assess it correctly with regard to its natural ability and potential. This requires good theoretical knowledge concerning – amongst other aspects – its conformation and, of course, also basic gaits. There are indeed close connections here, nevertheless sometimes amazingly good quality of movement can be observed in a horse despite significantly less than perfect conformation. Vice versa, not infrequently one comes across horses which are not able to do full justice to their potential of movement on account of deficiencies in their training (an indication of this is poorly developed muscles of the upper neck, for example).

In order also to be able to apply this knowledge, it is important to train the eye accordingly by means of frequent observation and naturally this can be done best under the auspices of an experienced expert. In these observations of as many different horses as possible it is of great advantage – on the basis of one's own experience and activity as a rider and trainer – to be able to comprehend and fully appreciate much of what is to be observed and make a projection accordingly

2.1.1 Preliminary remarks

Before going into detail on the individual basic gaits, I should like to make a few preliminary remarks concerning the prerequisites for good observation and judgement, also concerning the perspective and the external conditions:

- **Ideally the observer should stand at the level of the riding area in question, if he wishes to sit, a slightly higher place is better so that in this case his eye is also at the appropriate level.**

---

[1] In the English text we have used the term basic gaits as a translation of "Gangarten", i.e. as a collective term describing walk, trot and canter. We have used the term paces as a translation of "Tempi", i.e. to describe the different "Tempi" within the gait, e.g. working trot, collected trot, medium trot and extended trot.

- Ground conditions which are not ideal will restrict a horse in the full development of its movement, or even impede it if the conditions are really poor; this applies particularly on a curved line. A relatively slight slope can also have a negative effect.
- A wet or even just very cold horse will have great difficulty in becoming supple, as a consequence its movements will be tensed.

Very significant in this context is also the comparison of movements in hand or loose and under the rider. When the horse is running loose the observer can gain a good impression of the horse's balance and, hopefully, its natural suppleness. Occasionally under the rider allowances have to be made for hindrances caused by a lack of ability on his part.

Correctness of the gaits can be assessed most reliably in hand and on firm ground. Confident and firm steps, even on the circle, should also be apparent here, otherwise a vet should be consulted. Deficiencies in the correctness of the gaits are often caused by faults in the conformation of the legs.

Quite fundamentally, the quality of movement in the case of an uphill horse is initially different, better than that of a horse of more horizontal conformation. A horse's inner qualities are also very important for the quality of movement, however: for example as far as the agility and liveliness of the stepping off, particularly of the hind legs, and the expression is concerned.

Of similarly fundamental significance is the degree of natural crookedness (or in the case of a more advanced horse the state of training regarding straightening). Naturally in the case of sport horses, depending on the discipline in which they are to compete, it is possible to apply different standards of assessment, particularly also with regard to possible concessions. Three fundamentally good gaits, however, always form an excellent basis. In this context I should like to give three examples – concerning a dressage, jumping and eventing horse respectively:

Florencio, by Florestan I by Weltmeyer, 5 year old Dressage Horse World Champion in 2004.

- For a dressage horse intended to perform at a high level great, secure regularity of rhythm (also at walk) combined with good cadence (recognizable e.g. in the form of a clearly defined moment of suspension at the trot and canter) and distinct ability to collect of prime importance.
- For a show jumper the trot is not of decisive importance; as far as the canter is concerned no major concessions should be made with regard to the canter, however, particularly the aspects of ground cover and economy.
- In the case of an eventer the economy of the sequence of movement at canter is of even greater significance; nevertheless good scope and sufficient elasticity should also be recognizable.

2.1.2 Detailed comments on the three basic gaits

Before proceeding to go into more detail on the individual gaits, i.e. walk, trot and canter, I should like to explain the following terms:

- The description in the German riding theory of the trot and canter as **"schwunghaft"** (**swinging**) simply expresses the fact that there is a moment of suspension in each of these gaits. This moment of suspension, on the other hand, is a pre-requisite for being able to develop "impulsion" (Schwung), in other words that the horse can step off actively forwards-upwards and swing through far forward with its hind legs **(schwungvoll: with good thrust)** at trot and canter.

Attempt at an extended trot, contracted neck, not swinging through properly in the hindquarters, toe flicking with the forelegs ("in front a lion, behind a mouse"), rider leaning too far back

Good working trot of a young horse; unfortunately slightly tilted in the poll

Trot extension with good frame and in good self-carriage

Collected trot with good bend and carriage

er's training. The trot is therefore also the gait which can be improved most by means of optimum gymnasticizing in accordance with our training scale.

In trotting work careful attention to the working pace, as well adapted as possible to the individually appropriate basic tempo, is particularly important and valuable. At the working trot every horse should step with its hind hooves at least completely into the tracks of the fore hooves. If this is not the case in the suppling up phase and relaxation intervals, the problem is due to faults in training. Unfortunately at trot the working tempo is frequently exceeded (this is commonly seen especially in dressage tests at novice level), which ultimately is to the detriment of suppleness and impulsion.

Almost more significantly than at the walk, a lack of straightening is clearly reflected in rhythm faults at the trot, if the horse does not step forward evenly to both reins, for example. In turns this – not infrequently – can even become as serious as "rein-lameness".

Genuine trot extensions, i.e. medium or extended trot, only become possible gradually with improved collection. Only then is it possible to allow the horse to expand its frame appropriately in the extension, only then will it have enough strength, for example to present a medium or extended trot in well-balanced self-carriage and good regular rhythm on the long side or diagonal of the 60-m dressage arena. The improved cadence (a more significantly emphasized and expressive moment of suspension), which is desired at the latest from medium-level classes upwards, e.g. in lateral movements is dependent to a great extent on the horse's natural talent and on an appropriate innate sequence of movement. This talent should be considered as an essential pre-requisite for advanced-level dressage training working towards piaffe and passage. Horses with some disposition for knee action have distinct advantages here.

The canter

After the walk, the canter is the gait most used by horses living free, and usually corresponds very strongly with the walk as far as the sequence and "transmission" are concerned, in other words in the aspects of speed and scope.

It is a sequence of strides in three-beat rhythm, with a moment of suspension between each of these, i.e. "schwunghaft".

The hoof sequence begins with the outside hind leg, then follows the diagonal pair of legs – inside hind leg and outside fore leg simultaneously, followed by the inside fore leg and the moment of suspension.

The following six phases ensue:
- one leg support outside hind leg,
- three leg support outside hind leg together with the diagonal pair of legs inside hind leg and outside fore leg,
- two leg support inside hind leg and outside fore leg,
- three leg support inside hind leg, outside fore leg and inside foreleg,
- one leg support inside fore leg, followed by
- the moment of suspension

Good but not too large scope is required, the hind legs striking off actively and in a lively way.

Good working canter

A horse with very large transmission at canter makes the shortening and collection of the strides more difficult. This will also involve problems regarding handiness for the average dressage rider on the 40-m dressage arena and in the context of jumping. In the show jumping ring horses with this large "transmission" need to be ridden by a very competent rider, particularly also with regard to the ability to find a good distance to jump off. They have to be ridden at a relatively calm pace between the fences, on no account, however, this should be at the expense of the activity and diligence of the hind legs.

The better the horse moves naturally uphill, the better conditions it offers to the rider. The ability to do this is normally linked to the horse's conformation, in other words it is dependent on its "construction" (physical build).

If the horse is supple, particularly in the back, the movement goes through the whole body and the better and more confidently the horse goes forward to both hands, the more easily it can be straightened even at canter. On account of the diagonal sequence of movement going from the outside hind leg to the inner foreleg horses tend to go crooked at a canter on both hands, in order to bring the leg striking off first (outside hind leg) and the leg which strikes off last (inside fore leg) more or less on one line, in the direction of movement.

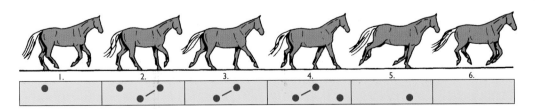

The six phases of the canter

Genuine extensions, as it is the case at trot, require at least a certain degree of collection and can only be of value and controllable if the rider has his horse well on the driving aids, in other words in front of him.

The more naturally balanced the horse is at canter, the easier it is to have good contact and the more confident the self-carriage will be e.g. also in turns.

The nodding movement which is frequently to be observed here is, in contrast to the nodding movement at the medium and extended walk, most definitely not desirable. It leads to the assumption that the horse is not striding up confidently enough to the rider's hand, is not "pulling" (in the positive sense) enough and is thus not in reliable self-carriage.

In spite of all desirability for uphill, the canter should, however, not be too exaggerated in the uphill sequence; the reliable impulse forward is of very fundamental significance, once again, however, this depends very decisively on the suppleness.

On the other hand, too flat a canter also tends to be a disadvantage for a sport horse:

In the case of dressage work the expressive collected canter, e.g. in the case of flying changes, would be made more difficult for horses with such a flat canter, in the context of showjumping these horses are not expected to have such a quick front leg.

Particularly in the disciplines in which speed is decisive, such as jumping and even more so in eventing, the economy of the sequence of movement is also an important criterion.

The four-beat rhythm, which unfortunately can be observed all too often, sometimes people even talk about a "four-beat canter", ensues as a consequence of the diagonal pair of legs no long-

Canter extension in good uphill motion

er landing and striking off simultaneously but rather subsequently to each other. This is usually caused by too strong influence with the hand, particularly the inside hand, as a result of which the inside hind leg is prevented from coming far enough forwards and therefore lands again somewhat more quickly. Also in the case of exaggerated or incorrectly understood collecting work, this fault in regularity can occur because the horse lacks the strength and/or balance required for this work. In extreme cases simultaneous landing of both hind legs can even be observed.

And now for the sake of completion, just a few words on the subject of the rein back.

2.1.3 The rein back

The rein back, of course, is not one of the basic gaits, nevertheless it is by no means an unnatural movement, young horses can be observed doing this movement when they are playing together in the field. The horse always moves a diagonal pair of legs simultaneously.

Crookedness at the canter

Sequence of footfalls in rein-back

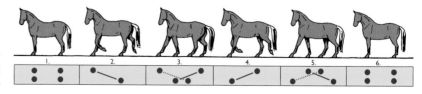

The rein back gives a very good indication of the degree of suppleness and back activity.

When a horse stubbornly refuses, even in hand, to step backwards it may be quite definitely assumed that something – either concerning the training or even the horse's health e.g. with the back – is not in order.

→ Straightening; Riding at walk; Canter work; Extensions; Rein back

2.2 Takt – Rhythmus, Pace (Tempo) – Speed (Gangmaß)

What is the difference between Takt and Rhythmus?
Initially I would like to use the English words regularity and rhythm for these two German equestrian terms (unfortunately the translation for Takt in the Scale of Training is rhythm).

I am sorry to say that frequently these two expressions are either confused or considered to be almost inter-changeable (also by German people).

By Takt we understand in our riding theory the spatial and temporal regularity of the movements in the basic gaits walk, trot, canter as well as in the rein back. This means that the length of the steps and strides within a pace remain constant and also that the speed of the sequence of movement does not change. For example at the working trot one step should have as much ground cover as another and the sequence of movement should remain regular, as if determined by a metronome.

Also in the transitions from one gait to another, e.g. from canter to trot, the canter should be regular through to the last stride and the trot from the first step onwards. The individuality of the basic tempo which obviously varies from horse to horse remains independent of this.

The term rhythm (Rhythmus) by contrast is of interest principally in connection with transitions within a gait and in turns.
Two examples: When lengthening the strides out of the collected trot or canter into medium trot or canter a horse can become more hurried, without making a real mistake in Takt (regularity), in other words without changing the rhythm.

When riding a jumping course, it is very important, for example within a sequence of fences (distance) or a combination, to lengthen or shorten the length of the canter strides so subtly that reliable evenness of rhythm is maintained. If the rider does not succeed in this, it becomes difficult to get the right distance to the next jump, furthermore the horse would also be subjected to unnecessary extra strain, physically as well as psychologically as a result.

Particularly in tighter turns, the rider has to apply the driving aids to ensure that the horse does not – unintentionally – come back too much, or even begin to hesitate, but rather canters on confidently in even rhythm. Only in this way is it possible, to ride on accurately to the next fence without any loss of impulsion and time.

Naturally there are also situations in which the Takt (regularity) as well as also the rhythm are disturbed. For example, turning on a diagonal within a jumping course it is possible that problems may arise in the Takt and rhythm if the rider does not have the horse well enough on the driving aids, in other words in front of him, and instead rides the turns incorrectly with the rein-aids.

What is the difference between pace (Tempo) and speed (Gangmaß)?
In German equestrian language there are very precise definitions for these individual terms. Unfortunately these have sunk partially into oblivion or tend to be confused, which is to the detriment of accuracy. In English – particularly on account of the many different countries where English is spoken – however, such a distinction does not exist in the first place. (This section may therefore be superfluous for the English-speaking reader because the nature of the confusion and equivalence discussed applies specifically to the German language:)
A typical example for this are the two terms pace (Tempo) and speed (Gangmaß) which are

Good ground-covering walk, stretched well forward-downward, the slight poll control required for walk "on long reins" is, however, lacking.

sometimes treated as synonyms or are confused in their application.

By pace (Tempo) we mean the differently ridden step and stride lengths within the three basic gaits, e.g. in the trot – working trot, collected trot, medium and extended trot. Naturally this also includes the appropriate frame and degree of collection in each case. It has nothing to do with the actual speed which the horse develops in the process. When judging a horse on the basis of speed (Gangmaß), two aspects are to be considered.

One is the ground cover or scope, we could also say the "transmission" within a pace (Tempo), e.g. the working trot. The other aspect is the frequency, in other words (the tempo (Geschwindigkeit) of) the frequency of movement. This can vary quite considerably from horse to horse and it is important to find as perfect a tempo as possible for the individual horse in question, particularly in the working trot or medium walk. The horse should be brought on to a good degree of suppleness. It is also a question of this frequency of sequence of movement when we talk about the individually suitable basic tempo.

The combination of the two means that two horses which are both trotting at a working pace, which is ideal for each of them individually, will move forward at different velocity.

This can best be explained on the basis of an example:

When a trainer separates a group into classes, he also has to stipulate an order within these. In this context, in addition to the level of training or the riders and horses concerned, the size, possibly also the colour and attractiveness of the latter, plays a role. When selecting the head horse, however, its speed (Gangmaß), particularly in the gaits used most often when riding in classes, the working trot and working canter, should be the decisive criterion. For a well-ridden sequence with well-kept distances for example, the actual velocity in each case is of particular significance. For this reason the horse which is most suitable is certainly the one which has a medium speed as compared with the others, in other words at working trot is neither too "fast" for the horses with smaller "transmission" nor too "slow" for those with larger transmission.

Unfortunately in common usage speed (Gangmaß) and pace (Tempo) are frequently treated as synonyms. This, however, is incorrect because in the language of the riding theory the different pace descriptions, such as working, collected, medium and extended trot, for example, are indeed not intended to express the different velocity – which may actually vary somewhat – but rather they are intended to communicate the different ground cover or scope, frame and/or degree of collection.

2.3 Riding at walk: "Don't touch me!"?

Although the walk is the first of the basic gaits and is normally done at the beginning and end of every training unit, very often at a walk horses are more or less allowed to go as they please. They are almost always ridden with loose reins which are usually not shortened and taken until immediately before trotting on. This, however, means a loss of valuable time which could be used in a more effective way for the training of horse and rider. Particularly in the case of horses which have an especially long "transmission" in the walk and step over very far, many people think that any riding at walk with contact, in other words on the bit, must be damaging and have a detrimental effect on the walk. Provided the rider knows what he is doing and has learned to ride with understanding and feeling, this is not correct, however.

In the following I should like to explain how the rider can and indeed should influence the sequence of movement of his horse.

Anyone who is unsure whether they know enough about the basic gait walk should refer back to the chapter "Basic Gaits" and refresh his knowledge there before continuing.

The walk is a marching movement in four-beat rhythm, which always involves an alternating three-leg or two-leg support phase, it therefore has no moment of suspension. This is often described as without impulsion ("schwunglos") as compared to the basic gaits with impulsion ("schwunghaft"), i.e. trot and canter. Unfortunately this expression conveys a rather incorrect impression of slowness or lack of sufficient activity, although at walk, just as the other basic gaits, the appropriate activity and liveliness is a very important criterion.

2.3.1 Riding at walk

The walk is the basic gait in which tensions, in other words a lack of suppleness – also on the basis of psychological problems, are reflected in the first place. This, for example can also be recognized by the fact that very frequently in dressage tests one and the same horse shows a significantly better walk after completing its test than during the test when it knows that demanding collected movements usually follow the walk section.

It is important to take careful note of this knowledge and to use it in daily work: also at walk, particularly in the suppling work, it is of decisive importance that the rider finds and chooses the right individual basic tempo for the horse in question. He will only succeed in doing this if

he has the appropriate concentration right from the beginning and is prepared to have his personal chat – which can sometimes get rather out of proportion – with the trainer or other riders either before or after, but not during the session. Unfortunately in these first minutes many riders ride in pairs or even more alongside each other. This automatically forces the horses to go at the same tempo, therefore there is always one which has to move more slowly and the other has to hurry more. The same applies with regard to riding in a class (Abteilung – i.e. 3 or 4 riders separated by a specific distance), which is why the walk interludes should either be kept relatively short or it should be ridden with a considerably longer distance between the horses.

The driving aids at the walk are applied to the horse's sides in alternation, according to the sequence of movement of the hind legs. On no account, however, the rider should try to apply pressure with his legs, alternating between left and right at every step, rather, from a supple, correct seat, he must apply the calf of his leg calmly to the horse's side. He will then feel how the ribcage curves slightly more to the left and right in alternation, and in this way he will drive in the right rhythm to a certain extent automatically. The rider only has to give a driving impulse when the activity and diligence of the walk subsides. This impulse, however, should be applied decisively and precisely, possibly even with the spurs; the desired forward reaction of the horse has to be allowed by means of the rider accompanying the horse accordingly in the movement (by sitting a little forward) and becoming light

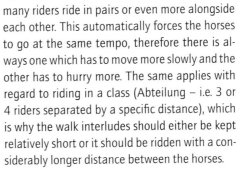

A supple walk with completely given reins

Also at ◄ walk, particularly in the suppling work, it is of decisive importance that the rider finds and chooses the right individual basic tempo for the horse in question.

in the hand. If the horse is sensitive enough to the leg aids, it is quite sufficient to take the lower leg or even the whole leg away from the horse's side a little and apply it again gently (renewing the leg) (> Illustration p. 26) in order to achieve more active marching again.

In the case of horses which tend to rush, either on account of over-eagerness or due to a lack of composure, the rider should never attempt to counteract this by pulling on the reins as this will make the horse feel constrained. Instead the rider must think about sitting supply, elastically and driving gently and steadily in order to encourage a calmer tempo. Often in such cases it is a good idea to make frequent brief stops in order to get the horse to reflect somewhat and then to ride on again calmly.

And now to the question of contact whilst riding at walk: Riding with loose reins at walk only makes sense and is correct if the surroundings and also the mental state of the horse permit a relaxed marching in regular rhythm with a convex top line. However even then it is recommendable to take up the reins soon and feel with the hand to the horse's mouth. If contact to the horse's mouth is taken up with sufficient feeling and, thanks to good suppleness and elasticity in the shoulder and elbow joint, the correctly positioned upright hand with constant, light connection, can permit or "join in" the nodding movement, the horse will step into the bit trustingly and step over farther forward with the hind legs. The better the horse has gained confidence in the rider's hand in this unconstrained work at a walk, the more willing it will be, with a yielding poll, to drop the neck. Naturally attention has to be paid to ensure that the horse does not come too deep here and that it does not try to use the contact as something to lean on, as this would restrict the free stepping of the forelegs out of the shoulder.

In the case of horses which are very interested in everything around them and particularly like to have a good look at their surroundings especially at the beginning, the rider should not try to completely forbid this right from the start. Such horses have to learn that they can look at everything and take it in but at the same time they have to keep going forwards. Such a procedure produces advantages in further training, also in a competition context. **As the willingness to perform and sensitivity of horses is usually also connected with greater powers of perception and receptiveness to outside influences, they are usually also more easily distracted. Therefore if the rider wants to maintain and make use of the former characteristics, he must also learn to handle the other ones and to direct them in the right way.**

This riding at a walk on a long rein is also quite consciously recommended and required in the first competitions for young (three and four year old) riding horses because this is the way in which the quality of the walk can best be shown. In demanding dressage tests at medium and advanced levels this fact is often confirmed. It is by no means rare for horses to show less ground cover in the extended walk than previously in the medium walk if the rider incorrectly believes that he has to give the reins too much at the extended walk.

If through riding at a walk on a long rein horses have got to know contact as something pleasant and supportive, rather than as something restrictive (backward influence) and constraining, this also facilitates the work in the other gaits and in the collected movements. Then a horse later, for example when shortening the walk before a turn on the haunches or a walk pirouette will continue to march forward actively, "pull" positively instead of hesitating, which unfortunately can very frequently be observed, it will also keep the four-beat rhythm better in the turn. When, for example, the rider gives half halts before cantering on, the horse will remain calm and not fidget (jog) or anticipate.

In the case of serious horse training, riding in stretch position is always done at the beginning, at the end and also in the recuperation breaks during the lesson unit; this not only serves for re-

➢ Suppleness refers to the physical as well as the mental state of the horse.

laxation, reward or recuperation, but rather particularly for the improvement and strengthening of the entire trunk extensor muscle system, thus particularly the upper neck and back muscles. As there is usually still something to be desired in this respect, it would be a pity not to use the time of riding at a walk for this purpose. Within a few days of correct training of this aspect, every horse can learn to accept this kind of work at walk, to step willingly into the bit whilst at the same time yielding at the poll and always to chew the rein which is adjusted again out of the hand (the rider has to take and to give the reins). Valuable training of the muscle system mentioned takes place as a result, at the same time the horse will also be positively conditioned as far as contact is concerned. In the relaxation phase at the end of a work unit this, however, also prevents the back which has – hopefully – become very supple during the session, from tensing up again immediately because on account of the loose reins, the horse, with its head raised to a greater or lesser extent, makes the back hollow.

The young rider can learn this work best on a "schoolmaster" horse which goes correctly and in this way by feeling and going with the nodding movement, do a lot for his hand position and in particular benefit with regard to the independence of his hand from the seat. Vice versa the young horse or horse requiring correction can only be familiarized properly with this extremely valuable work by an experienced rider who has learned all these things correctly. If this constellation is not possible, a young, fairly talented rider on an unspoiled young horse can be helped by a good trainer.

Naturally there are also very well-known and experienced trainers who quite consciously ride themselves or ask pupils to ride with loose reins at the beginning and end of a training unit, sometimes also in a walk break. This, however, only makes sense and is of value if – thanks to good training experiences – the horse in question is trusting in the rider's hand completely and has been worked in such a way for a long time so

Working trot with good suppleness, the horse could, however, push off more energetically and swing through better.

that it drops the neck and moves with an curved, convex top line. If, on the other hand, in the walk breaks or at the end of the session, the horse raises its head, relieved, the moment contact is released, even walking on the long rein will not help very much. Rather the work as a whole must be done differently, in particular with less constraint.

➔ **Suppleness of the rider; basic gaits**

3. Suppleness (Losgelassenheit) – First and Final Aim in the Training of a Riding Horse

3.1 What do we understand by suppleness?

Suppleness refers to the physical as well as the mental state of the horse. From a physical point of view, by suppleness we understand the most economical use possible of the entire locomotor system without any tension or cramping, whereby the back must always be considered the central area.

As mentally supple, we consider a horse which is experiencing pleasure in working to-

3. ➢ Suppleness

Stretched well forward-down-ward at trot

Good, supple working canter with enough scope

gether with the rider (freedom of anxiety) and **is relaxed and at the same time concentrated in the task it is performing.**

The physical and mental aspects together form the prerequisite for optimum ability as well as willingness to perform. Progress in training, for example in connection with muscle development and learning, also becomes possible as a result.

3.2 The significance of suppleness

Every rider and trainer who is seriously concerned about riding in a horse-friendly way knows about the fundamental significance of suppleness. Therefore the question constantly occurs in connection with our training scale of why suppleness is only listed in second position. The fact that in daily training it has to be seen as of at least equal importance to rhythm is beyond any doubt. Nevertheless it is perfectly justified for rhythm (Takt) to be in first position in our riding theory:

Also for the competent expert, e.g. trainer or judge, it is easier to judge objectively whether a horse moves rhythmically/regularly in every ex-

ercise, movement or other task imposed on it in all three basic gaits. The maintenance of the reliable four-beat, two-beat and three-beat rhythm in walk, trot and canter always has to be the highest criterion in training. When rhythm/regularity problems occur, this should always be a clear and immediate warning for the rider and/or trainer that something is wrong. In this way the initial stages of suppleness problems can be recognized even earlier because they are often reflected in rhythm/regularity problems.

Supling work with the horse must be done anew every day at the beginning of every riding sessions and every work unit. It is only through a reasonable and individually structured suppling phase that the horse – as well as the rider of course – attains its full ability and also willingness to perform. Therefore this phase is an indispensable prerequisite for any successful work. For this reason it is important, even on days when little time is available, not to make any compromises here in order to gain more time for the work phase.

In the case of a young horse which is at the beginning of its training as a riding horse, it is indeed the very aim of every work session to bring the horse into good balance and suppleness, also together with the rider.

As the two terms ability to perform and willingness to perform already imply, the physical and the mental aspect are of equal importance here. In practice the two are inseparable:

- **If a horse does not get a chance to bring its circulation into "operational frequency" (to get its circulation going properly), to warm up its muscle system accordingly, to make its joints with their cartilages more elastic and therefore able to take more strain as well as to "run up" its entire metabolism, or if it is restricted in its movement on account of any health problems, or is even suffering pain, it will certainly also not be mentally capable of good suppleness, in other words not be able to attain its full willingness to perform.**
- **Vice versa, a horse which – due to lack of confidence in the rider – in his hand or due to bad experience, possibly even becomes afraid when the saddle is put on its back, will hardly be able to become mentally supple, even simply on account of the cramped breathing this causes.**

In daily work, even during the working phase, it is not possible to demand a consistently high level physical and mental performance. This is why the good rider or trainer will always try to be aware of the state of the horse and, by means of appropriate exercises, check to find out whether the horse is still able to move in a relaxed and supple way. For this reason little breaks for recuperation have to be made approximately every 5-10 minutes. The more demanding the performance being required, with regard to collection for example, the easier it becomes for the necessary positive tension to become negative and the horse to cramp up.

In the little breaks mentioned it is possible – but not necessary – to ride just at a walk. The decisive point is that the horse has the opportunity to relax physically as well as mentally, in order then to be all the more able and willing to perform afterwards. Always to find the right point for this, and not to wait to react until after the horse has started to lose concentration or even become unwilling, requires good feeling, experience and self-discipline and is one of the decisive points which distinguishes really good riders.

Particularly in the case of horses which, by nature, are very willing to perform, the situation frequently arises that too much is demanded of them at a time, that the right measure of strain for them is not found. Tenseness, however, leads to premature tiredness and therefore has a restricting effect on the ability to perform. Furthermore, it has a negative effect on the horse's wellbeing and can even cause pain, which naturally restricts its ability to perform as a consequence and the horse then has considerably less pleasure in working together with the rider.

Unless this is reacted to immediately and measures are taken to reduce the tension, serious – and even permanent – damage can ensue. In a tense muscle system the blood does not circulate properly and therefore the metabolism also cannot function as required so that, instead of strengthening a weakness, it can actually lead to disintegration of the muscles in question.

Moving in a tensed up way on the more longterm, e.g. with tense steps, which may in fact even look very spectacular, leads to excess strain on the locomotor system and damage, particularly of the joints.

And the psychological defects which can be caused by such incorrect training are almost more serious. Unfortunately it is not such an infrequent occurrence for horses to "lose their nerve" as a result and their willingness to perform is restricted on the long-term or even for ever as a result. Particularly the mental aspect of suppleness requires a well thought-out training plan which is regularly controlled, also by the rider's feeling.

This means: it is not only a question of paying heed to this imposing and relieving strain in in-

> ➢ **The more variety that is offered here, the greater the success will be and the more valuable it is particularly for the mental state of the horse (and rider).**

be tried out. In any case it should take place in the form of many transitions with (particularly in the case of horses with large canter transmission) not too long canter repeats. In this context active, lively forward movement can be encouraged right from the beginning, nevertheless each canter stride has to be controlled.

• From the first minute onwards attention has to be paid correctly and with consideration to the horse's natural crookedness, which has to be dealt with appropriately. The experienced rider and trainer will do this almost automatically without giving much extra thought to the matter.

The following exercises and movements, in my experience, are particularly suitable for achieving suppleness:
• simple transitions walk-trot-walk and trot-canter-trot
• full halts from walk
• large, especially curved and circular tracks, such as circle, simple serpentine loops along the long side
• serpentine loops through the arena (old form), 3 or 4 loops (40-m arena)
• extending and shortening steps and strides
• leg-yielding on the long side
• turn on the forehand (less valuable for the horse)
• riding into and out of the circle (in contrast to reducing and enlarging the circle, this is ridden on one track)

and with more advanced horses and riders:
• leg-yielding away from and back to the track
• reducing (in travers-like movement) and enlarging (in shoulder-in-like movement) the circle
• stepping over (leg-yielding) on the open side of the circle
• change through the circle
• figure of eight
• shoulder-fore and riding in position

Naturally the suppling work need not and indeed should not always take place in an enclosed arena or indoor school, not even for dressage horses. The more variety is offered here, the greater the success will be and the more valuable it is particularly for the mental state of the horse (and rider).

In this context there is one possibility which I feel is particularly worthy of mention, and this is riding in the light seat. Especially also in the case of particularly sensitive horses with a rather fine back, this is not only a wonderful method of doing the rising trot for a longer period, it is also a good idea to start cantering work in the light (forward-)seat. In order to relieve the horse's back, the rider leans forward slightly out of the hips. Consequently the balance changes somewhat for horse and rider. Therefore the rider must be experienced and well-balanced in this type of seat in order to be able to achieve a positive outcome. He must nevertheless still keep his point of gravity close to the horse, be in a position to hold and apply his hands independently of the seat and be able to keep his horse reliably in front of him.

Other possibilities are:
• hacking out
• hill-work (gently up- and downhill)
• climbing
• cavaletti work
• jumping gymnastics
• work on the lunge etc.

In some cases it may make sense to lunge first of all. The value of work on the lunge should not be over-rated however. Moving constantly on a curved track can easily lead to wrong or excess strain being imposed on the locomotor system, particularly when the ground conditions are not ideal and lunging is done on a small circle.

No-one should believe that good work on the lunge is easier to learn or do than riding.

As horses, by their very nature, are herd animals, it is a great advantage if several horses can work together in daily riding.

3.7 How do you recognize a supple horse?

For the rider and attentive observer there are many signs which are a very certain indication of a horse's degree of suppleness; every genuine horseman will want to take careful note of these and sharpen his awareness of them:

- the contented facial expression (eyes, ear movements, upper and lower lips),
- the good activity of the mouth (closed, but not pulled tight by the noseband, chewing calmly with light foam formation),
- contented gentle snorting, not excited puffing and blowing,
- an actively swinging back, movements going through the whole body so that the rider is taken along better with the horse and can sit well; at walk (except collected walk) the clear nodding movement forwards-downwards,
- the relaxed, swinging tail,
- the increasing throughness, particularly also in transitions, without phases of tenseness (passage trot)) when reducing to a slower tempo from trot extensions,
- the willingness to drop the neck at any time and take up the stretch position,
- the ability to show the working pace at any time,
- the horse's behaviour at walk is particularly indicative: consistent regularity of movement, the horse's willingness to stretch, the supple, genuine nodding movement (forward-downward) and the involvement of the whole body, including the back in the sequence of movement.

3.8 Summary

First of all a rather critical – but also perhaps thought-provoking – comment:

Anyone attending a normal horse show nowadays who takes a critical look at the horses competing there and tries to assess their suppleness and freedom from constraint will realise that it is not possible to award many good marks. Really good, competent work in this respect is not often to be seen, even at the beginning of warm up riding in the practice area. Nevertheless, the majority of horses are quite obedient and confident in the movements.

It sounds almost paradoxical to make the excellent average quality of our modern riding horses responsible for this situation. Nevertheless, it is indeed the case that much less talented horses, which had not been specifically bred for good rideability, as were widespread 40 or 50 years ago forced riders and trainers to much more attention to suppleness and to work over the back; otherwise such horses would very quickly lose their pleasure in working together and put an end to their collaboration.

By contrast, our modern warmblood horses, usually highly moulded by thoroughbred, have such quality of movement and willingness to perform that, even with a stiff back and little inner suppleness, they are still able to move amazingly actively and expressively. **The real state of affairs, however, becomes very clear to the competent and interested observer when he looks carefully at where the hind legs step, whether they really swing through in a forward direction, and when he looks into the horse's face and onto its mouth.**

At the beginning of this chapter on the subject of suppleness some consideration was given to its position on the scale of training, and now at this point we may conclude that any dispute about this is senseless. Training of a horse is such a complex matter that a classification of this is indeed theoretically possible and valuable for the sake of understanding, in order to be successful in the practical implementation, however, it is essential to have good knowledge and good understand-

Horse with mouth chewing contentedly

➢ **A young horse needs an experienced rider and an inexperienced rider needs a sufficiently trained and settled horse!**

ing of the mutual dependences and connections in order to be able to take a holistic approach.

Therefore I should like to repeat once again the demand from the foreword of our Principles of Riding Volume I.:

A young horse needs an experienced rider and an inexperienced rider needs a sufficiently trained and settled horse!

Suppleness is not only of elementary significance at the beginning of every work unit and in fundamental basic training. Anyone who would like to ride well in a horse-friendly way, also in order to have a horse which remains physically and mentally healthy on the long-term, which – irrespective of the equestrian level – presents itself willing to perform, free of constraint, lively and "attractive", will always – at the beginning of every riding session, during the work phase and subsequently in the recuperation phase – pay due attention to good suppleness.

➔ Riding at walk, Chewing the reins out of the rider's hands, Breaking-in

Stretched position, forehead nose line slightly behind the vertical, but nevertheless acceptable

4. Contact – A Matter of Trust

Contact as the third point on the training scale is indeed one of the most frequently misunderstood training aims. It fundamentally means the constant, soft and elastic connection between the rider's hand and the horse's mouth, initially irrespective of the frame.

Only when, by means of appropriate training, the horse has learned, also under the rider, to move in a well-balanced, more closed and also slightly elevated way, can it take up the carriage of a riding horse, the so-called "Beizäumung", that means a posture with a round outline (well arched neck and yielding poll). At the same time the horse also gains in self-carriage and the connection to the hand becomes increasingly lighter.

Such connection only comes about, however, when in training the rider always allows himself to be guided by the concept that the hand, in other words the restraining rein aids, may only be the counterpart for the driving weight and leg aids. Therefore he always has to aim to achieve this desired carriage by maintaining the horse's pleasure in working with the rider, by encouraging the thrust and optimising the mutual balance together with the rider so that, with a yielding poll, the horse steps trustingly onto the bit / hand and seeks the contact. He should, however, never try to use compulsion or strength – possibly involving draw reins or a double bridle – to force this.

To train a horse in such a way requires good balance and suppleness on the part of the rider. Only then is he in a position to fine tune his driving and restraining aids to suit each other and, above all, to apply his hands completely independently of his seat. He should offer and allow contact, but not mislead his horse in the process into looking for the so-called fifth leg, in other words leaning on the reins.

A horse with correct contact may be recognized by

- **the external posture: upper neck line evenly arched, brow-nose line as much as possible slightly ahead of the vertical[1], neck in no way short or narrow, poll highest point (in the case of a horse at a more advanced stage of training),**
- **good mouth activity: slight chewing, gently closed mouth and slight formation of foam**

---

[1] In phases, in which horses are consciously ridden in a slightly lower position, e.g. during suppling up, the brow-nose line occasionally comes somewhat behind the vertical. That should not lead to the horse going behind the bit or leaning on it.

on the relaxed, gently closed mouth and slight foaming on uncramped lips in natural position,

- appropriate throughness; this can be tested, for example, by demanding simple transitions[1] and by letting the horse chew the reins out of the rider's hand; only a horse which is in reliable contact, in other words well on the driving aids, stretches calmly and contentedly forwards-downwards at the end of the test. [2]

Riding with reins in one hand is not required in competitions at the present time, apart from the salute. In freestyle tests some riders also present short repeats holding the reins in one hand, which increases the level of difficulty and emphasizes the horse's good degree of throughness. Previously more attention used to be given to this method of holding the reins, in the cavalry and mounted police, in order to keep the right hand free for hand signals, to salute, to carry a standard or flag, to lead a second horse or to use a weapon. After all, this was also the reason why the usual way of holding the reins with a double bridle was 3:1 ("three reins in the left, one in the right hand"), in order to be able to change as easily as possible to reins in one hand.

Naturally when holding the reins in one hand, this hand – the left one – must be positioned centrally in front of the rider's body, directly over the withers.

Also in normal riding training, it is worthwhile to take the reins into one hand from time to time, and indeed to do this alternately – sometimes into the left hand and sometimes the right. This can be done very well in connection with letting the horse chew the reins out of the rider's hand at the end of the supling phase, in every little break for interim relaxation and in the recuperation phase at the end of the training unit.

Particularly in the case of horses which are

This very low head position neither promotes the activity of the back nor the swinging through of the hind legs; most horses tense up in the process and come on the forehand.

very sensitive in the mouth and light in the poll, and therefore tend to become too light in the contact, indeed even to go somewhat behind the bit, it can be very helpful to take both reins into the outside hand and to praise the horse with the inside hand on both sides of the neck. As the rider has less strength with one hand, however in particular no longer has the possibility to move the bit to and fro in the horse's mouth, the horse usually immediately steps forward better onto the hand and comes slightly ahead of the vertical (> Illustration page 40).

4.1 Faults in contact

Unfortunately a wide variety of different faults frequently occur in the work. Ideally of course, on the basis of good knowledge and riding ability should be prevented and avoided in the first place. When contact problems occur, however, it is important to recognize them already in the initial stages and, if possible, start to correct them immediately. Otherwise serious physical as well as psychological problems can result.

As usually more or less fundamental faults of the rider are at least part of the cause here, it is

---

[1] By simple transitions we mean: walk-trot-walk, trot-canter-trot.
[2] Also in the stretch position the horse has to step onto the hand. If the connection becomes too light or the horse comes behind the bit, the activity of the hind legs gets lost (> Page 158/9).

4. ➤ Contact

Even going slightly behind the vertical, as is the case here, should only be accepted at the most for a very brief period.

well as keeping the hands completely independent of the seat (out of a supple shoulder- and elbow-joint). On no account should he become stiff or blocked in the arm (elbow and shoulder) as a result of his efforts to hold his hands still. This would cause a flapping rein, which is naturally also not in the interests of good contact. Equally wrong, indeed counter-productive in this connection would be the wish to hold up a horse which comes too low by means of raising the hands.

In the correcting work the first step is to re-establish the horse's confidence in the rider's hand. A good recommendation here is to ride more suppling exercises in stretch position (more often the reins in one hand!). Energetic canter work, particularly in the natural countryside, and lunging with relatively long side reins have also proved successful here.

If driving on to the elastic hand held deep does not bring about sufficient success, it can also on an occasion be correct to give a "provocative halt", as I call it. For this the rider gives a driving impulse with weight (stomach muscles tensing!) and leg to a non-yielding or even taking and yielding hand, which is still held low. If the horse reacts to this impulse in the desired way, and steps forward more onto the hand, then the rider must clearly yield, possibly even lean slightly forward, in order to give the horse a positive reward for reacting in the desired way, but not sit behind the movement and hang in the reins.

In individual cases it also helps if the rider makes this carriage uncomfortable for a horse going behind the bit by means of increased taking and non-yielding in order, however, to become lighter with the hand as soon as the horse shows its willingness to step forward onto the hand better again.

Horses with a very fine, sensitive mouth and/or with a very light poll are particularly prone to this fault. This is why only experienced riders with fine-tuned application of the aids and very skilful hands can do justice to such horses, particularly when it is a question of their training or correction.

important for the rider to check his seat and correct it – if necessary with the help of a trainer. A genuine and lasting correction of the contact fault will only be possible if the rider improves and corrects himself first of all. Otherwise he will hardly be in a position to improve the horse again himself (> also Part 1, Chapter 4. "Instinctively – correct?")

Parallel to looking for causes with the rider, consideration should also be given as to whether any changes how the horse is kept, relating to its equipment or health in general may also be contributing to the problem. Mouth and teeth problems in particular, immediately restrict the horse in stepping confidently onto the bit.

• **Behind the bit**

A horse going behind the bit is not only behind the vertical with its brow-nose line, it also no longer steps onto the bit properly. It evades the rein aids in a backward direction as a result of exaggerated yielding in the poll or "by tipping down" so that it can hardly be controlled or accept the half halts; this is also described as "hiding behind the bit or curling".

The most frequent cause of this is a rider's hand which is too hard, not calm and still enough or held too high. Therefore the rider particularly has to ensure that he keeps his hands in a calm, elastic and correct position, i.e. carefully observing the straight line - elbow-hand-horse's mouth, as

A good method also to prevent this problem or to deal with it, if it already exists, is to ride with the reins in one hand and to let the other hand hang down or use it to praise the horse (> box page 125). Horses usually then immediately step forward better onto the bit.

• **Behind the vertical**

As the expression already indicates, the horse moves with its brow-nose line behind the vertical, however without evading the contact and going behind the bit. Nevertheless it is important to avoid this mistake because the position the horse takes up will restrict the activity of the back so that the hind legs can no longer swing through in an optimum way, and because the shortened neck means the horse is restricted in its balance.

Providing this fault is only to be observed occasionally and to a minimal extent, the reason for it is usually only a fleeting fault in the application of the aids: if the rider has temporarily exercised too strong or too long non-yielding influence with his hands, and at the same time not had it enough on the driving aids, i.e. had his horse in front of him. In such a case it usually helps, to give a correct (i.e. with all aids), somewhat clearer half halt, whereby particularly the immediate yielding is decisive. For this purpose the hand actually has to go forward somewhat, the reins may even have to be lengthened slightly.

If this fault occurs to a greater extent, more frequently or even continuously in collecting work, there is certainly a fundamental mistake in the training. This usually begins with the rider trying to pursue too quickly with collection, in the process paying too little attention in the coordination of the aids to the absolutely essential domination of the driving aids and holding too much and too firmly with the hand or even exerting a backwards effect. Horses which particularly enjoy working together with the rider and are naturally willing to perform sometimes induce the rider into doing this, particularly as – thanks to their wonderful conformation and interior qualities – they can nevertheless still move surprisingly actively and expressively.

False "longitudinal flexion", – poll not the highest point of the neck

"Strong" riders sometimes even risk this deficiency in order to disguise a lack of training or lack of movement potential. The competent observer is not to be deceived by this, however; he recognises the poor swinging through of the hind legs and the unsatisfactory self-carriage of the horse.

Particularly horses with well-constructed necks and fine gullets can very easily come behind the vertical and become rather short and therefore particular attention is to be accorded to this point in their training.

• **Broken neckline (poll is not the highest point of the neck)**

A broken neckline describes the situation when the highest point of the horse is no longer between the ears, i.e. in the poll, but considerably further back, roughly between the third and fourth cervical vertebra. Thus the upper neck line is no longer evenly arched, but is rather "broken". This fault occurs principally in connection with one of the two contact problems mentioned above.

It usually comes about when the rider – due to a wrong concept of contact and longitudinal flexing ("Beizäumung") – tries to force the horse into apparently elevated carriage mainly with the hands and reins. The horse tries to come to terms with this compulsion in the upper part of the neck, however it cannot open and drop the neck out of the shoulder and thus also cannot

The horse leaning on the reins, is not yielding at the poll and opens its mouth.

become supple in the back. If this fault is not dealt with immediately, an extremely negative training effect ensues. The lower neck muscles become increasingly strengthened whilst the upper neck and back muscles become cramped and even waste away (atrophy).

Horses which are of rather horizontal conformation and have a low-set neck are unfortunately incorrectly treated this way quite frequently because their qualities and possibilities due to this not having been recognized properly.

In order to counteract the "broken neckline", the rider has to drive forwards decisively with elastic hands, independent of the seat, thus with optimally coordinated application of the aids prevent over-hurried forwards movement and the faults in regularity which this involves. Here the aim must be to give the horse so much stretch and frame that it can arch its upper neck line evenly again. The horse's confidence in the rider's hand has to be re-established so that (half) halts, even on a long rein, become possible again. Frequent "chewing the reins out of the hand" in all three gaits is particularly helpful. Initially work should be done mainly with the horse positioned lower, in reliable forwards-downwards.

• Leaning on the bit
Here the horse leans on the bit as a kind of support, it looks for the so-called "fifth leg". Consequently the rider has a lot in his hands, in particular, however, it shows that the horse is not willing, perhaps also not able, to close in with the hind legs and take up the load.

This fault is due to a lack of, or incorrectly applied, driving aids, usually in connection with a stiff hand (non-elastic arm). Inexperienced but physically strong riders with relatively long levers either do not notice at all, or notice too late, how – often due to an incorrect understanding of contact – they really offer this "fifth leg" to the horse. This can be avoided by riding more with the concept

Even if the noseline appears to be correct here, this horse is resisting the hand and tensing up in the back so therefore it can not swing through with the hind legs.

of the hand just being a counterpart for the driving aids and of the giving or becoming light at the right moment being the most important rein aid.

In addition to decisive, rhythmical forward driving with a feelingly yielding hand, all exercises which mobilise the hindquarters and encourage the horse to more self-carriage can be helpful with this problem, for example: trotting from the spot, cantering on from walk, lengthening and getting back in trot and canter or full halts, whereby in the full halts the driving aids always have to prevail and the rein aids must be applied in as short and precise a way as possible.

Even the slightest attempt on the part of the horse to lean, has to be responded to with a decisive half halt, whereby of course the driving aids are important, but also the taking may have to be done quite heartily and energetically but briefly, followed immediately by clear giving.

This fault occurs more easily in the case of horses which are of rather horizontal built or even those which stand with their quarters rather too high (downhill); particularly if they have a less sensitive mouth and/or are less light in the poll.

• Above the bit / against the bit

Horses which go above or against the bit find themselves significantly in front of the vertical, do not yield in the poll and move with tense lower neck muscles as well as a stiff back.

Accordingly, it is important to place particular emphasis on supplying work on large curved tracks in an energetic but in no way exaggerated basic tempo. In the case of horses which tend to have this fault on the basis of back problems lunging work with relatively long side reins (initially also with running side reins on the girth) is highly recommendable. In working with such a horse the rider should try under no circumstances to force the horse's head down with the reins held too low, or use a German standing martingale. Both methods would only provoke increased counter-pressure and therefore strengthen the lower neck muscles. The rider has to drive strongly into the non-yielding hand in order to get the horse to push itself off the bit and yield in the poll. If it then, even just slightly, yields and begins to drop the neck, the rider must confirm this to the horse immediately by becoming correspondingly light and show that the lower position is more pleasant. The position of the hand in this situation is always determined by the horse's carriage on account of the straight line elbow-hand-horse's mouth. The driving should be done principally by the legs; a "heavy" sitting into the horse even with leaning back, is normally counter-productive. It is not until the horse has found the way into the stretch position and has noticed that the movement, also under the rider, is easier as a result, will it yield in the poll and generally cooperate with more composure, instead of fighting against the rider. In this work on curved tracks the sideways-leading rein aid with the inner hand can indeed be helpful, under no circumstances however the nose should be pulled around with the inner rein (possibly with the hand across the crest), as this could only lead to a false impression of success.

As in the case of all training faults, faster correction results will be achieved if action is taken to remedy the fault before a horse has been moving incorrectly for long enough to develop muscle deficits or malformations.

In the case of a horizontally constructed horse with slightly lower set neck, the low positioning in stretch position is not to be exaggerated; the nose should not come much lower than the point of the shoulder. Otherwise the horse comes too much onto the forehand ("on the head"), which only makes active stepping off and swinging through of the hind legs more difficult.

As going in stretch position is to some degree assured, all exercises are indicated which promote the activity of the hind legs and the self-carriage (see above).

4.2 Stiff and difficult side

A problem which is particularly connected with straightening, should be mentioned at least briefly at this point, the problem of the so-called stiff and difficult (hollow) side:

The majority of horses are more difficult to flex and bend on the left due to crookedness on the right side, as a result of which many riders are mislead into wanting to work principally more on the left rein.

It is, however, very important to try to encourage such a horse increasingly to accept and "trust" the right rein, by means of increased driving with the left leg to the right rein and by alternately leading sideways and becoming light on the left rein.

The difficult side here, and this description in itself makes the situation easier to understand, would be considered the right side, on which the horse falls out with the hindquarters, and tries to make itself concave in the turns and on which sufficient ability to stretch is lacking. (for more information see chapter Straightening!)

4.3 Notes on correction of faults in contact

The value of variety in the organisation of training should actually not just be recognized and accorded attention after faults have already occurred. Particularly however also when it is a

As in the ◄ case of all training faults, faster correction results will be achieved if action is taken to remedy the fault before a horse has been moving incorrectly for long enough to develop muscle deficits or malformations.

Tongue
positioner

a higher inner hand and increased strength as this would make the horse short in the neck and make bending in the neck without becoming tilted in the poll even more difficult. The outside, i.e. left hand, may be taken slightly to the left, away from the shoulder, in this guarding function so that the left rein continues to lead straight to the mouth in an unbroken line, even when the horse starts to bend in the neck as required. This resolute flexing must be followed as quickly as possible by becoming light with both reins, in order to reward the horse positively for what is hopefully a positive reaction to this aid.

According to the principle "Ride your horse forward and straighten it!", attention has to be paid to good, lively activity during this work. So that the horse also accepts the right bending in the ribs, as already mentioned, the right well forward driving rider's leg has to ensure that the horse does not push to the right with its shoulder, the rider's left leg has to make sure that the horse does not push away with the hindquarters and try to evade the bending aids.

In the entire work it is important not to overdo the amount of work on the right rein. When riding on the left rein care always has to be taken to ensure reliable contact, also on the left inside rein. Frequently riders tend to ride almost exclusively on the outside rein during riding on this "hollow" rein. The bit is usually pulled significantly to the right in the process, which means that on the left side the horse's lips are pulled onto the teeth and this most certainly does not increase its willingness to step more trustingly onto the left hand. If the horse tries to use the right rein too much, tries to lean on it, it may well be correct once, even once abruptly, to give, to yield more significantly on this rein.

It has also proved very useful to ride the horse in counter position on the left rein on the long side, in other words to flex it to the right and, just as on the right rein, to drive it forward increasingly with the right leg to the left rein; here also the left leg has the important task of preventing the hindquarters from pushing out to the left.

When flexing to the right, the left rein should always be held low on account of the fact that the horse always steps onto the hand better when the rein is held low.

This work will be all the more successful, the better the rider is able to exercise influence from a correctly balanced and supple seat, with elastic and feeling hands which are independent of the seat. The hands must be positioned upright, closed and with slightly angled thumbs, this is essential in order for all the rein aids to come feelingly from the wrist. Furthermore, the hands have to reliably follow the horse's mouth insofar as they always, depending on the posture of the horse, take up a position whereby the rider's elbow, hand and the horse's mouth actually form a straight line.

When tongue faults are recognized in good time, preferably right at the outset, and dealt with in an appropriate way, following a correct analysis of the causes, the problem can always be controlled.

As a tongue positioner can only deal with the symptoms, its use can only be of benefit in an individual case, when it is also handled by an experienced and competent person.

➔ Contact; Straightening; Crookedness; Self-carriage; Position of the hands; Hand faults by the rider

4.6 Teeth grinding

Unfortunately there are a relatively large number of horses which, some of them at a very young age, grind with their teeth, sometime this is barely perceptible, frequently it can be quite clearly heard, however. There can also be considerable variations in the point and period of time when the horse actually makes this noise.

At any rate it is a bad habit which is undesirable because it quite clearly indicates some kind of discomfort on the part of the horse.

The first step, therefore, is to find out what the horse is experiencing as unpleasant. Frequently the horse is feeling some kind of disturbance directly in its mouth so that it lacks confidence in the rider's hand and there is a faulty connection. Possible causes can be problems with the teeth, the bit or even incorrect rein aids on the part of the rider.

Sometimes there is a general lack of suppleness because the horse does not feel generally at ease under the rider and too little attention is given to freedom of constraint in the work.

If this expression of discomfort is ignored over a lengthy period and nothing is done to change the situation, teeth grinding can become a habit to such an extent that the horse grinds its teeth without there being any actual reason for doing so.

Therefore it is important that this vice also should be "nipped in the bud", immediate steps should be taken to discover the causes and appropriate action undertaken to remedy the problem. Attention is to be accorded to the following points in particular:

- **Teeth and the inside of the horse's mouth have to be examined and, if necessary, treated by a competent and qualified person.**
- **The bridle has to be checked to find out whether the bit and the rest of the bridle have been correctly selected for the horse and fit properly.**
- **A badly fitting saddle can also be responsible.**

If the above are all in order, it is important to check and improve the influences of the rider, in other words his seat and application of the aids.

More attention – and possibly also more time – has to be accorded to the daily suppling work. The horse has to be worked better through over the back and ridden onto the hand with well coordinated driving aids.

The better the rider will get the horse on his driving weight and leg aids, the more finely he can exercise influence with his reins and the more the work is characterized by a freedom of constraint.

If you have the feeling that the grinding starts particularly in sitting trot, i.e. through the in-

fluence of the weight on the horse's back, it makes sense to do some of the suppling work on the lunge, when riding to do the rising trot for longer, and also to sit in the forward seat for somewhat longer at canter.

Nevertheless the rider must also take care at the rising trot and canter in the forward seat to have the horse in front of him so that he manages with increasingly fine rein aids.

If the grinding occurs principally during dressage-type work in the outdoor arena or indoor school, it makes sense to start the suppling work either in the open countryside or in the jumping arena, but naturally also already to get the horse reliably on the aids, to frame it in between the driving and restraining aids, and in such a way to prepare it for this work. It is essential that the horse does not start to connect dressage training with monotony, compulsion or even confrontation.

Avoiding boredom and offering variety to the horse is the surest way of preventing bad habits or even stereotypes.

→ **Contact; Straightening; Crookedness; Inside – Outside**

5. Impulsion (Schwung) and what the Rider wins by it

"Contact" and "impulsion" as the third and fourth points on the German training scale in a way represent its centre and are also almost as closely and intricately interlinked as rhythm (Takt) and suppleness (Losgelassenheit). Both are of decisive importance in the training of a horse with regard to improvement of the thrust (Schubkraft).

This is how a flash noseband should be fastened.

Avoiding boredom and offering variety to the horse is the surest way of preventing bad habits or even stereotypes.

6. ➤ Straightening

Very clearly flexed horse

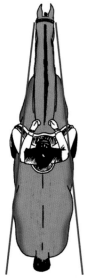

A horse is naturally more slimly built in the shoulder area and initially often moves in such a way.

6. Straightening

6.1 Why no "natural straightness"?

There are a variety of different answers to this question:
- On the one hand, there is the asymmetry of the physical build, with which we are also familiar in the case of human beings. Perhaps at some stage you have noticed how different the portrait of a person looks, depending on whether the right or the left half of the face has been symmetrically doubled for the photo composition.
  - the fact that the forehand has a narrower track than the hindquarters so that one hind leg steps outside the track of the fore leg further contributes to crookedness.
- A decisive reason for the natural crookedness of a horse is also considered to be the fact that, similarly to a right-handed or left-handed person, there is a cerebrally caused (i.e. in the brain) uneven dominance or aptitude of both sides.
- Finally in this connection the rider also often plays a not particularly praiseworthy role. There are in fact riders whose horses all, sooner or later, become crooked on the same side – because they themselves are not able to sit straight and well-balanced and to apply the aids equally well with both legs and hands.

It is commonly asserted that most horses are "crooked on the right", i.e. that they evade somewhat to the right with the hindquarters, are more hollow on the right and stiffer on the left. According to my observations, however, the distribution nowadays of crookedness on the left and on the right is not (any more) so uneven. Generally speaking, horses with very distinct crookedness have become rare nowadays in our warmblood breeds. This is probably thanks to selection, amongst other aspects, according to rideability values. Already at a young age, horses undergo tests with different riders (e.g. in all stallion and mare performance tests), and the horses which are more successful in such contexts are those with less crookedness.

6.2 Why straightening?

If the horse is not straightened by nature, why should, indeed why must we riders try to counteract this "natural crookedness", to minimize it as much as possible by means of straightening gymnasticizing work?
- A horse which is crooked on the right side, for example, takes up more load on the left fore leg, has to take over more load with the left hind leg, which steps under the body more, and it has to produce more thrust with the right hind leg. This uneven strain is further reinforced when the horse is being ridden and would lead to premature wearing on one side if it were not given appropriate attention in training. Particularly in the extensions, crookedness further increases if the horse is not straightened enough. I am quite sure that many horses which constantly make mistakes in rhythm or even are really lame ("rein-lame"), for reasons which initially may seem incomprehensible, in fact suffer from gradually increasing crookedness when being ridden, which initially "only" causes sore muscles due to constant crampedness, ultimately however leads to defects in the muscles and even to changes in the joints and bones.
- Only in an increasingly straightened horse the thrust of the hindquarters can have an optimum effect in the direction of the horse's centre of gravity and thus be available in its entirety. The more crooked a horse still is, the more its thrust gets lost and the more the rider has to interrupt to correct this, which also involves an unnecessary expenditure of energy. Straightening is therefore also a question of economy and as such particularly valuable wherever stamina is required.
- Only a horse which is familiar with straightening work and accepts the relevant aids willingly, will allow itself to be collected well; otherwise

it would increasingly evade to the side with the hindquarters and thus avoid taking up increased weight. All arguments in favour of collection apply all the more with regard to straightening.

• Consequently straightening is also an essential pre-requisite for gradually improved throughness.

The better a horse accepts straightening aids, the more precisely it can be "controlled" and guided. And this is highly advantageous for every purpose for which the horse may be used: The **dressage horse** can present clean school figures and all exercises and movements equally well on both reins – which hopefully will then be appropriately recognized and appreciated by the judges.

The **show jumping horse** can be turned more reliably on both reins without pushing outwards via the shoulder or inwards against the rider's inside leg. This also makes it possible to ride precise courses between combinations and sequences of fences as well as to come to the jump accurately (also to a narrow 2-m jump).

The same also applies to the **cross country horse**, whereby even more frequently here a horse has to take very narrow jumps precisely at a certain point (corner jumps, for example).

Also the normal **"happy hacker"** is better balanced and can be ridden more reliably in difficult countryside if it knows and accepts the straightening aids.

According to the philosophy of our riding, every rider is obliged to make his horse's use under the saddle as easy as possible. This involves a minimum of training for rider and horse including at least a certain amount of ability on the part of the rider to do straightening work and on the part of the horse, to accept the straightening aids. (> "Ethical Principles of the True Horseman", published by the German Equestrian Federation)

6.3 When can you start with straightening?

Although straightening is only in fifth position in our training scale, the experienced rider and

trainer will also have a straightening influence on the horse at as early a stage as possible. This can start as soon as it is possible to work in all three basic gaits without help from the ground and without a lead horse. Nevertheless the straightening work only becomes really valuable and productive when, thanks to good suppleness, particularly also in the back and thanks to confident stepping onto the hand, the horse goes forward rhythmically and swings through well forward with the hind legs.

In this connection it shows in a wonderful way how important it is to keep looking at the six training aims of our scale of training with their cross-connections and to understand them. They are certainly not to be seen as a strict line of progression. Just as a horse only allows itself to be straightened well when it has the relevant "positive pull", i.e. it is capable of sufficient development of impulsion, it must also be asserted that economic and expressive, optimal development of impulsion is only possible for a well-straightened horse.

6.4 How can you straighten a horse?

The first point to take into account is always to guide the forehand before the hindquarters when doing straightening work. Many riders instinctively, however, try "simply" to push the hindquarters over. In individual situations this may well be acceptable on the short term. If, however, a rider tries to counteract crookedness in this way on the long term, the horse will only learn to constantly evade with the hindquarters. The more receptive a horse is to the sideways-driving aids, the more this fault will occur. With the help of serpentine loops, double half voltes or in the valuable but also very demanding exercise, the eight (> Part 4, Chapter 2.) a rider has a very

A crooked horse at trot

A straightened horse on a curved line

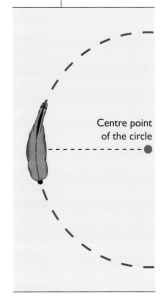

Centre point of the circle

Shoulder-fore canter, the poll comes rather low here.

or shoulder-in like at canter, and this is indeed quite correct. This correction can only be valuable and effective if, thanks to reliable driving forward with both legs, particularly with the inside leg positioned close to the girth, and the horse trustingly striding onto the hand, the horse allows itself to be led with the forehand ahead of the hindquarters. Too strong influence with the inside rein has to be avoided, because otherwise the striding through of the inside hind leg would be reduced.

Equally counter-productive on the long term would be the attempt to push the hindquarters out with the rider's inside leg positioned further back; in time the horse would press increasingly strongly against this. No attempt should ever be made to reduce, to shorten the horse at canter too early, too much and in too long repeats. If this kind of work is overdone, a lack of strength and balance often leads to crampedness, which restricts the striding through in clear three-beat, the expression and the willingness to work together with the rider, indeed it can even lead to resistance.

This applies particularly in the case of horses with a large transition, i.e. a very long canter stride. Here also the rhythm, a very clear three-beat, is the principal criterion.

At a very early stage of straightening at canter, it is possible to use the counter-canter; on the long side the wall or arena rails can be helpful. This also functions very well in the extension. Nevertheless riders should never forget that a genuine counter-canter always requires a certain amount of collection. On a large arena counter-canter can be ridden by waiting until the long side to canter on and then already changing into trot again before the next corner, in order not to have to ride the turn at counter-canter. In individual cases it can occasionally be

helpful and useful, also at canter, to practise riding in position on one rein, usually on the horse's stiff side (compulsion side), i.e. to think a little about travers. If the horse does not bend well to the right, for example, in the right canter it will try to push to the right with the shoulder and to evade to the left with the hindquarters. The rider has to oppose this with the right driving leg close to the girth and an actively guarding, indeed almost sideways-driving left leg positioned slightly further back, thinking here in terms of demanding "shoulder-out" and "croup-in".

Simply for the sake of completion, I should also like to make brief mention of lunging work with regard to straightening:

Anyone who believes that lunging is considerably easier than riding is quite definitely under an illusion. Particularly, however, as far as straightening is concerned, valuable improvement through lunging is hardly possible, because in lunging there is no way of completely replacing the rider's inner leg, which is of such decisive importance – it can never by replaced by the lungeing whip, even in the case of optimum application of the aids; and this applies equally for work on the double lunge.

6.5 The significance of straightening

After these considerations it should be clear why straightening work is so important, and that the natural crookedness which is innate in every horse to a greater or lesser extent, remains – at least as far as the natural disposition is concerned – for the horse's entire life. This situation hopefully generates sufficient motivation and ambition for the serious rider and trainer first of all to learn the correct way of dealing with this natural crookedness, and subsequently to exercise appropriate influence consistently during riding.

An essential criterion of the good rider is to work on straightening every day anew, with every horse, regardless of its level of training, instead of merely trying to compensate for the crookedness.

For the attentive observer, and therefore certainly also for every judge, it is very significant, for example in a dressage test, to see a horse doing exercises and movements on both reins and to be able to compare these accordingly.

A lack of being straightened can be reflected, for example, in the different quality of the canter, the turn on the haunches or walk pirouettes, the half-passes, the flying changes of leg at canter on the left or right rein but, in addition, irregularities in the full halt, walk, trot extensions, canter pirouettes, piaffes and passages are also often caused by deficiencies in the correction of crookedness.

Therefore exercises and movements for dealing with the horse's crookedness will constitute a significant element in almost all the following chapters, despite the fact that a certain amount of repetition will become unavoidable as a result.

→ **Inside and outside; dealing with the natural crookedness; riding of turns; lateral movements**

6.6 Dealing with natural crookedness: stiff and difficult side

As already mentioned at the end of the last chapter, the importance of understanding the problems of natural crookedness and learning how to deal with them on an individual basis cannot be estimated highly enough.

On the basis of a concrete example, I should like to explain here how to handle the natural crookedness of a horse in training, in order to minimize this gradually. This work should be started at a very early stage with a young horse.

It is a question in this example of a horse which is indeed active and willing to perform, but which constantly stiffens up on the left side. Particularly before it becomes supple, it always tries to flex to the right whilst on the left it remains quite unyielding.

Such a problem occurs, to a greater or lesser extent, with almost every horse. Therefore it is

highly advantageous for every rider, who would like to have a horse which goes well and is easy to ride, to have learned how to handle this properly.

When you think about the scale of training in this connection, it concerns the contact first of all, however it is directly connected with the horse's natural, innate crookedness and/or the lack of having been straightened..

It is often possible to recognize how crooked the horse is by the way the bit is pulled through to one side

Before trying to find a solution from the riding point of view, it should be checked to ensure that the bridle fits and is in good order and that the horse has no injuries to its mouth, e.g. through "hooks" on the teeth, which obviously have a negative effect on its well-being.

Such a problem is always particularly evident before the horse is properly suppled up. This is why, at the beginning of each session, suppling exercises have to be ridden carefully and extensively, of course evenly on both reins. In doing this at trot and canter a brisk working tempo, which is nevertheless adjusted to suit the horse in question should be chosen: It cannot be said often enough that particularly the trot should never be hurried. The aim has to be, already in this work, to ride the horse forward quite evenly on both reins, to offer it constant, elastic contact with both rein fists, which should come out of supple shoulder and elbow joints. Here the "Beizäumung" (the German expression just of the well positioned head and neck > p.130), perhaps made only by a strong or even forceful "pressing into position", should never be in the forefront, rather it is a question of showing the horse that everything is easiest when it steps trustingly onto both reins and yields in the poll. Rider as well as horse can learn this particularly well working at walk on the long rein (> Riding at walk). A pre-requisite is that the rider concentrates on his horse at walk, allows the natural forward-downward nodding movement and accompanies it well with his hands out of the shoulders and elbows.

Particularly in the case of horses which are somewhat spooky, no attempt should be made to prevent them looking at and taking in external influences during the suppling work. They just have to learn quite consistently always to continue moving forwards, and that they are "perfectly safe" on the rider's aids.

In order now to get the horse bending and through to an equal extent on both reins, consciousness has to be created for the real problems in question:

Of course the horse has to become more yielding and able to bend on the stiff side, in this case the left side, particularly, however, it has to learn on the other side, in this case the right side, to step forward more confidently and reliably onto the bit. In order, however, to be able to flex and bend better on the left, the stretching ability of the muscle system on the right side has to be improved.

Counter-flexed horse at a trot, verging on exaggeration here

When riding on the left rein, this means driving on more with the left leg to the outside right rein, in order to come away from the inside left rein. When flexing to the left, the horse's nose may be brought around by means of a slightly more energetic sideways-leading aid with the left rein, at the same moment, however, the right outside rein, must be held well deep in a guarding function, in order to prevent the bit being pulled through the horse's mouth. The inside hand should also not be held too high in the process because then the horse would make itself narrow and it would become even more difficult to achieve a bending in the neck without the horse becoming tilted in the poll. The outside, i.e. right, hand may also be taken somewhat to the right away from the shoulder in this guarding function, so that the right rein continues to form a straight, unbroken line to the mouth, even when the horse takes up the desired bend in the neck. This resolute flexing must be followed as quickly as possible by becoming light with both reins in order also to respond positive-

ly to what has hopefully been a positive reaction by the horse.

According to the fundamental principle "Ride your horse forward and straighten it!", attention always has to be paid to ensure good activity during this work. In order for the horse then also to take on the left bending in its ribs, as already mentioned, the rider's left leg has to drive well forwards to ensure that the horse does not evade to the left with the shoulder, with the right guarding leg attention has to be paid to ensure that the horse does not evade with the hindquarters and withdraw.

In the context of the work as a whole, work on the left rein should not be overdone. When riding on the right rein, careful attention has to be paid to ensure that a good connection also exists on the right inside rein. Frequently on this "hollow" side, riders tend to ride almost exclusively on the outside rein. The consequence is that the bit is usually pulled, in this case to the left, so that on the right side the horse's lips are pulled onto the teeth. This obviously does not exactly increase the horse's willingness to come trustingly onto the right rein. If, of its own accord, the horse looks too much for the left rein and wants to lean on it, it is correct to yield somewhat more clearly, even abruptly, with this rein.

It has also proved very beneficial, on the right rein on the long side, sometimes also to ride the horse in counter position, in other words to flex to the left and, just as on the left rein, to drive the horse forward more with the left leg to the right rein, whereby here also the guarding right leg has the important task of preventing the horse from evading to the right with the hindquarters.

When flexing to the left, the right rein is to be kept very low.

In difficult cases another way of proceeding which can be of additional help but should only be used, however, by experienced riders with good feeling, or under supervision:

When riding, in this case on the left rein along the long side of the arena, the horse is also – and in this case very significantly – counter-flexed, in other words on its hollow side. For this purpose, the rider takes up both reins more, particularly the right rein however, and consciously makes the horse short in the neck, to such an extent that it is indeed rather unpleasant for the horse. At the end of the long side the rider becomes lighter again gradually with both reins and, of its own accord, the horse will then position itself at least in a straight-on position again. The "counter-overflexing" may only be attempted if it is completely ensured that the horse is well on the driving aids and remains reliably forwards.

The idea in this variation of correction is based on the horse getting the feeling itself that it is more pleasant and comfortable when it steps more evenly onto both reins or, conversely, that moving with right-hand flexion on one side and exaggerated contact on the left rein is unpleasant.

The entire straightening work will be all the more successful, the better the rider is in a position to exercise influence from a correct, well-balanced and supple seat, with elastic and feeling hands which are independent of the seat. A prerequisite for this is that the rider holds both hands upright, closed and with slightly angled thumbs, in order to be able to apply all rein aids feelingly out of the wrist. Furthermore, he has to follow the horse's mouth with his hand to the extent that he always carries his hands, adapted according to the horse's posture, so that the elbow, rider's hand and horse's mouth indeed do always form a straight line.

The ability to deal correctly with the horse's crookedness, to do valuable straightening work, is one of the most important criteria of a good rider.

A book on this subject which is particularly to be recommended is "Von der Koppel bis zur Kapriole" (title English "Horsemanship") by Waldemar Seunig.

➔ **Application of the aids; straightening**

7. Collection and Elevation

Collection is the sixth and last point on our training scale. As far as the first five training aims are concerned, it is perfectly possible to talk about a modification of the order, possibly even to argue about it; in some cases the aims have to be regarded and treated as parallel. In the case of collection, however, its position as the last point on the scale is virtually beyond discussion. Genuine collecting work assumes a certain standard of the preceding points, in particular straightening. This in no way means, however, that work indirectly towards collection can not be done already at the stage of improving suppleness, when riding in good (forwards-downwards) stretched posture the horse's hind legs can be activated to swing through forwards better by the driving aids. A certain amount of collection, however – although this is often not realized – is important together with the ensuing elevation, not only in higher

This is how you can imagine the relative elevation.

7. ➤ Collection and Elevation

This horse is raised too much at the front, in other words its neck is absolutely elevated. It can no longer swing through via the back.

➤ On no account should collection be confused with riding slowly, it should never be at the expense of liveliness and activity.

dressage training; it is also advantageous for every riding horse, even for a "happy hacker".

7.1 What is collection?

On account of its physical build, a significant larger part of the horse's body weight is carried by its forehand. When being ridden this weight distribution becomes even more unfavourable due to the rider sitting a short distance behind the shoulder. Therefore the horse's hindquarters, which have a primarily pushing function on account of their construction, have to be encouraged to take over more of a carrying function, to take on a weight load. This means they have to be brought forward more in order to come under the point of gravity; which means they have to bend more primarily in the hip and knee joint (we call this the "haunches"), in order to relieve the forehand of some of the load. On account of their construction, furthermore, the lower joints of the hindquarters also bend to the same extent as the hips and knees. This indeed makes the steps and strides shorter, however they should become more elegant and cadenced.

On no account should collection be confused with riding slowly, it should never be at the expense of liveliness and activity.

7.2 What is elevation?

As the forehand by its very nature is formed as a support, the shoulder always remains at the same height. If we imagine the horse as a set of scales (illustration p.145), the forehand forms the point of contact, so that the lowering of the croup – due to the bending of the haunches – brings the entire top line from the tail to the poll increasingly into an uphill position, and results in an elevation in the neck and head with the poll also actually coming somewhat higher. **Because this "getting taller" is in relation to the lowering of the hindquarters, we speak of relative elevation and only this kind of elevation is beneficial and desirable.**

In contrast to this is the absolute elevation. In this case the rider works from the front to the back and exercises influence mainly with the hand. The head and neck are actively taken up, irrespective of what "is happening behind". This necessarily leads to the back being held stiff, or even pushed away, so that the hind legs, instead of closing in more, rather work out to the back without any bending of the haunches; in German this is described very visually in an old expression: "Das Pferd zeigt die (Hinter-)Eisen." (The horse is showing its (hind) shoes.)

In the case of a normal average horse the hind legs will then only move sluggishly; in the case of horses with particularly active hind legs, they sometimes nevertheless continue to step off significantly upwards and thus deceive semi-competent "experts", they will no longer swing through forwards, however. This has nothing to do with collection, causes discomfort to the horse, particularly in the back, and on the long-term it restricts its pleasure in working together with the rider and its willingness to perform; this absolute elevation is therefore counter-productive and to be rejected completely.

Correct elevation is always the result of correct collection.

To what extent a horse can and should be collected and thus elevated, depends on the one

Collected trot, correctly elevated. Unfortunately the rider is sitting somewhat behind the movement and leaning backwards.

Hubertus Schmidt on Engard shows here, with very slight contact, how a horse in collection and with good self-carriage can exude composure and contentment.

hand on the qualities of its exterior, but almost even more on the qualities of its interior, on the other hand, of course, also on the duration and quality of its training so far.

7.3 Why is it advantageous for every horse to have a certain amount of collection?

The aim of the entire training in accordance with our riding theory is to make being ridden as simple and pleasant for the horse as possible, whilst at the same time making the horse able and willing to perform for the rider to an optimal level; good health – as far as possible throughout the horse's entire life – and thus the ability to be ridden up to an advanced age is equally advantage and desirable for both parties concerned. All training aims have to stand up to this requirement.

As already explained, by the very nature of the horse, more weight (approx. 55%) rests on the forehand, and this "top-heaviness" is further reinforced by the position of the rider close behind the shoulder. Therefore, if we wish to keep our horse healthy and ridable on the long term, we have to train it to take up more weight with the hindquarters, in other words to collect it. A horse which constantly goes on the forehand will

experience early signs of wear and tear and go lame. On account of their supporting construction, the fore legs principally carry the weight with the skeleton plus joints, ligaments and tendons. However ingenious and sophisticated the training, it is almost impossible to strengthen them.

By contrast the hind legs bear the weight imposed on them principally with powerful muscles which, as we are aware, can be relatively easily trained.

There are also a few further points which make collecting work worthwhile:

The aim of our gymnasticizing training is a ridable, i.e. pleasant horse which can also be handled with precision. Thus a rider, who has learned to ride accordingly, will also value a horse which can collect somewhat when riding out in difficult terrain, because this makes it easier to direct with precision, and also more-sure footed.

The same also applies, of course, when out hunting or riding a more demanding jumping course.

Also in the dressage arena, contrary to commonly expressed opinion, already at novice level a not insignificant degree of collection is necessary in order to be able to participate successfully. Only then, for example, will it be possible to do half halts and, more particularly, full halts reliably and successfully, to lengthen and shorten steps and strides in a controlled way, without the horse coming onto the forehand in the process.

7.4 Training aim: what can be achieved with collecting work?

When the horse has actually learned to accept the collecting aids sufficiently, it can then successfully

- bring the hind legs more in the direction under the centre of gravity so that they take up more load.
- As a result of this closing of the hind legs, the area which the horse covers with its four legs, standing as well as in movement, becomes smaller. This makes the balance situation more instable, so that the horse becomes more receptive and sensitive to the rider's aids, particularly the weight aids.
- Even through just a small degree of collection and the elevation which ensues from this, the horse's tendency to come onto the forehand under the rider is reduced. Consequently the horse is able to move more freely out of the shoulder,
- Additionally it will become more mentally attentive and circumspect. Consequently it will also become significantly more surefooted also on rough or uneven ground, e.g. on a cross-country course, or even just being ridden in the open countryside.
  - The increased activity of the hindquarters, the bending of the haunches and the freedom of the shoulder already mentioned above, are what make it possible for the horse to make full use of its (impulsion) potential in extensions and, for example, to show an extended trot or canter impressively and in self-carriage.
  - After every extension it will be able to take the impulsion (Schwung) into the collection, to convert it again into carrying power and elasticity. With-

"Überstreichen" (giving and retaking the reins) – incorrectly– but as it is often demonstrated; if it is done correctly, the rider moves his fists along the crest of the mane, in other words deeper.

out any loss in liveliness and activity, it will move more elegantly and impressively with distinct cadence in collected exercises and, in so far as its exterior and interior qualities permit, will be able to be trained to do movements requiring highest levels of collection (piaffe, passage and canter-pirouettes).
- And when jumping, irrespective of whether on the jumping course or cross country, a more closed, in other words somewhat collected horse has significant advantages: Necessary lengthening or shortening ("coming back"), in order always to have the suitable distance for take-off, is made easier; this also makes the horse more skilful at the jump itself. In the case of higher jumps or more closely positioned combinations the horse is consequently able to convert the forwards movement and take it with it without any loss of impulsion and rhythm, even in a steeper flight over the jump.

7.5 How is collection achieved?

Collecting work is a very demanding matter. It requires a great deal of skill and the coordination of all aids, fine feeling and a great degree of patience.

Horse in good collection at canter

A showjumper (thoroughbred), well on the aids

As additional muscles have to be developed, the time factor is of irreplaceable value here; overdoing the work with too long collecting repeats only leads to detrimental effects such as loss of pleasure in working together with the rider, crampedness and even disobedience. It is important to respect this to exactly the same extent also in the case of horses which only come into work at an age when they are indeed already "of age".

The rider or trainer must also take into account difficulties related to the horse's conformation e.g. rather steep hindquarters or a longer middle section. Decisive, however, is the right systematic progression (from easy to difficult) and the right feeling for the optimum dosage of work, to introduce strong enough stimuli to make progress possible, on the other hand not to exaggerate in any way as this would otherwise be counter-productive.

In order always to find the right degree here, it is of an advantage which is in no way to be under-estimated when the rider, or at least his trainer, has extensive experience with many different horses.

7.6 Exercises and movements to improve collection

Fundamentally speaking, every correctly ridden half and full halt improves the collection.

What is the meaning of "correctly ridden" in this context?

All the aids have to be applied, especially also the driving aids, whereby in the course of training it has to become possible to gradually manage with increasingly fine rein aids. These will ultimately only be necessary in the form of a very calm non-yielding hand (nevertheless with an elastic arm) as a vis à vis to the driving aid.

Only the rider who has learned to feel his horse's movements very precisely will be in a position to coordinate his entire application of the aids regarding dosage and timing in an optimum way.

Particularly in the case of horses which are very light in the poll, which tend to become short and/or have a deep-set neck, the aim must be to be able to give halts without making the horse shorter. This will make it easier for the horse to close in behind and take up weight.

Before coming to the following list of exercises and movements which are of value for collection and are divided into collecting on the one hand, and collected on the other hand, it is well worth devoting some thought to this division.

The first, as the name already says, are beneficial for collection and serve to gradually build the horse up with regard to carrying power, physically as well as mentally. The latter already assumes a certain degree of collection, naturally however, they should also further optimize the horse's ability and willingness in this respect.

Which exercises and movements still belong to the collecting and which, in concrete terms, already belong to the collected is a matter of individual judgement and depends completely on the pre-requites concerning natural ability and level of training of the individual horse, to a certain extent also on the skill of the rider. Many exercises can be adapted to suit different levels, depending on the degree of collection they are ridden in and what is required.

Thus, for example, the rein back, can be ridden with more frame and in somewhat lower position

Poetin by Sandro Hit, by Brentano II, 6 year-old German and World Champion Dressage Horse in 2003

with a less advanced horse, than apply as a collecting exercise. If, on the contrary, it is required in medium or advanced level dressage, for example, with good collection, elevation and self-carriage, it is without doubt a collected exercise.

Collecting exercises and movements:
- The figure of eight
- Trotting on from the spot
- Turns in the trot and canter, which can gradually be reduced in size
- Full halts out of trot
- Lengthening and shortening at trot and canter (also on a large curved track)
- Cantering on out of walk
- Double or treble serpentine loops on the long side (depending on length of the arena)
- Serpentine loops across the arena with four to six loops
- Exercises in preparation for the lateral movements – "shoulder-fore" and "riding in position"
- Reducing and enlarging the circle (travers-like and shoulder-in-like)
- Rein back
- Rein back followed by trotting on

- Turn on the haunches from walk and between two halts (initially only around 90°)
- Preliminary exercises for the counter-canter

Collected exercises and movements:
- Collected trot, canter and walk (in so far as genuine collection is possible at walk)[1]
- Cantering on from halt
- Transition from canter to walk
- Walk pirouette
- Rein back in collection and with elevation, possibly with a certain number of steps
- Rein back followed immediately by cantering on
- Counter-canter
- "Schaukel" (Rein-back series)
- Lateral movements at trot and canter: Shoulder-in and counter shoulder-in, travers, renvers, half-passes
- Flying change at canter
- Canter pirouette

Although in training clear differentiation is made between suppling, collecting and collected exercises and movements, it has to be considered that transitions between them are quite fluent and therefore no strict and clear delimitations exist. Thus exercises which are ridden for suppling purposes on an experienced dressage horse represent the aim of the work phase in the case of a younger horse; the figure of eight is a good example of this.

These overlaps exist in the same way concerning jumping horses, e.g. with regard to the requirements for the jumps in the suppling phase

7.7 Where is the difficulty in collecting work?

With all these exercises, the rider constantly has to be aware of the problem, on the one hand of having the horse well with him and "picking up" the thrust of the decisively mobi-

---

[1] As there is no moment of suspension at walk, genuine collection is not possible in this gait. There are also only very few horses which show a bending of the haunches at walk without any detriment to rhythm (Takt) and activity.

lized hind legs, so that this does not simply disappear to the front, on the other hand to apply the restraining aids so skilfully that the hind legs are not prevented from swinging through and stepping forward, which would make bending of the haunches impossible.

Only when the extent and intensity of the collecting repeats are measured correctly and the training stimuli are well measured, is good training progress possible.

Variety and frequent lively forwards riding is of tremendous importance in connection with this work. Because this is the only way of guaranteeing that the closing (up) of the horse in reducing the pace within a gait takes place by closing of the hindquarters rather than by holding back of the forehand.

The best exercises for checking correct work in this respect are
- transitions, particularly reducing from an extension,
- "Überstreichen" (Giving and retaking the reins) with one or two hands by way of checking the self-carriage,
- "Zügel-aus-der-Hand-kauen-lassen" (allowing the horse to chew the reins out of the rider's hand) in contentedly stretched posture in small breaks, for relaxation and by way of reward during work phases as well as at the end of every session.

Riders who always allow themselves to be guided by the idea of reducing the horse (riding the half-halts) from the rear to the fore will make the fewest mistakes in collecting work. Every rider of the fact that he can only achieve this stepping and striding forward in an optimum way if he can succeed in using the horse's pleasure in working together with the rider and willingness to perform for this purpose, if necessary to re-awaken them in the horse, and to maintain them appropriately – but under no circumstances to try and force them by exaggerated, even "forceful" driving. The horse has to step or stride forward trustingly to the rider's hand and "pull positively".

7.8 Optimum evolvement of the horse's natural potential

Only a horse which is worked according to the entire scale of training, including collection and the elevation which results from this, can develop fully with regard to ridability, manageability and, not least, expression and beauty in carriage and movement, and make optimum use of its natural potential.

At the same time this makes it possible for the horse, despite being used for riding, indeed even for competition purposes, thanks to good physical and mental health, to remain able and willing to perform until an advanced age.

7.9 Self-carriage of the horse

The fact that according to our riding theory, an important aim of the training of a horse consists of making it a reliable as well as pleasant and easy-to-manage riding horse, makes the significance of self-carriage automatically clear.

By self-carriage we understand that, on the basis of correct training, the horse has learned to balance in an optimal way under the rider, to carry itself, and is consequently in a position to accept the most subtle of rider's aids and to follow them.

In this connection, we tend to think initially of a horse at an advanced level of training which already moves in good collection and with the appropriate elevation ensuing from this.

The experienced, good rider, however, already during the basic training, where the horse needs more clear support through the rider and still goes in a clearly wider frame, will take due care constantly to remind it to carry itself. Thus in this phase of training, but also in the case of the advanced horse, more work will be done in the stretched position every day during the suppling phase. This stretched position is particularly valuable when the horse simultaneously steps up trustingly to the bit and pulls a little in a positive way. Also in this posture, the horse should

Rein-back – an exercise which usually does not look as good on photos: Here in correct diagonal hoof sequence, stepping off well, in confident self-carriage, perhaps not quite yielding at the poll, however.

move in reliable balance with its hind legs swinging through well and indeed go in self-carriage, under no circumstances the horse should be allowed to lean on the reins.

Any correct training according to the training scale also promotes self-carriage. The better the horse moves in natural balance due to a harmoniously well-balanced physical build, but also corresponding motoric disposition, the more easily it will learn to move in self-carriage under the saddle.

In order to check the self-carriage, the rider can "sound this out" with both hands, i.e. become so light that the contact is almost given up.

In tests this is required in the form of "Überstreichen" (Giving and retaking the reins).

➔ **Halts; all collected and collecting movements mentioned here; "Überstreichen" (Giving and retaking the reins)**

8. Throughness (Durchlässigkeit) – The Superordinate Training Aim for every Riding Horse

"Ultimate happiness on earth is only to be found on horseback" – This famous quotation can only apply in its full dimensions if the communication functions well between horse and rider. It is hard to imagine anything more beautiful than a ride in which both merge almost into one unit, but hardly anything worse than a ride which takes the form of struggle and tension. In dressage, jumping, out in the country, hunting, even on a quiet trek it is necessary for the horse to accept the rider's aids confidently and reliably; this is the only way in which the desired harmony between animal and human being can be achieved.

Basically the term "throughness" is not so difficult to understand because the word really almost speaks for itself.

The horse should allow the aids of the rider to permeate through its whole body, and follow them willingly, not only register them, but also respect them. Unfortunately in this connection many people only think about the influence of the reins, usually because this is also the way they ride, in other words predominantly "backwards". In the fore, however, throughness is primarily the accepting and following of all driving aids, forwards as well as laterally. Only when the horse willingly accepts the impulses of the weight and leg aids, can the flow of the impulsion, originating from the hind-legs, flow through freely to the hand and be regulated appropriately.

Throughness is by no means to be equated with obedience, however. Naturally, from when it is a foal onwards, a certain fundamental obedience should be demanded of a horse; otherwise any handling, even in the stable or out in the field, would involve difficulties. It would, however, contradict the entire philosophy of our equestrian theory, to see the requesting of exercises and movements in the first place as a test of obedience. It is a very definite advantage of our riding system to understand dressage training as careful gymnasticizing but not as drilled training. Thus in dressage-type work it must always be recognizable that the horse – due to correctly structured and dosed training – is easily in the position to perform in the way demanded of it and therefore also does this willingly, that it is also prepared, however, to wait for the rider's aids. The more a horse tends to anticipate the rider's aids, the more important it is to avoid any drill in the training.

As nowadays our horses usually have very good neck and poll formation, and therefore relatively rarely have serious gullet problems, the majority of them are unfortunately made very short in the neck.

This becoming narrow in the neck, however, particularly with regard to throughness, is very counter-productive, because then the rein aids no longer come through as far as the hindquarters but instead disappear to a certain extent in the poll. This may be compared with a water pipe which runs from the mouth via the poll, the neck and the back, into the hindquarters, and as a result of this "kink" has forfeited its throughness. An additional point is that this getting short in the neck almost always leads to the fact that the horse can no longer balance well and becomes "elevated absolutely". Instead of moving with a supple back and optimally engaged hind legs, it will cramp up in the back, even make the back hollow and consequently show little willingness to take up the load with the hindquarters. This is why the rider must always have the following aim in mind when riding half-halts and halts:

The horse has to be so trusting on the driving aids, i.e. in front of the rider, that, with good yielding at the poll and corresponding sensitivity in the mouth, it steps forward so trustingly to the bit that the rider can ride halts without the horse becoming visibly shorter in the neck. The better this works, the easier it will be for the horse to swing through and forwards from behind.[1]

The riding training necessary for this can only be successful if the horse has learned, from when

Horse with a very shortened neck and clearly behind the vertical

it was a foal onwards, in daily handling, i.e. in the stable, being lead, groomed, tacked up etc. to respect the human being as the leader animal and recognize human "dominance". Under the saddle the training aims of the scale of training then have to be worked on systematically, with enough time and patience, in other words, correctly and competently. It is only after rhythm (Takt), suppleness (Losgelassenheit), contact (Anlehnung), impulsion (Schwung), straightening (Geradrichten) and at least a certain degree of collection have been achieved that genuine throughness without coercion is possible. In all performance sport orientated disciplines it is an essential prerequisite for safety, enjoyment and success in sport. However, even the pure leisure rider will feel safer and more at ease when he knows that the accelerator as well as the brake function all the time and do not have to be forced using tricks and special equipment.

How closely connected the individual training aims of our training scale (> Graphic of Training Scale p. 98) are with throughness, and are interlinked with it, can be well recognized by means of the following examples:

It is a very ◁ definite advantage of our riding system to understand dressage training as careful gymnasticing but not as drilled training.

---

[1] The closing in with the hind legs poses increased demands on the horse's balance, in a state of collection it has to move on a smaller surface area with its four feet. This is easier, particularly for a horse which is still learning, if its balancing pole is in no way curtailed, i.e. the neck is not shortened or even fully contracted.

- Only with increasing throughness is it possible for a horse to move continuously, in other words also in all transitions, for example, in reliable regularity (Takt).
- A lack of suppleness will always mean either the impulse from the hindquarters cannot go through the entire horse, or the restraining rein aids "get stuck" in the poll, neck or back, in any case they do not reach the horse's hindquarters.
- Every contact problem, i.e. instability or rigidity in the connection between the rider's hand and horse's mouth or lack of trust on the part of the horse in the rider's hand has a directly restricting effect on the throughness.
- Only a horse which can swing through well with its hind legs out of a supple back, will be able to be through and submissive for the driving and restraining aids.
- Only with being increasingly straightened can a horse react with throughness to (half-) halts and, thanks to the forward-driving aids applied here, step forward better to the rider's hand, without evading with the hindquarters.
- This, in turn, is an essential pre-requisite for collection and the relative elevation which ensues from this which, thanks to the supple back with good bending of the haunches, enables increased thrust impulses and taking up of the weight in the hindquarters.

Every horse, even the young horse, can and indeed must have a certain amount of throughness if it is to be used as a riding horse. If the young horse reacts willingly and supply to the driving aids after the very first phase of breaking in, if it begins to swing in the back, taking the rider with it well, stepping forward to the bit and trustingly looking for the rider's hand, then it is appropriately through for this level of training. In the course of further training, e.g. after elementary level, this all has to be refined, impulsion, straightening and also a considerable amount of collection and the raising of the forehand ensuing from this have to be worked on. Only then can the throughness be described as appropriate to this level.

Particularly in dressage tests, a degree of throughness which is appropriate to the level in question is a decisive criterion in the assessment whereby some uncertainties in the form of temporary slight resistance can never be completely excluded.

Also in jumping and eventing competitions, however, success is not dependent solely on cantering and jumping ability and on jumping technique, but also to a great degree on throughness. Throughness is of particular significance especially also in the case of increased demands (e.g. in combinations, sequences of fences, in a jump-off or in demanding cross-country stretches). Only a horse which has a fairly confident command of all training aims can be through at any time and without any restrictions.

Thanks to modern breeding of riding horses, most horses today, due to their good exterior and – almost more important – interior, as well as good basic gaits, can be brought very quickly to an attractive throughness, provided they are given competent training. This is quite certainly due to the fact that for many generations of horses, one of the most important selection criteria has been the ridability. This is tested and evaluated already in the case of very young horses, e.g. in the context of stallion and mare performance tests as well as competitions for young riding and dressage horses when external riders try out these horses. Here all the above-mentioned features of the exterior and interior are scrutinized once again. But also less obviously visible quality features such as balancing ability and more or less distinct natural crookedness are accorded appropriate acknowledgement.

Thus a horse which moves well in natural balance and has less natural crookedness, will certainly be able to receive the higher mark for riding qualities.

In the case of horses which do not correspond to the ideal in all points, it is, however, possible with careful and more patient training for the normal requirement level of most average riders, also to achieve a very acceptable result.

Anyone who would like to train a horse must have already acquired a considerable level of equestrian ability, if possible on suitable school horses; and if any doubt exists, assistance should be sought from an experienced rider or trainer. **Only someone who has pleasure in pursuing the course of training in harmonious collaboration with his horse, and actually pursues this aim at least once a day, will achieve throughness.** The throughness makes it easier for the horse to be obedient, it becomes easier for the rider to handle, and quite generally more pleasant. Consequently conflicts with the rider are avoided which means that the horse's position as the rider's partner is also positively influenced.

With an appropriately through horse it will be possible – regardless of the stage or level of training, to enjoy the hours spent in the saddle and to indulge in our sport in easy harmony with your horse.

> **Exercises and movements which provide a particularly good indication of the degree of throughness achieved:**
>
> - **Every full halt in which the horse closes well with the hindquarters, shows self-carriage and balance and does not become short in the neck.**
> - **All transitions from one gait to another and also within a gait, which correspond to the same criteria and take place fluently. This applies particularly with regard to the transitions from the higher gait or higher pace to a lower one.**

> - **Rein back, reliable diagonal, with good stepping off and collection and elevation appropriate to the level of training, with subsequent full halt or riding on, as far as "Schaukel" (rein-back series).**
> - **Walk and canter pirouettes, ridden as well on both reins as possible.**
> - **Zig-zag half passes, also at canter, whereby the change in flexion and bend (with flying change) is particularly indicative.**

→ Training scale; riding of transitions

8.1 Tilting at the poll –
   a typical problem of throughness

Tilting at the poll is a fault which occurs particularly in the riding of turns and lateral movements.

The horse holds its head – to a greater or lesser extent – crooked, it comes lower with one ear, e.g. with the right one and evades to the other side with the nose, in this case to the left side.

Tilting at the poll can be observed particularly frequently in the case of horses which have been made short in the neck.

First of all a distinction has to be made, whether a horse only tilts at the poll to one side or whether the problem occurs in the same way to the left and to the right. The former is usually related to the natural crookedness, lack of even contact on both sides[1] and insufficient straightening. The latter is usually caused by technical deficiencies.

In order to be able to correct such a fault in a permanent and reliable way, it is – as always – necessary to find out the exact causes. Particularly with regard to tilting at the poll, attempts are frequently only made to deal with the symptoms.

---

[1] It is important to ensure that the horse is not suffering from teeth problems.

Tilting at the poll with a somewhat tight right rein

The following technical faults on the part of the rider very frequently cause tilting at the poll: If the rider

- in order to achieve a more significant bending in the neck, pulls the rein across the crest of the mane with his inside hand, or
- does not allow the longitudinal bending enough with the outside regulating rein, in other words does not yield enough.
- presses over the crest of the mane with the outside hand, in order to turn the horse better and/or to push it sideways to a certain extent, or
- guides the horse with his outside hand positioned too high, or
- in an effort to make the horse bend more significantly, turns in the seat and pulls his inside hand in front of his thigh or in front of his stomach.

All technical faults described, particularly concerning the height of the hand, have a particularly serious effect on horses ridden in a double bridle, because this has a stronger "beizäumend" effect in the case of most horses, in other words they can be made short even more easily. Furthermore, any incorrect use of the curb bit, e. g. when a curb rein is either too tight or is hanging completely loose, can cause tilting.

Unfortunately the causes are not always such faults in riding technique, which can indeed be relatively easily avoided or corrected by means of concentration and as frequent reminding as possible by a trainer.

Very often tilting at the poll is an indication for the fact that the horse, as mentioned above, still has general deficiencies in its training which have to be improved or corrected, particularly with regard to suppleness, contact and straightening.

The rider can then feel that the horse does not go forwards willingly, does not step trustingly onto both reins equally and is crooked.

The necessary method of procedure can then be read about in the appropriate chapters.

➔ Instinctively – correct?; position of the hand; contact; crookedness; straightening; lateral movements (half passes)

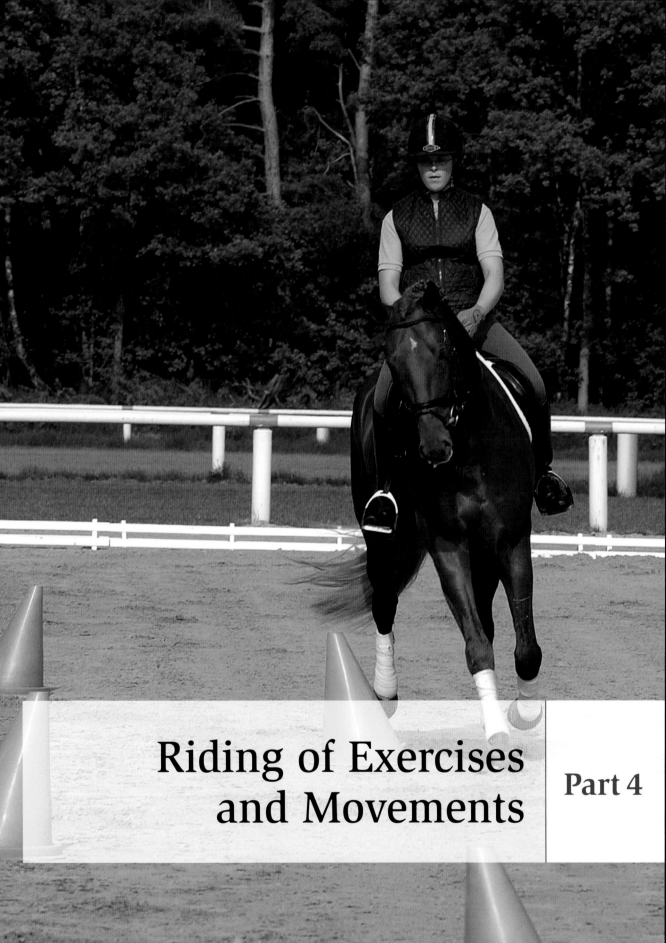

Riding of Exercises and Movements

Part 4

Good extended posture in confident self-carriage with active stepping off

Too little stretched **forward**-downward, as a result the horse comes on the forehand

1.1 Letting the horse chew the reins out of the rider's hands

The exercise "chewing the reins out of the rider's hands" provides a wonderful way of testing the horse's suppleness. It is a very pleasing development that this exercise is now also being asked for in our present dressage tests much more frequently than was previously the case. Unfortunately, however, quite a few of the people concerned – including some judges – are not fully informed about the exercise.

The horse is required to stretch forward-downwards to the bit, with the rider gradually lengthening the reins to "long reins". The horse should stretch at least so far that its mouth comes to the level of the point of the shoulder, but not further than is compatible with the balance of the horse in question. The brow-nose line should remain ahead of the vertical.

The well-suppled horse executes the exercise in complete balance, maintaining gait, rhythm (Takt) and tempo; the rider can increasingly drive and sit better. In this exercise the rider's hands should move forward somewhat in the direction of the horse's mouth so that the subsequent adjusting and shortening of the reins can be done more easily and softly. As far as the position of the hand is concerned, the rider should always follow the horse's mouth so as to maintain the straight line elbow-hand-horse's mouth. This is particularly important when riding in a double bridle because simply the lowering of the horse's mouth makes the effect of the curb bit sharper, i.e. more forming (overflexing) the head-neck position. This is why, when yielding the reins, the curb rein should be yielded significantly more than the snaffle. In order to keep the hindquarters active, the rider must apply particularly good driving aids just at the moment of stretching, because in the stretched position the horse initially has the tendency to reduce the tempo and the ground cover. This is connected to the fact that the trunk extensor muscles from the occipital bone via the neck, the back and the hindquarters to the hocks have to be seen as one inter-connected unit, – and they have to stretch more in this position.

When "chewing the reins out of the rider's hands" is ridden at trot, this can be done either sitting or rising. When the horse really becomes supple and the rider can therefore sit well, he should do sitting trot (except in the case of a young, green horse), whereby it can be advantageous to sit somewhat forward. Many riders manage better to drive on accordingly and to notice changes in the tempo immediately using this form of seat. The rising trot, if used, has to be absolutely balanced, smooth and possible with a fine hand independent of the seat; otherwise it is extremely counter-productive.

The repeated tensing and relaxing of the muscles involved is particularly valuable. Therefore it is not so important for the horse to remain in this same stretched position for longer repeats, it is much more valuable when the rider repeatedly lets the horse chew the reins out of his hands, and then shortens them again somewhat in order to let the horse stretch again. It is only when also in this stretched position, thanks to good confidence in the rider's hand, the horse steps reliably onto the bit, in other words "pulls positively", that the entire exercise is really of value. Because it is only then that the hind legs step or stride off actively and swing through forward and thus also stretch and strengthen the rear area of the trunk extensor muscles accordingly. In the process the rider thus still always has to have some feeling of pull in the hand and above all to have the feeling that he has the horse in front of him. This also has to be reflected in his seat, in the degree to which he sits forward. Exaggerated leaning forward is detrimental here.

How far the individual horse should be allowed to stretch depends ultimately on its physical build, its state of training and ability to find balance with the rider. Anyone who is lucky enough to actually own the naturally "uphill horse" which, on account of appropriate conformation, but also due to a good degree of willingness to perform, is always well balanced, can allow stretching with a good conscience until the horse's nose almost touches the ground and the rider is holding the buckle of the reins in his hand.

However, in the case of the majority of horses which are available to the average riders, this allowing to stretch very deep, referred to as "chewing the reins out of the rider's hands as far as the buckle", should only be permitted and required at the end of the suppling work in very short repeats. Otherwise the horse would only come unnecessarily onto the forehand and in all probability have problems in balance and rhythm.

"Chewing the reins out of the rider's hands" is not only a wonderful exercise for testing the suppleness, at secondary level also the rhythm (Takt) and the contact – it is also specially suitable, for example, for rewarding and praising a horse after a successfully completed movement, or simply as a positive response to its good collaboration and performance.

This is why every lesson unit, regardless of what discipline or class, should end with the horse being ridden into a stretched position. In what gait this is done varies in each individual case. It is best to begin with it at canter, e.g. on a large circle, then riding a flowing transition to trot in stretched position (either in the forward seat or at rising trot), changing rein at trot, cantering in stretched position or with only slightly shortened reins once again on the other rein and then repeating the whole. Also the concluding transition to walk must flow and function easily on the long rein if the exercise has been ridden well. **Such a conclusion is an excellent way of checking the entire work of the training unit; at the same time, however, this positive conclusion is also optimum preparation for the commencement of work the following day.**

1.2. "Überstreichen"
(Giving and retaking the reins)

"Überstreichen" is an exercise for testing a horse's self-carriage; its purpose is to show whether a horse is reliable on the rider's weight and leg aids and is independent of the support by the rider's hand. In dressage tests it is asked for in different forms, at trot as well as at canter. The rider should ride a repeat of two to three horse's lengths pushing both rein fists along the crest of the mane and then bringing them back again into their original position. Normally he should go a distance forward of about two hands' widths, thus really giving up the contact tempo-

> "Chewing ◄ the reins out of the rider's hands" is not only a wonderful exercise for testing the suppleness, at secondary level also the rhythm (Takt) and the contact.

rarily. Riders with relatively short arms may naturally only go as far forward with their hands as it is possible without coming out of the correct dressage seat.

When the horse really is reliably on the driving aids, it will come somewhat more ahead of the vertical, remaining in self-carriage however, i.e. not following the rider's hand as in "chewing the reins out of the rider's hands". The horse remains unchanged in its tempo.

Frequently in this exercise riders take their hands significantly upwards, in other words do not give up the contact to the horse's mouth when going forward. This is incorrect because in this way no genuine test of self-carriage can take place. When riding in a double bridle the hand coming higher will automatically reinforce the "beizäumende" effect of the double bridle, the horse will thus be forced to become short in the neck.

Occasionally "Überstreichen" can also be done just with one hand. This is asked for in large turns, for example, and of course it is to be done with the inside hand. This is intended to test whether the clearly flexed and bent horse is reliable on the outside rein, whether the rider is coming away from the inside rein. In addition a reliable seat is required and correct influence with the inside leg, which drives the horse increasingly onto the outside rein. The outside hand should be held low as the horse steps more willingly up to the rein when it is held low.

Contrary to popular opinion, "Überstreichen" is not particularly suitable for checking whether the horse is stepping trustingly onto the rider's hand. Even a constricted horse going behind the bit can pass this test quite plausibly. More suitable for exposing such a fault in contact would be "chewing the reins out of the rider's hand" or simply the riding of extensions and transitions.

➜ Suppleness; riding a test; self-carriage

2. Riding of Turns in Movement

(Here it is intended to describe and discuss riding turns in movement as opposed to riding turns out of halt e.g. turn on the forehand.)

Correct riding of turns requires practice; it serves the purpose,

- of being able to ride school figures precisely, even under increased requirements e.g. in tests or quadrille riding,
- when riding a show jumping or cross country course of being in the position to follow exact tracks in order to come to the jump quickly, at an optimum angle and in an good distance.
- Turns ridden correctly with all aids also serve to gymnasticize the horse evenly on both reins, in other words to straighten the horse, and so create the necessary conditions for all collecting work.

How tightly the turns can be ridden depends on the level of training, above all on the horse's bending ability. Also in daily work tighter turns should only be demanded gradually with increasing suppleness. In order to be able to ride turns almost equally well on both reins, the rider has to be aware of the problem of natural crookedness and to have learned to deal with it, also adapting appropriately from horse to horse depending on the individual requirements. (> Part 3, Chapter 6. "Straightening"!)

The aim always has to be for the horse to bend around the rider's inside leg and step reliably onto the outside rein, the rider's outside leg being used to prevent evading with the hindquarters. The weight aid increasing the weight on one seat bone, which only results from the position of the rider's leg, supports the flexing and bending. Only when the horse accepts the diagonal aids, accepts the driving of the rider's inside leg to the outside rein well, can the rider become light on the inside rein. This in turn is a pre-requisite for regularity of rhythm and self-carriage in all turns.

A frequently made mistake results from the exaggeration of the weight aid, when increasing the weight on one seat bone. Through the collapsing in the hip, the rider's weight is shifted outwards so that the common balance is disturbed.

All turns can be practised at walk first of all and then, in accordance with the level of training and degree of collection, ridden in appropriate size at trot and canter.

The so-called "straightening bending work" does not, however, demand a constant, even exaggerated riding of turns and "curls". Even the young rider and young horse can be familiarized with the very valuable exercises shoulder-fore and riding in position (> Part 4, Chapters 10.1 and 10.2) at an early stage.

Here a few examples:

Riding corners
Such a simple exercise as riding a corner in the arena or on an enclosed area seems to be hardly worth mentioning. Nevertheless, it is indeed a valuable subject which deserves consideration. Previous generations of trainers described the corners as "the rider's allies". This applies in so far as in a corner it is most easily possible to ensure bending mainly with the inside leg and not to be mislead into exerting too much influence with the inside rein.

Most riders think about the flexing and bending before and in the corner whilst frequently forgetting, however, that – in contrast to a car – a horse does not have automatic straight-running stability. This is why they omit to finish the corners, the riding of the turn, properly and to give the horse the aids for going straight ahead. This problem, moreover, can not only be observed after corners at the beginning of the long sides but also often when turning onto the centre line or a diagonal.

For the corners also, it applies: how deeply can be ridden into the corners depends on the bending ability and elasticity of the individual horse; faults in rhythm due to unreasonable demands being imposed on the horse are to be avoided at all costs.

The simple serpentine loop on the long side
This exercise is unfortunately not quite as easy to do as its name makes it sound. As before every exercise, the rider first of all has to make himself aware of how it should look and what the criteria of good execution are.

As with all turns, an important prerequisite for successfully executing these with the required precision is that the horse steps trustingly onto the hand, swings through well and thus has enough "positive pull". In a similar way to turning on the diagonal, many horses tend to turn too abruptly and at too great an angle when leaving the track. This is why the rider must quite consciously remain on the track coming out of the corner until the point of change and then remain bent for approx. two horse lengths still around the left leg, when coming from the left rein. Only then does the rider start very gradually to change the flexion, for which now the other leg – the rider's right leg – is primarily responsible, by driving onto the new outside rein, in this case the left one. The reins are adjusted (the new inside one has to be shortened somewhat), on no account the hands may be pressed across the crest of the mane.

During the entire middle part of the serpentine loop, the horse remains bent – in this case to the right – in order to be re-positioned again approximately two horse lengths before the point of change and now to be ridden back again to the track with the rider's left leg. (> Illustration on next page)

The more precise the rider's mental vision of the line to be ridden is, including the points for changing flexion and the vertex at the level of B-X-E, the better he will succeed in riding simple serpentine loops. The use of cones can be a great help when practising (> Illustration p.162). The size of the serpentine loop can gradually be increased and should normally be as a maximum to the quarter

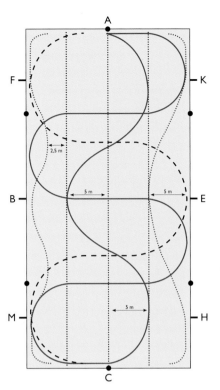

Serpentine lines: Single and double along the long side, across the arena, three and four loops, along the centre line (between the quarter lines)

A

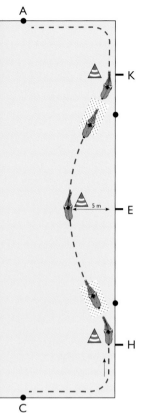

K

5 m

E

H

C

Simple serpentine loop, the areas where the change in flexion and bend has to take place are specially marked

line, in other words five metres into the arena. In training riders of an appropriately advanced level can also ride them larger sometimes.

The volte

Even in dressage tests at medium level well described, circular voltes are a rarity. The size of the volte depends on the level of training and within the training session, the degree of suppleness and bending ability of the horse in question. In novice tests 10-m voltes are required, in elementary tests 8-m and from medium level upwards upwards 6-m voltes.

First voltes are best ridden in one of the corners, particularly because, as described above, these make it easier to bend the horse and are already a quarter volte. Only when the horse is already so reliable on the rider's aids that he can become somewhat light on the inside rein in the turn, does it make sense to start riding (large) voltes.

Another good preliminary exercise is "riding into the circle". This involves starting with the large 20-m circle and gradually riding into it. In contrast to "reducing the circle" (riding the circle progressively smaller), the horse continues to move on one track. The rider can become light with the inside rein every two to three horse lengths; the trainer standing in the middle helps him with the orientation so he can describe the circles concentrically. When working without a trainer, a cone can also be used for orientation purposes.

Even the young rider should learn at an early stage how to deal with the horse's crookedness in this exercise: on the rein on which the horse is more stiff, the "compulsion side", the rider has to pay particular attention with his inside leg to ensure the shoulder does not push over into the circle, and with the outside leg to prevent evading of the hindquarters.

On the rein on which the horse seems to be able to be bent better (on the hollow side), he has to ensure with the guarding outside rein that the horse does not lean on this and "fall out" with the shoulder. As a prophylactic measure he can even bring the horse into counter-flexion; i.e. flex it outwards. For this purpose the outside rein fist

is turned inwards, the rein is taken somewhat and yielded again. He has to drive well onto the outside rein and even think a little in terms of "croup-out", without putting his inside leg further back for this, however.

All in all, this exercise should not be prolonged too much, it is better to begin with riding out again too early than to wait until the horse comes onto the forehand.

Subsequently the volte is then practised on the long side, ideally at a particular point, e.g. in the middle of the long side at B. In any case a point should be selected which is far enough from the short side, because otherwise the horse will try to push over in this direction. Already when riding towards the marker, the

This is the flexion with which a horse should go into the volte.

horse should already be flexed for the turn approximately two horse lengths before B and indeed also already bent somewhat, so that at the marker only a half halt is required as a signal to the horse to turn – it must be possible to become light on the inside rein.

In order to be able to execute a volte which is of true circular form, it is possible to imagine the connecting line between B and E as the straight line dividing the circle into two halves, it is even possible to position a jump pole on this line, approx. one metre away from B (see Graphic p.163 below). The rider's inside leg has to be used in connection with the outside rein to ensure that the prepared horse does not turn too abruptly, which would make the first half of the volte too flat. In the second half, by contrast, it is important to prevent the horse pushing out of the volte and/or making it too large. On the rein on which the horse is somewhat hollow it is important to limit the shoulder well with the guarding rein, which should be held low, sup-

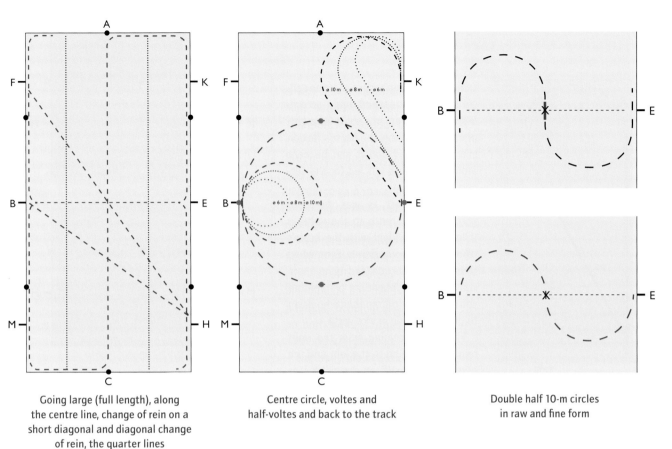

Going large (full length), along
the centre line, change of rein on a
short diagonal and diagonal change
of rein, the quarter lines

Centre circle, voltes and
half-voltes and back to the track

Double half 10-m circles
in raw and fine form

ported by the outside leg which in this case is positioned relatively far forward. On the rather stiffer side (compulsion side) by contrast, the falling out of the hindquarters has to be prevented more; the rider's outside guarding leg, positioned well behind the girth, is responsible for this.

When the volte in the middle of the arena is asked for in higher level tests, the rider has to imagine the relevant line and markers and try to orientate himself carefully, with his head remaining in supple posture.

The half-volte back to the track

The half-volte back to the track either comes in the form of "turning in a circle out of a corner and back to the track" or on the long side. It can be imagined simply as a volte ridden to about two thirds, out of which the horse is then re-positioned (change of flexion and bend) and ridden back to the track (> Graphic p.164).

The double half 10-m circle

The double half 10-m circle is a very worthwhile exercise for gymnasticizing purposes. It is

an easy way of testing both the suppleness and equal smoothness of the horse on both reins and also the skill of the rider. It is asked for in quite a lot of tests, usually crosswise to the centre line.

It is ridden, for example, from the right rein, starting in the middle of the long side at B, in a half 10-m circle to the centre line to X and with a second half 10-m circle to the left to the E marker back to the track. In more advanced training the aim is for the horse to do a flowing change of flexion and bend at X, without riding straight on, i.e. to join two genuine half circles together.

When practising, it is recommendable, in order to gain enough space and time for careful changing of flexion and bend, not to turn precisely at B but rather slightly later, thus doing the first half volte

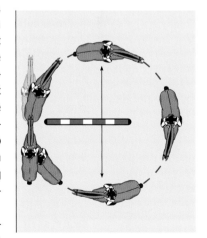

A pole makes
it easier to
calculate
a volte.

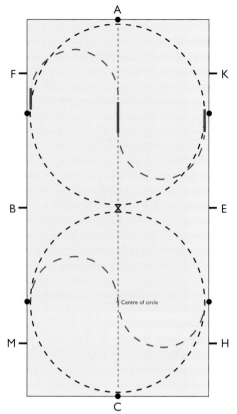

Changing through the circle: raw form and fine form

Cones make it easier to ride two serpentine loops correctly.

Cones or poles can also be very helpful practising serpentine lines through the arena, each loop touching the long side of the arena.

ridden on the long side from marker to marker in a collected, at least shortened, working trot and should be ridden with its vertexes 2.5 m into the arena. Analogous to the simple serpentine loop, the horse has to change the bend four times here, this has to be done much more skilfully and quickly. For that reason already before starting, the reins have to be shortened so much that no more adjustment is necessary during the serpentine.

As the loops are very flat, the horse only has to be bent slightly; too strong bending of the neck in particular is to be avoided. Two serpentine loops is an exercise where the rider can feel in an exemplary that it can only be done correctly with finely coordinated interplay of all aids and precise navigation controlled by the rider's mind.

In contrast to the simple serpentine loop in which riders frequently reach the dividing point vertex too early, in other words before the connecting line between B and E, they usually change the flexion too late in the double loops, particularly in the first one so that there is no longer space for the second loop. The use of cones can work wonders here!

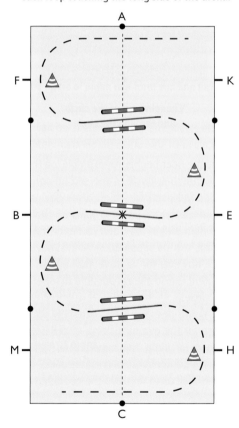

Serpentine loops across the arena (touching the long side)
Serpentine loops across the arena can be done in different ways: one of these is the form which is required in dressage tests, in which the centre line is crossed in the right angle. In the second,

older form this is done in a slightly S-shaped way (> Graphic p.140 and p.166). Originally the corners were to be ridden normally and the loops started at the changing point.. More harmonious to ride and at least as valuable is the form illustrated here, in which the first loop is already started on the short side, and the last loop finished on the short side again; in this respect it corresponds to the form required in dressage tests.

In daily work this form (some call it pear shape) should also be ridden more, because it is more valuable from a gymnasticizing point of view.

Depending on the size of the arena, 40 or 60 metres long, between three and six loops are usually ridden. The number of loops ridden should depend on how supple and able to bend the horse is.

In order to be able to calculate them well and ride them correctly, a kind of plan has to be worked out beforehand and then the loops "navigated" with clear foresight.

In the case of four loops on a 40-m arena for example, the centre line is always crossed at the centre points of the circles and at X.

Concerning precise riding, particularly as far as change in flexion is concerned, more precise information was already given in the chapter "Straightening".

For the precise riding of very different tracks, also in jumping – incidentally – cones and poles can provide valuable help and also create some variety in the training of horses as well as of riders (> Graphics!).

→ Straightening

3. Transitions – Moments of Truth

There are a variety of different transitions to be used in equestrian training:

- **On the one hand there is the change from one basic gait to another. In this context there is a further distinction: the so-called simple transitions, in other words the changes from one gait into the next higher or lower gait, walk-trot, trot-canter, canter-trot and trot-walk, which count amongst the suppling exercises.**
- **Considerably more demanding, and already belonging to collecting work, are the transitions walk-canter and canter-walk.**
- **Also described as transitions are the changes within a basic gait from one pace to another, e.g. from collected trot to medium trot or vice versa etc.**
- **The term transitions is also used in relation to the lateral work, e.g. from travers to shoulder-in and/or to renvers etc.**
- **Finally, at Grand-Prix level, there are the transitions from the piaffe to the passage and vice versa as well as from the passage to the extended trot and vice versa.**

Transition to medium canter: The rider is relieving the horse of some of her weight in order to merge well with the horse's movement.

4. ➤ Turn on the Forehand

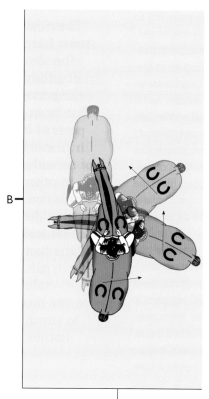

B —

Turn on the forehand

4. Turn on the Forehand

The turn on the forehand is very rarely required in a competition context, it is frequently discussed, however – often in controversial terms: what exactly is its purpose and what is the correct sequence of the movement and application of the relevant aids?

The turn on the forehand is a suppling exercise, however when executed correctly, it is a very difficult movement.

Occasionally it is also ridden in order to familiarize the young horse with the sideways-driving aids, for this purpose the experienced rider and trainer, however, are more likely to use leg-yielding or the preliminary exercises for the lateral movements (shoulder-fore and riding in position).

Nevertheless, it can be quite valuable for the training of the young rider. On a suitable schoolmaster, the young rider can practise and learn the entire application of the aids and, above all, the coordination of the aids particularly well, because the sequence of movement here is slow and the movement can even be executed in sections.

The ideally executed turn on the forehand should be done as follows: out of a good, confident halt, the horse flexed in the direction of the turn, describes a half-circle around the forehand with the hind legs, whereby the turning point should be as close to the inside fore hoof as possible. The outside fore leg steps around the inside fore leg on a small half circle whilst the outside hind leg always just steps slightly to the side, so that subsequently the inside hind leg in question can step over or cross clearly forwards-

sideways. The undesirable turning with the inside fore leg grounded does not happen so easily if the turn is not kept too small. The horse should in fact be slightly flexed only, under no circumstances, however, be bent too much out of the shoulder, because otherwise it will fall out over the shoulder. In order to avoid provoking any stepping back or a raising of the neck and the head, the turn on the forehand should not be executed at the rails of an enclosed riding arena.

For the turn on the forehand the rider applies the following aids: He gives a gentle weight aid increasing the weight on one seat bone and takes the somewhat shortened new inside rein slightly to flex the horse, simultaneously with the guarding outside rein, held low, he prevents the neck being bent too sharply. With the inside leg positioned slightly back, he drives the horse round in the rhythm of the sequence of movement, step by step forward-sideways and, with the guarding outside leg, which is also positioned slightly back, he prevents the horse from stepping too much sideways with the outside hind leg and/or hurrying around with the hindquarters. During the entire turn the rider has to use his weight aids and both legs to keep the horse well in front of him ; this is the only way to ensure that the horse remains on the rein and does not go against the hand. The fact that, contrary to popular opinion, an even slightly backward tendency during the turn on the forehand is certainly a more serious mistake, is due to a variety of reasons: **Throughout the entire riding theory the stipulation that the rider should always have his horse in front of him features – quasi as a recurrent principle – and naturally this also applies with regard to this exercise. This concept is especially important for less experienced riders because they very frequently tend to sit in a forward-leaning position prior to commencing a movement and, above all, to deal with contact problems by using rein aids with a backward-pulling effect.**

In the case of horses which regularly only step beside with the inside hind leg , instead of crossing over forward-sideways, it is recommendable even with a slight forward-sideways tendency, to ride rather like leg-yielding, thus promoting and facilitating the stepping over and crossing of the hind legs. In order to further increase the learning effect for the rider, the turn on the forehand should be ridden at a different point every time. If it is ridden too often on the second track many horses no longer wait for the rider's aids but rather complete the turn of their own accord. It functions much better either on or across to the centre line; the horse then waits better for the rider's aids. The trainer can also increase the learning effect further by giving the rider a sign with his voice each time when the inside hind leg should step off and move sideways, when the rider has to drive sideways with the inside leg. **All in all, it is less important for the horse to turn as quickly as possible – the very important aspect is that it indeed clearly responds to the rider's aids but really waits for these, however, rather than anticipating them in advance.** Therefore it is perfectly acceptable for the exercise to be done in sections, i.e. after every second step a halt for a short moment may be integrated.

As the ridden horse should follow the weight of the rider, in other words should always try to be in balance with the rider, in the case of the weight aid increasing the weight on one seat bone, indeed only the pressure on the inner seat bone should be increased slightly. This happens simply as a result of the outside guarding leg being taken back somewhat out of the hip and made as long as possible in the process. On no account the rider should move, even slightly, to this side with his upper body and trunk.

Although the turn on the forehand does not play a direct role in the further training of a dressage horse, every horse which is well on the aids should always be able to execute this exercise correctly.

➜ Application of the aids; suppleness

5. Leg Yielding

The leg yielding exercise, and the different possibilities it offer, is subjected to a wide variety of different judgements by trainers. In the following I should like to clarify when and how this exercise can be executed usefully, and what specific aspects deserve attention.

Leg yielding counts among the supplying movements. It is intended to familiarize the horse with the sideways-driving aids and altogether make it more through. For a rider in the learning stages it is an excellent exercise for improving the coordination of the aids, because it can be done at walk, therefore giving the rider more time by the slow sequence of movement. In this context the rider can experience that a horse, which initially hesitates in responding to the sideways-driving aids, accepts these much more easily when he coordinates the timing of these better. Frequently then, with a more subtly applied sideways-driving leg aid, i.e. with less strength, he can achieve better success.

In leg yielding the horse moves slightly flexed, but without a bend in the ribcage forwards-sideways on two tracks. Here the inside legs step ahead of and cross over the outside legs. The four-beat rhythm of the walk must be maintained. The flexion always takes place to the side of the sideways-driving leg, which thus becomes the inside leg, even if it is positioned towards the rails. Leg yielding is normally done at walk and only ever ridden at a working trot by advanced riders on appropriate horses. It should only be done over not too long stretches.

> The following aids are to be applied:
> • The rider applies a weight aid, increasing the weight on one seat bone which should, however, only ensue as a result of the outside guarding leg being taken back out of the hip in its guarding function; the upper body should remain upright in the process.

Leg yielding with head to the rails

Leg yielding with head facing into the arena

5. ➢ Leg Yielding

➢ Leg yield-
ing away
from and
back to the
track should
always be
practised
in sections
and, in the
first place,
separately.

- The inside leg is positioned slightly behind the girth and drives forwards-sideways as well as possible in rhythm with
the stepping off hind leg, the rider's outside leg, as already mentioned above, in
a guarding position behind the girth,
thus preventing the horse stepping
round too far with the hindquarters; simultaneously it is also responsible for
the forward movement.
However it is not possible to prevent
the horse evading over the shoulder
with the outside leg in a guarding position.
- The inside rein is taken slightly in order
to give the horse flexion.
- The outside rein is given as much as is
required for the flexion, without surren-
dering reliable contact to the horse's
mouth. On the other hand it prevents
too strong bending of the neck and thus
falling out over the shoulder.

Leg yielding can be ridden in the following different forms:

For the learning rider it is easier initially to use
the leg adjacent to the wall to get the horse to
yield ("head to the wall"). This way the rider can
concentrate more on his forward-sideways driving and, on account of the delimitation by the
wall, will be less inclined to apply too many rein
aids.

This is the form in which first attempts will certainly be made with the young horse.

The second corner of the short side is cut
slightly so the long side is approached at an angle, thus representing the desired angle. Similarly, it also functions well out of a half-volte and
back to the track. It is finished by the horse being re-flexed and brought back to the track in a
flat curve.

In the further training it is more valuable, but
also more demanding, to ask the horse to yield
to the leg away from the wall, In other words fac-

ing the inside of the arena ("head into the arena"). Here, starting at the first marker on the long side, the horse is very gradually guided inwards with the forehand, whereby the sideways-driving leg in connection with the guarding rein has to show the horse in good time what is required of it, that it should remain along the rails and not turn into the arena. To finish, the forehand is guided back onto the track, keeping the horse flexed, however.

Furthermore, there is also the exercise "leg yielding away from and back to the track" which simply involves leg yielding along a diagonal line. For this exercise the horse is re-positioned (the horse's flexion is changed) out of the corner at the beginning of the long side as it is still going straight and only then it should be ridden forwards-sideways into the arena. At a maximum of five metres' distance to the track, the horse is positioned and ridden straight, with a gradual change of flexion, and only then rid-den back again forwards-sideways to the wall.

Leg yielding away from and back to the track should always be practised in sections and, in the first place, separately. That means in the learning stage, and also occasionally in further practice, only leg yielding away from the track

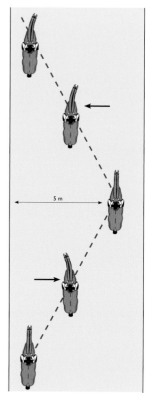

5 m

Leg-yielding away
from and back to the track consists of performing the
leg-yielding along a dia-
gonal line and back again.

or only back to the track should be ridden. Particularly in a larger arena or space, some steps forwards-sideways can then be required in alternation with some steps straight ahead, only forwards, and then again some steps forwards-sideways.

"Letting the horse step over on the open side of the circle" is already a very difficult exercise and should only be done by more advanced riders. This exercise is only meaningful when the forwards movement is properly maintained whilst at the same time the circle line can be followed with great precision.

All these exercises are only of value as long as the regularity of rhythm is guaranteed in the flowing and active forward movement of the walk. Depending on the extent of this, the rider or trainer decides how much angle, and thus how much crossing of the legs, he may require. If leg yielding is practised frequently, it is important to make sure that the horse does not begin anticipating and starting to move sideways more, or yielding sideways, of its own accord; on the one hand it should respond in a through way to the rider's aids, on the other hand however, it should always wait for the aids to be applied.

And now a few frequently made mistakes, which every rider should try to avoid:

When applying the weight aid increasing the weight on one seat bone, the rider must on no account lean over with the upper body, as this would irritate particularly the ridden horse as it has, after all, learned to follow the rider's weight. Exaggeration of this aid occurs frequently because the rider has the incorrect conception of being able to push the horse sideways in this way. Responsible for this, however, is the forward-sideways driving leg, which is positioned approximately one hand's width further back.

If the horse does not accept this aid enough, it makes little sense to put the leg further back or even to exert constant pressure, instead the aid must simply be applied more precisely as an impulse at exactly the moment in which the inside hind leg steps off.

It can frequently be observed here that the rider, without noticing, also uses the guarding outside leg more at the same time as giving the impulse with the inside leg. This is completely counter-productive, especially with the guarding leg quite far back, because, as a consequence, the horse knows even less that it is intended to cross with the hind legs. Rather here, once again, the so-called diagonal application of the aids is extremely important. That means at the moment in which the inside leg gives more impulse, the guarding outside rein has to ensure that the horse does not evade over the shoulder.

When the horse constantly tries, by becoming rushed and evading over the shoulder, to avoid crossing with the legs, it has proved useful to halt once, in the position and with the angle where the horse is at that particular moment. In this way the horse learns better to wait for the rider's aids.

If, when pushing away via the outside shoulder, the horse bends its neck too much, the rider has to hold his hand with the outside guarding rein somewhat lower and, by clear taking and yielding, prevent the horse from leaning on the rein. Unfortunately in such cases many riders push across the withers with the outside hand, as a result of which the horse is restricted in the forwards movement and is virtually forced to tilt at the poll.

When limiting the outside shoulder, it can indeed be quite helpful to position a whip against this shoulder. Under no circumstances the outside leg should exercise a stronger guarding influence on the hindquarters; possibly however, in

Leg yielding with head to the rails: At the beginning it is a good idea to be content with a slightly less angle than is shown here.

The horse shows correct leg-yielding away from the track with correct flexing. At this moment the rider is exerting influence slightly too far back with the right leg.

6. ➤ Rein Back... With Patience

This is a very good way of helping a horse to rein-back.

be thinking of buying, it is important also to test the rein back. If it is not possible to get the horse to rein back just two to three steps, even with assistance, and even leading the horse in hand, investigations should be conducted to find out whether health problems, e.g. in the back , may be the reason for this.

Occasionally, with regard to horses which have difficulty in doing reining back, one hears the recommendation, by way of introduction to the exercise, to get them to step sideways as in a turn on the for hand. For psychological reasons, this idea is not acceptable; as far as the motorics are concerned, it is senselesss – if not impossible – to learn a sequence of movement by making a detour via a false pattern of movement.

In further training, from approximately elementary level upwards, the rein back should be so familiar and natural to the horse that it can complete this movement with the elevation and head position (Beizäumung) appropriate to the class in question.

6.1 The rein back with an advanced horse

The rein back always has to be commenced out of a reliable, closed halt, depending on the demands posed by the test, it ends either in halt again or it is followed on immediately by moving forward in walk, trot or canter.

In the Schaukel (rein back series), in dressage tests as from advanced level, moving back a certain number of steps is followed by a certain number of steps forwards, again a certain number of steps backwards and then immediate moving forward in walk, trot or canter; the horse should not actually halt during the rein back series and should move smoothly, without any hesitation on a straight line, the entire ex-

Reining-back against the hand

ercise should be executed with good bending at the haunches and collection.

In the case of a trained horse which is familiar with this exercise, the rider applies an aid as in riding on, in other words slightly forward-driving with weight and legs and intercepts the forward movement as it starts with a non-yielding or taking and yielding rein aid and re-directs it into backward movement. As the horse starts to take the first step backwards with a yielding poll, the rider becomes slightly light with the hand without giving up the contact. Each further step backwards is accompanied by the same application of the aids, both legs of the rider are slightly back in a guarding position in order to prevent the horse from becoming crooked.

Whether the reins have to be used in a non-yielding or asking and yielding way, depends on the horse's level of training. If the horse has good throughness, a very fine non-yielding aid will be sufficient, the rider will drive the horse on to this and the horse will push away from it to a certain extent. If it is still necessary to work with taking and yielding, riders should be aware of the very realistic danger that the horse will become increasingly short in the neck with every step it takes – until it becomes stiff in the back and starts to hesitate.

The more through the full halt was, the more willing and supple the rein back will turn out.

In any case, the first step backwards should not be asked for – or allowed – until the horse yields in the poll and is concentrating well on the matter in hand.

It may sound somewhat paradoxical, but even when reining back, the rider must have the horse on the driving aids and well in front of him; otherwise it is hardly possible to control every step and, later on, also to ride a specifically stipulated number of steps.

6.2 Incorrect rein back

Rein back with resistance against the hand

If the horse has learned to do the rein back correctly and without compulsion so that it has a good command of the principles of the exercise, resistance really only occurs when the rider does not allow himself enough time at the beginning, does not wait until the horse yields in the poll and begins to pull backwards with the reins.

If this fault occurs in every rein back attempt, the entire exercise must be started anew, and built up again just as with a young horse.

Rein back in a hurry

The reason for this fault is usually that the horse is not sufficiently on the driving aids, is not in front of the rider enough. Therefore it is important to prevent the fault already when halting and, if necessary, not even to begin the rein back at this moment. Great attention should generally be paid to ensure that the horse in no way anticipates, in other words begins the rein back of its own accord.

When the rider notices that the horse is beginning to hurry during the rein back, he has to apply his legs, which should be positioned slightly behind the girth, rather more strongly and think more about driving forward. He should not make the mistake, caused by the instinct, as soon as the horse starts to rush backwards, of yielding too much or even giving up the contact. Otherwise the horse will learn very quickly that by starting to hurry, it can cause the rider to give up the contact, it learns to evade the aids.

Faults in the sequence of steps

Problems relating to the diagonal sequence of footfalls usually occur when the horse, due to a lack of throughness, either begins to hurry or steps backwards, dragging, with resistance. Occasionally it is also caused by the fact that it begins the first step with the fore leg only without taking the diagonal hind leg with it too.

This occurs particularly if, already when halting, a horse has closed in too much with the hind legs and the rider has not allowed it to correct itself by taking half a step forwards with its fore legs.

A further reason for the problem can be that the rider is imposing too much pressure with his guarding legs in a backward position, frequently also specifically because the horse hesitates somewhat to step backwards, and it therefore does not feel confident about stepping back immediately with its hind legs.

Crooked rein back

When a horse has a tendency to become crooked, normally valuable correction can only be achieved by an improvement in how the horse is straightened.

When practising on the first track, i.e. along the wall or rails of the arena, it is possible that the horse may become crooked on both reins if, due to a lack of balance and collection, it also becomes wide at the rear.

Problems in the rein back followed by moving forward immediately in the required gait

If the test asks for "Rein back, followed by moving forward in walk, trot or canter", the first step or stride in the required gait should be regular in rhythm and free of tension. On the one hand, the rider has to permit the forward movement well, i.e. to become light with the hands, on the other hand he must not give up the contact and has to keep the horse closed; particularly when cantering on, the necessary positive body tension must be maintained.

The forward-driving aids should be applied resolutely, without taking the horse by surprise or making it hectic. With a horse which enjoys working together with the rider and is sensitive

to the rider's leg, this exercise does not pose any great difficulties.

In the case of all problems which occur in connection with the rein back and occur frequently in more or less the same form, a step back must be taken with regard to the demands, the horse must be adjusted better again forward-downwards over the back, more attention must be given to the suppleness as a whole in order to be able to correct the horse effectively.

➔ Basic gaits; suppleness; straightening; crookedness; collection

7. Turn on the Haunches from Halt, Turn on the Haunches from Walk or Trot, Walk Pirouette

The turn on the haunches from halt and turn on the haunches from walk or trot are collecting exercises which pose increased demands on the horse and rider, walk pirouettes already require a higher degree of collection and are not required until medium level tests.

The sequence of movement in all three exercises is, in principle, identical. The horse, in reliable contact, is evenly bent around the rider's inside leg, it turns 180° around the hindquarters with the forehand, the turning point should be as close as possible to the inside hind hoof, which steps down and steps off almost on the spot, the forelegs step forward-sideways and cross, the entire turn should be executed in

Turn on the haunches: At the movement sequence of a walk, the horse moves around a set point which is close to the inner hind hoof.

the four-beat rhythm of walk and be characterized by a slight forward tendency.

As, on the basis of the sequence of movement around the inside hind leg, the horse leaves the original track by a body's width, it has to be brought back onto the track at the end with a travers-like forward-sideways step. Only in this final step the outside hind leg should step over forward-sideways. A crossing of the hind legs would otherwise be incorrect because in this way the horse evades taking up the load with the inside hind leg.

When the turn on the haunches is done from trot, a half-halt to walk has to be given one to two steps beforehand. The walk pirouette is ridden out of the collected walk and differentiates itself from the other two exercises only by means of the high degree of collection.

The following aids are applied:
- The weight aid increasing the weight on one seat bone (without leaning over to the side or even collapsing in the hip) ensues from the re-positioning of the legs for the leg aids.
- The rider's inside leg is in a forward-driving position on the girth.
- The rider's outside leg is taken back slightly out of the hip in a guarding position, it prevents a falling out of the hindquarters, it should not drive sideways, however.
- The inside rein has a sideways-leading function, contributes to the flexion and directs the horse in the direction of the turn.
- The outside rein permits the flexion, limits it and the bending of the neck and prevents the horse falling out over of the shoulder.
- The sum of all aids together ensures the necessary longitudinal bending, whereby the inside rider's leg is of prime importance.

- **Both rider's legs are responsible for the slight forward tendency and the regular stepping off and stepping on.**

In order to apply all aids correctly, the rider should have the following conception:

He has the horse, stepping trustingly onto the hand, reliable on the driving aids and in front of him, he is sitting slightly in the direction in which he would like to turn and, using his weight and leg aids, takes the slightly forward-thinking ("positively pulling") horse with him. In order to avoid collapsing in the inside hip and thus sitting to the wrong side, he can try slipping slightly towards the middle of the saddle with his outside seat bone.

A pre-requisite for the turn on the haunches (from halt and from walk or trot) is that the horse already allows itself to be more or less straightened and, to a certain extent, be collected. As the turn on the haunches from walk or trot has already begun in movement, it should be practised first of all, initially just in small stages – i.e. with a turn of 60° or at the most 90°.

A useful preliminary exercise is any correctly ridden turn in which the horse is correspondingly bent and moves reliably on one track (tracking up well), i.e. does not evade or fall out to the inside or outside, either with the forehand or the hindquarters. It has to be reliable on the outside rein and altogether step well and trustingly onto the rider's hand. In most cases this is particularly difficult at walk. Therefore, it is important in training to ride precise turns at walk in which the horse learns, always in the half halt prior to the turn, not to hesitate but rather to step forward trustingly (> Part 3, Chapter 2. "Riding at Walk"). In order to come off well from the inside rein in the turn, as emphasized above, it is advantageous to flex the horse appropriately, possibly also already bend it, a few steps beforehand. This riding straight ahead with slight flexion and bending corresponds to the familiar preliminary exercises for the lateral movements, i.e. shoulder-fore and riding in position (> Part 4, Chapter 10.2 and 10.3).

As indeed, on account of their natural crookedness, all horses are somewhat stiff on one side and tend to make themselves rather hollow on the other side, it is of advantage to ride accordingly, even before the turn. In this context the rider should think more in terms of shoulder-fore on the rather hollow side, if necessary even a little about "croup-out", in order to avoid the horse either evading over the shoulder or coming in with the hindquarters in the turn.

On the other side, the rider should think more about riding in position, perhaps even a little in terms of travers or "shoulder-out". This prevents the horse either falling out with the hindquarters or, however, pushing into the turn with the shoulder and thus avoiding the required longitudinal bending.

A good preparatory exercise is a large volte (approx. 10 m) at walk, which ideally should be ridden around the trainer, if no trainer is available, around a cone or an imaginary fixed point. Here again the rider should think of shoulder-fore on the hollow side (see above), i.e. the hindquarters move precisely on the line of the circle, the shoulder approx. two hand widths within the circle. If during this exercise, going evenly forwards, with a slight "positive pull", the horse steps trustingly onto the hand, the rider can guide it two steps with the forehand into the volte, and subsequently – whilst maintaining the longitudinal bend – ride ahead, again on one track and return to the circle track.

On the stiffer side, the so-called compulsion side, the rider has to ride somewhat travers-like so that the forehand moves precisely on the circle line, the hindquarters one or two hand's widths inside this. If this succeeds well, the turn is to be tried again in the same way as on the other rein, and just in small sections.

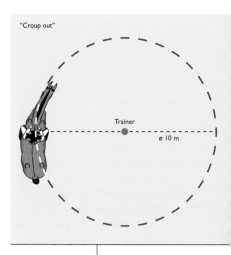

"Croup out"

Trainer

ø 10 m

"Croup out":
The imaginary line of the track is exactly between the fore-hooves, the inner hind hoof follows approximately along this line.

7. ➤ Turn on the Haunches from Halt, Turn on the Haunches from Walk or Trot, Walk Pirouette

The square volte: Riding along each side with flexion and a slight bend, a short turn out of the corners then at 90°. When riding on the horse's difficult (concave) side, shoulderfore is to be recommended, in the stiffer compulsory side, riding in position.

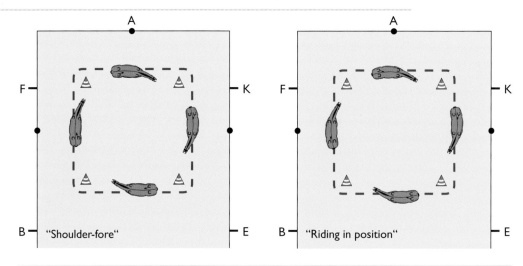

"Shoulder-fore"

"Riding in position"

Cones help the rider to calculate the turn accurately.

On the hollow side a possible coming inwards with the hindquarters has to be prevented by means of slight "croup out", on the stiffer side a pushing in with the forehand by "shoulder-out" (possibly with the whip on the inside shoulder!).

Unfortunately these turns are frequently ridden with the wrong impression of wanting to "push" the horse around with the weight and leg aid. Of course the horse has to be sensitive to both legs, it not only has to accept the forward-driving but also to have good respect for the guarding leg, which should always have a forward-driving effect, too.

Only when the horse reacts against the guarding leg and tries to evade with the hindquarters the outside leg should react with active impulses in order to re-establish respect. A rider's outside leg which is constantly too active causes the horse to step sideways, sometimes even to cross the hind legs. On the one hand the turn will become too large as a consequence, on the other hand, however, the collecting purpose of this exercise gets lost because the horse evades taking up the load with the inside hind leg.

The first exercises should always be done out of walk, ideally away from the track, because then the horse concentrates best on the rider's aids. It is recommendable, as mentioned above, to be satisfied initially with one or two steps in which the horse accepts the turn. This can then be continued, e.g. in the form of a so-called square volte (> Graphic), in which (in the inside of the arena,) the horse is always turned in the corner in the form of a half turn on the haunches from walk or trot by 90°. On the sides of the square in question, the horse is ridden straight ahead with flexion and slight bending.

The first complete turns on the haunches from walk or trot by 180° can be ridden particularly well on a line across the arena, always turning the horse shortly before reaching the long side. The wall or rails help the rider to close the horse without having to exercise too much influence with the reins.

These exercises should be done successfully before it makes sense to ride a turn on the haunches from halt. Also from halt, the horse should start off with a step forwards. In the further progression there is no difference to a turn on the haunches from walk or trot, only that a full halt should be done immediately afterwards.

If the turn on the haunches from halt is ridden on the track at the wall, in the middle part of the turn the rider should have the conception of wanting to ride half a step forwards away from the wall because in this section most horses have the tendency to push backwards and lean on the wall. In the last third of the turn on the haunches from halt the rider has to keep the horse well with him by means of correctly ridden half halts, because in this section the horse tends to want to go forwards too much and rush back to the track.

As soon as the horse begins to step no longer evenly in the sequence of movement of the walk, also with the hind legs, the turn has to be ridden somewhat larger, to a certain extent in half steps, in a forward direction. Too active influence with the outside leg is to be avoided here, as this would again provoke the incorrect crossing of the hind legs already mentioned above.

Some horses hesitate when they know this exercise well and begin to anticipate, i.e. they begin to turn of their own accord and the necessary forward tendency gets lost. This has to be counteracted immediately otherwise problems ensue ranging from mistakes in rhythm (Takt) to an ambling sequence of movement:

The turn is ridden more in forwards, e.g. in half steps. In the preparation the horse is closed somewhat more significantly, approximately two horse's lengths beforehand (with good, even further driving aids), in order with somewhat more frame again to remain more clearly in forwards during the turn.

If the horse tries to rush around in the turn, the rider has to apply all the aids somewhat more resolutely, however in particular he has to try and intercept this with the inside leg in connection with the outside rein. This fault usually occurs on the horse's stiffer side because, as described above, this is how it tries to escape the longitudinal bending. If the horse does not accept the turn enough, the turn has to be tried again in more clear forwards, because then the crossing with the fore legs is easier for the horse;

touching on the outside shoulder with the whip may be helpful. Under no circumstances the rider should try to push the horse around with the outside rein because this would impede the forward movement and the longitudinal bending. Tilting in the poll may also be a consequence.

On finishing the turn on the haunches from walk or trot attention must consistently be paid to ensure that this is done clearly and in good time with the inside leg so that the horse does not change flexion too early by itself and evade the aids.

In the turn on the haunches from walk or trot as well as the turn on the haunches from halt, it is always important as, in all such technical exercises and movements, to practise them often enough with correct and well considered application of the aids, ideally under supervision. Otherwise, particularly also with these movements, as already mentioned above, attention must be paid to ensure that the horse does not anticipate, but rather waits step for step to be given the aids; this is the only way in which to avoid faults relating to rhythm (Takt) and longitudinal bending. Therefore it is important also to use a little imagination and to ride the exercises for these movements at different points and in different contexts during training.

Thus it is recommendable occasionally to ride turns on the haunches from walk or trot, or at a more advanced level of training walk pirouettes, on the quarter line or at the end of a diagonal in the direction of the wall.

Touching with the whip on the outer shoulder can help to show the horse the direction of the turn.

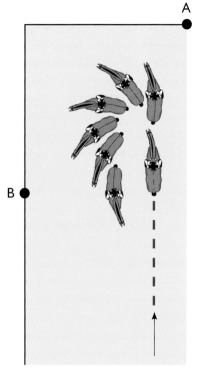

A

B

In the walk pirouette to the wall or into the corner the horse will wait better for the rider's aids.

When horse and rider have learnt the turn on the haunches from halt and turn on the haunches from walk or trot according to this system and have a good command of them, providing the horse has enough ability and willingness to collect at walk, riding a walk pirouette also does not cause any difficulties.

➔ **Riding at walk; riding turns; shoulder-fore; riding in position**

8. **Canter Work: Collecting Work, Simple Change of Leg and Counter-canter**

Concerning the canter as a basic gait, all important aspects relating to sequence of movement, rhythm, scope etc. have already been explained in the relevant chapter on this subject (> Part 3.2). In the following I shall give some special tips specifically about collecting canter work.

8.1 Application of the aids when cantering on

The aids for cantering out of walk and out of trot are basically the same:

The horse is prepared with half halts and increasingly closed, i.e. more framed in between the forward-driving and the restraining aids. This short process may be compared with the gentle bending of a spring.

The rider's inside leg is positioned on the girth, whilst the outside leg is moved approximately one hand's width further back and well lengthened.

As a result of this position of the rider's legs, particularly the moving back and lengthening of the outside leg, the inner seat bone has somewhat more pressure imposed on it (weight aid increasing the weight on one seat bone). Bending over with the upper body is superfluous, indeed it would disturb the balance.

The inside rein is shortened somewhat or leads somewhat sideways, in order to give the horse the necessary flexion.

The outside rein guards, i.e. it permits the flexion, but also limits it.

As soon as the horse starts to canter on, the rider becomes light, particularly with the inside hand, in order to allow the canter stride to emerge.

Unfortunately the impression is also conveyed to young riders that the most important, or even solely important, matter when cantering on, is to move the outside leg back. Initially this may also be enough to "jockey the well-behaved older horse into canter". For further, rather more advanced training this concept is in fact counterproductive however, because usually the rider's leg is moved too far back, pulled up and used too much in the process.

Thus the horse is indeed rather encouraged to do a crooked canter; particularly in work in the counter-canter and in flying changes it is important to request every canter stride with the inside leg.

When cantering on from walk it is particularly important that the horse remains on the one hand reliably over the back and yielding in the poll, that the rider however also manages to become light (without giving up contact) on the inside rein in order to permit good striding under with the inside hind leg. If it may be expected that the horse comes up in the transition, on no account should the rider try to push it down with his hands, however. Rather, already as a preventative measure, he must try to hold – particularly the inside hand – in a position which guarantees that he will keep the straight line elbow-hand-horse's mouth even at the moment of cantering on.

Very keen horses which have pleasure in working together with the rider tend, in expectation of cantering on (that means more up), to become tense and hectic. This can be avoided by quite consciously demanding the walk with the driving aid beforehand, on no account trying to exert restricting, preventative influence, however.

As it is usually difficult for less experienced riders to apply the canter aid precisely in the support phase of the walk, out of which the footfall sequence of the canter is immediately possible, they should not apply this too selectively and elaborately. If they move the inside leg back approximately one hand's width prior to cantering, in order then, at the moment of cantering on, to let it stroke along the hair again and then to ask for the canter, they give the horse a little more time to react. The moving back of the outside guarding leg should also not be done too abruptly and too extremely. This modified application of the aids can also be advantageous when cantering on out of trot, in case the horse is rather over-eager and is already anticipating the aid.

Transitions always present situations in which the rider-horse system is particularly prone to disturbances, e.g. in relation to the contact. The better the rider knows his horse, the more easily he is able to prevent such disturbances. Thus, when he expects the horse to raise itself when going into canter, he must hold both hands, particularly the inside-hand however, in a position that maintains the straight line elbow-hand-horse's mouth. If it is expected that the horse will come too low in the process, possibly even drops behind, then he must keep the rein fist considerably lower.

Particularly also in the cantering on from walk, the rider has to ensure that he responds appropriately to the change in tempo and balance, that he comes along well with the movement out of his seat, but does not sit behind the movement.

At the beginning it can be helpful to canter on at the same point: as soon as a certain sense of confidence and security has been achieved, however, it is important for this always to be done at a different point, the horse must not be given the opportunity to anticipate, (in other words respond before the aid is applied). In this case the horse must be ridden at trot or walk again until the horse waits for the aid again. It is then important to occupy the horse with half halts, particularly with the driving aids, or by riding with clearer flexion or even bending so that it does not even "have time to think about" cantering on.

In order to be able to ride a simple change of leg at canter, the horse already has to be able to allow itself to be collected well. Therefore I shall deal with that subject specifically in the section after next.

8.2 How can collection at canter be improved?

Naturally everything which promotes the training of the horse in accordance with our training scale ultimately also contributes to an improvement of the collection, irrespective of the basic gait. On account of the sometimes very different natural ability in relation to trot and canter, it is recommendable to plan and organize the training in a way which is differentiated appropriately.

This horse is easily and naturally on the aids immediately after cantering on.

Counter-canter with good flexion; the rider's right inside-hand could be somewhat lighter, however.

The indications "inside" rein or "inside" hind leg always refer to the canter and its flexion, i.e. in the case of a horse cantering on the left rein in counter-canter, in other words, leading on the right leg, the right side is the inside.

In the case of correct work in the counter-canter the horse's ability to balance itself and to take up weight with the hindquarters is initially improved, then also reviewed, the attention to the rider's aids is increased; it is also very suitable for improving the straightened cantering in the extension. Particularly in an indoor school, the wall is a great help in keeping the horse straight when extending in the counter-canter. Concerning the training system, it should be mentioned that the training of the counter-canter and the learning of the flying change can, and indeed should, take place on a parallel basis. Nevertheless it would not be particularly intelligent to practise flying change immediately prior to riding an elementary test.

Before the rider can begin work in the counter-canter, the following pre-requisites must be fulfilled:

- In the case of the rider and horse, the application and acceptance of the aids for the canter should be so refined that in the first place the inside, forward-driving leg asks for the canter, no longer so much the outside guarding leg (> Part 4, 8.1).
- It must be possible, at any point, to canter on leading on the left or right leg, in response to relatively subtle aids.
- Transitions within the gait, i.e. lengthening and shortening to "shortened working pace" already succeed reasonably well on one track, in other words without any significant crookedness.

- Horse and rider must have a relatively good command of cantering out of walk as well as, if possible, also the transition from canter to walk.
- For valuable work in the counter-canter a very considerable degree of collection (in good self-carriage) is necessary. The rider must already have developed a good feeling for collection in the canter as otherwise there is the danger that the stride through deteriorates, in other words loss or irregularities in rhythm (Takt) or other mistakes occur.

Exercises which lead to counter-canter

- A very appropriate first preliminary exercise is in transitions walk-canter-walk on a straight line alternatively also to canter in counter-canter (For this purpose the arena should be at least 40 m long.) If, during the work, the horse begins to anticipate, the walk repeats must be extended over a longer period.
- When riding initially very flat (approx. 1 m from the track) simple serpentine loops without change of leg at canter the horse can become acquainted with the first beginnings of counter-canter.
- Next, either by means of a large half volte back to the track or by a change of rein on a half diagonal to come properly to counter-canter, in order then to do a transition to trot before the following short side or, with a simple change of leg, to return to the true canter.
- Only when these exercises can be executed reliably it does make sense also to ride around the corners in counter-canter; initially these will be very rounded, becoming less as the horse becomes more practised.
- A very demanding exercise is the counter-canter on the circle with the change from counter-canter to counter-canter.
- Very similar and even slightly more demanding are the serpentine loops in canter through the arena, in parts then without

change of leg at canter or also with change from counter-canter to counter-canter, as is required in some tests.

If the counter-canter is ridden over longer stretches, the rider has to pay particular attention to maintaining the impulsion and the striding through.

Faults

- As mentioned above, in the entire cantering work, on straight as well as on curved tracks, the horse is ridden with slight flexion (in the poll). On the one hand this serves as reliable control of the poll, on the other hand it thus counteracts the horse's natural tendency to make itself crooked at canter on both reins and to push inwards somewhat with the hindquarters. This flexing can only fulfil its purpose, however, when it can reliably be achieved with the diagonal application of the aids, inside leg – outside rein, with the horse being well on the outside rein. If there are problems with this and the rider then exercises too much influence on the inside rein, the horse usually becomes even more crooked, however in particular the striding through of the hind legs is restricted.
- When flexed the horse should be bent slightly to the side in the poll and neck. As a rough guide, the recommendation still applies here only to require flexion so far that the inside eye and edge of the inside nostril are recognizable within the rider's field of vision. Unfortunately, particularly in work in the counter-canter, the flexion is frequently exaggerated. (Some judges are also responsible for this exaggeration.) **Too sharp flexing in the neck is completely counter-productive, however because, as mentioned above, it prevents optimum striding through (springy canter) and taking up the load with the hindquarters because it also promotes crooked cantering.** Thus when the rider notices that the horse is pushing into the arena with the shoulder in the counter-canter, the first thing he normal-

ly has to do is to reduce the flexion. At the same time he has to check whether he has perhaps positioned his guarding, still outside leg (in the canter leading on the right leg this would be his left leg) too far behind the girth and is thus exercising too strong influence, possibly even driving sideways.

- This mistake with the guarding outside leg may frequently be observed when riding back towards the track from a half volte or in a change of rein on a short diagonal, for example. Riders then try with this leg aid to prevent the horse changing back to the true canter. As a result, however, the horse is literally forced to become crooked and to canter – travers-like – to the track. **It would be more correct in this situation to have the idea of maintaining the canter in question and carefully asking for each canter stride.**

Here the horse is clearly crooked at the counter-canter and is lowering its head too much.

- If the rider notices that, on arriving at the track, the horse tries to remain on the second track, this can also be due to too strong flexing and lack of being straightened at canter. The correction also has to be undertaken accordingly. The rider must try with (what is still) the inside leg, to drive forward increasingly onto the outside rein, to avoid exaggerated sharp bending of the neck and to keep the horse straight better on one track. The rider should not be induced into wanting to push the horse's shoulder over with the rein fists, particularly the outside fist.
- **Also in the counter-canter, the purity of the gait – in this case therefore the regular three-beat, is the ultimate criterion. Collection should never be at the expense of lively activity.** A slowed down sequence of movement, in which the stride through deteriorates, the motion even degenerates into four-beat canter ("tranter"), is grossly deficient. The mo-

➤ Also when riding extensions, the principle applies that on the one hand the horse should react as immediately as possible to the rider's aids, on the other hand that it really does wait for them.

opment of the impulsion (Schwung). Instead, at precisely the moment when the horse extends, he should have the idea of coming along particularly well with the horse, perhaps sitting slightly forward and, whilst maintaining constant contact, allowing the horse the necessary freedom to extend. The horse can only develop its full potential properly with good, regular rhythm and in self-carriage if it can extend its frame appropriately. It is surprising what some modern warmblood horses can present in spite of short necks. The suppleness of the horse's centre of movement, its back, is decisively dependent, however, on the neck posture, as is its ability to balance properly. Therefore horses which are short in the neck have to be supported by the rider in the extensions, almost carried in fact, if they are to be able to keep moving without mistakes in rhythm, or even canter on.

If a horse shows little pleasure in working together with the rider in the extensions, particularly at trot, it will certainly be necessary to think carefully about the effectiveness of the driving aids, much more however, about the elasticity of the seat and the quality of the rider's hand. Only when the horse steps and strides trustingly onto the hand and strides through, it will, with a supple back, swing through with the hind legs in an ideal way, thus having the necessary impulse and "positive pull" forward which is required for the forward movement.

This confidence of the horse in the rider's hand also plays a very decisive role, particularly in reducing out of the extensions (in downward-transitions): Only if, when collecting, the rider has mastered the correct interplay between taking and yielding with the rein aids or, better still, between non-yielding and becoming light, the horse can take the impulsion (Schwung) with it into the collection, can swing through and close in more with the hind legs. Also as far as his driving aids are concerned, he should not exaggerate: naturally he must sit swinging out of the elastic middle position "bracing and relaxing the back", in other words sit driving, keep his

legs well on the horse's ribs, i.e. give driving impulses. If he exaggerates these aids, he will make too much pressure, possibly also too much tempo and can no longer react elastically to the horse's sequence of movement, and this would result in the horse becoming physically and mentally tense and therefore not working together with the rider in an optimum way; this applies increasingly, the more sensitive and willing the horse is to perform. Only as long as, despite of all "forwards", the composure of the horse's sequence of movement is preserved, no hecticness is created, it will be possible to maintain the necessary suppleness (Losgelassenheit).

Also when riding extensions, the principle applies that on the one hand the horse should react as immediately as possible to the rider's aids, on the other hand that it really does wait for them. It should never develop the habit, coming out of the corner, onto the long side, or across the diagonals, of "setting off" of its own accord, of anticipating. In order to prevent this, it is recommendable always to ride the extensions in different places; such variations can be done particularly well on a large circle. This extending on a large curved track also involves other benefits: As a result of the flexion and slight longitudinal bending predetermined in this case, the rider has the horse even better under control, the reliability of regularity as well as the balance are improved and the inside hind leg is forced to bend more, thus also improving the collection. If, through practising tests for example, the horse begins to extend of its own accord each time on the diagonals coming out of the corner, a good method by which to correct this is, in between times, quite consciously to demand the extension only on the second half. In this context the medium trot or canter should sometimes be continued to the short side, or sometimes even along it, so that the horse does not start to reduce by itself ahead of time.

As in the canter, on account of the diagonal sequence of movement, from the outside hind to the inside fore, horses tend to become more crooked on both reins in the extension, in this gait it is important to begin and to ride this extension out of shoulder-fore. It must be assured here that the horse reliably accepts the diagonal application of the aids "inside leg – outside rein", because otherwise, as a result of too strong influence from the inside rein, particularly when shortening, the inside hind leg is prevented from striding through, occasionally even a temporary change of stride with the hind legs is provoked. For straightening in the canter, thus also in the extension, riding in counter-canter can be very valuable, initially on a straight track and then on a large curved track. However in this context the rider must avoid taking the guarding outside leg too far back and using it too much because otherwise this would be counter productive.

In the trot as well as in the canter extension, despite of the horse's much desired pleasure in working together with the rider and willingness to perform, it must be assured that the initiative for the pace and tempo to be ridden remains with the rider. Only when the horse is still prepared to "wait" to be told in what degree the extension is to be executed, is it still possible for the rider to drive somewhat and keep the horse reliably in front of him. Otherwise faults in rhythm can quickly ensue because the horse comes onto the forehand, the extended trot or canter thus no longer comes out of the collection, and can be presented closed enough and in the desired uphill style. Shorter repeats, done more frequently and at different points, can prevent this problem. Furthermore, in the first steps or strides the rider should have the idea of developing the extension to a certain extent through the reins, through the elastic contact in the first place, before he allows the frame extension accordingly. The further on the horse is trained, the more through it is, the fewer the steps and strides which will be required for this developing of the extension.

Generally speaking, in connection with the collecting exercises one point, unfortunately, is frequently problematic and cannot be mentioned often enough: the horse can only close with the hind legs in a through way, in other words be brought into collection if, thanks to the horse stepping reliably onto the bit, the necessary half halts can be ridden without the horse becoming short in the neck. Otherwise a kind of "kink" comes about in the invisible connection which runs from the horse's mouth through the poll, the neck and back to the hindquarters, which leads to the horse becoming stiff in the back, the connection between reliable contact and swinging through hindquarters gets lost and the horse, instead of bending the hindlegs better and closing, reacts with a high croup and its hindquarters working backwards out.

This is why particularly also the halts must be given precisely and with determination for every reduction of the pace, if in doubt even be given rather more heartily, decisive is to become light with the hand immediately, if necessary the halt must be repeated. The appropriately trained horse will then, whilst yielding, close the hind legs particularly well, a mere signal-like aid will be sufficient to inform the horse to end the extension. If instead, however, the rider "remains hanging" with the taking or non-yielding rein aid until the horse has reduced ("changed the gear"), it will come onto the (fore)hand.

By way of conclusion, I should like to mention one more point which is important with a view to maintaining the horse's health:

In order to prevent premature wear and tear on the horse, the extensions should be ridden and trained in a carefully measured dosage; as the extended trot imposes very great strain on the limbs. This applies to an increased extent when, due to a lack of suppleness, the movement does not go elastically through the horse's entire body and tensions are created during the "downward-transitions". In the case of very hard, deep, rough or uneven ground conditions the responsible rider will abstain from extensions and generally ride very carefully.

→ Impulsion; throughness

Really a very correct shoulder-fore with good bend and elevation; slightly too much angle.

10. Lateral Movements (Side gaits)[1]

In accordance with the definition of our riding theory, the lateral movements are to be understood as forwards-sideways movements in which the horse moves with even longitudinal bending and appropriate collection. They are normally ridden at trot and canter, initially they can be practised very well at walk, however. In dressage tests they are ridden in the form of shoulder-in, travers, renvers and various half-passes.

On the basis of the example of the lateral movements, it is possible to give an outstanding demonstration of what is intended with so-called dressage-like movements. In a competition context they serve to check and to assess the level and quality of the training. Unfortunately this is the reason why many riders have come to believe that they have to practise the lateral movements as an aim in themselves.

Primarily, however, they have to be seen as an important means of training, with the help of which valuable gymnasticing work can be done. **Under this aspect their value for the correct training of a horse, particularly with a view to straightening, cannot be esteemed highly enough.** In the further course of training the bending of the haunches, thus the collection, is also improved as a result of this work; the horse learns to balance better and consequently becomes more through, lither and also more obedient. Particularly with a view to higher collection as a pre-requisite for good quality extensions, but also for an expressive passage, for example, the improvement of the shoulder freedom is also worthy of mention.

Starting point for the riding of lateral movements is the straightening bending work, i.e. riding on curved tracks in as correct longitudinal bending as possible on both reins.

Before progressing to the preliminary exercises such as shoulder-fore and riding in position, I should like to remind readers that in this area also, the inexperienced rider can only learn successfully on a well-trained "school master", whilst the young horse can only be brought on carefully and effectively by a competent trainer.

10.1 Shoulder-fore

Shoulder-fore is ridden at a very slight angle (to the track) and relatively little – but as even as possible – longitudinal bending. In this movement the horse steps with its inner hind leg in the direction between the two forelegs, with the outside hind leg as exactly as possible on the track of the outside for leg, thus already having to follow a narrower tracking with its hind legs. The necessary longitudinal bending, particularly in the ribcage, gets lost if the hindquarters evade outwards. Shoulder-fore is also referred to as "First Position"; see Waldemar Seunig's excellent book "Horsemanship" on this subject.

The application of the aids: By way of preparation the rider ensures that he has his horse reliably under control in collected or shortened working trot, that above all the basic tempo is

---

[1] Side gaits are defined as movements with longitudinal flexion and collection. This is why the forward-sideways movement "leg yielding" is not to be described as a true side gait in the strictest sense.

absolutely appropriate. For this purpose, he accompanies every trotting step with a correct half-halt, in the context of which the driving aids are therefore also carefully applied. As the horse is intended to move with longitudinal bending, the rider maintains the weight aid increasing the weight on one seat bone coming out of the first corner from the long side, drives with the inside leg positioned on the girth step for step onto the outside rein, thus keeping the correct bending of the ribcage and ensuring the inside hind foot continues to step off and move forward actively. The outside leg is positioned slightly back in a guarding position and prevents the hindquarters from evading. The inside rein, which was already shortened a little to ride through the corner, possibly slightly sideways-leading, ensures the flexion. The outside guarding rein permits the flexion, but at the same time also limits it.

In any case riding through the corner should be completely finished before the rider starts to develop the shoulder-fore, in other words he should never try to push the hindquarters out when riding through the corner.

A pre-requisite for the success of this exercise, as well as for the following ones, is that the horse steps forward very reliably and trustingly onto the hand (the horse has to "pull"), whereby in this phase of training it may not yet be automatically assumed that the horse is already so straightened that it really does step completely evenly onto both reins. Therefore with a horse which is still learning, the – hopefully experienced – rider has to apply his aids in an appropriately differentiated way according to the horse's crookedness, depending on whether he is working on the side, or rein of the horse which is rather hollow or rather stiff.

Although the following passage deals principally with the application of the rein aids, it should always be remembered that these can only achieve something if the horse is reliably on the leg aids which, in whatever position, must always exercise forward-driving influence.

On the hollow side attention always has to be paid to prevent an exaggerated bending of the neck or falling out of the shoulder, which is done by keeping the outside hand upright but held well low. Frequently here the horse accepts the outside rein too much and tries to lean on it. The rider should deal with this first of all by short yielding or, however, by short but resolute taking and giving on this rein. Under no circumstances should the horse be offered support in the form of a firm outside rein. The inside rein is also not to be forgotten in this context – it has to prevent the bit being pulled through the horse's mouth. The outside leg in this case should remain almost in forward-driving position, in order to help with the limiting of the outside shoulder.

If the horse is being ridden on the other rein, the rather stiffer side, then the inside leg is required primarily. It has to ensure that, when the horse is being flexed, it does not try to escape the flexion and longitudinal bending by pushing against the rider's leg with its shoulder, in other words, moving inwards into the arena. The guarding outside rein, which the horse is not so keen on stepping onto in this case, has to be held reliably and low to maintain the connection, particularly when the inside rein is used briefly and resolutely with a sideways-leading purpose. Also this sideways-leading with the inside rein in order to flex the horse, should not be done with the rider's hand positioned too high. In any case this aid has to be applied so resolutely and so briefly that the horse is not provoked in any way into objecting. The more resolutely the rider applies this aid, the more important it is that, at the same moment, the guarding rein prevents the bit from slipping through the horse's mouth, and that immediately afterwards the rider becomes light with both reins so as to show the horse what is required of it. Naturally on this rather stiffer side of the horse, the rider's outside leg must probably also be applied in a more clearly guarding function, as the horse – due to a lack of sufficient stretching ability of its muscles on the outer side – will try to evade outwards with the hindquar-

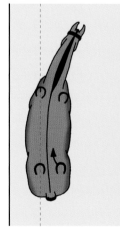

Shoulder-fore

Counter shoulder-fore: The rider should guard a little better with the outside right leg and keep the hindquarters better on the line; this would also improve the bend.

ters as a means of escaping the longitudinal bending.

Particularly in a (indoor) riding arena with a wall, it can be very valuable and effective when practising also sometimes to ride "counter-shoulder-fore". In the case of a horse crooked on the right side, which therefore steps more onto the left rein, and is thus also stiffer when working on the left rein, this would be done as follows: riding on the right rein, after riding through the corner, the horse is flexed in the way described above, but this time to the left, in other words towards the wall, so that the rider's left – in this case inside – leg can be further supported by the wall when the horse tries to push to the left with the shoulder in order to escape from the longitudinal bending. On the contrary, as a result of the flexing to the left, the shoulder will possibly come off the wall slightly, which nevertheless is only valuable when the right guarding leg keeps the hindquarters reliably on the track, in other words avoids any evading.

10.2 Riding in position

By riding in position the same training aims are pursued as with shoulder-fore; it is a further direct preliminary exercise for the lateral movements. Nevertheless, it is completely independent of the "higher" aims of a dressage rider, who would like to compete at medium level, just as shoulder-fore is one of the most important exercises for straightening. The difference between these two exercises could be described as follows for those who are already relatively competent in equestrian theory: **In shoulder-fore the rider has to think in the direction of shoulder-in and apply the appropriate aids, when riding in position, in the direction of travers.**

In shoulder-fore in the first place the inside hind leg is required to step forward more under the point of gravity, in riding in position more – or rather additionally – the outside hind leg, which in sum should lead to the narrower tracking of the hind legs, which are important for the collection and throughness. When executed correctly, in riding in position (also known as "Second Position"), the horse moves with its inside pair of legs on a track line which is parallel to the limitation of the arena. The outside hind leg steps lightly inside the track of the outside fore leg. From the front the observer can see the outside hind foot between the two fore legs, whereas in the shoulder-fore the outside pair of legs move parallel to the wall and accordingly, when observed from the front, the inside hind leg is visible between the fore legs.

The difference in the application of the aids for these two movements is only very minimal. The rider's outside leg has to limit the hindquarters more in order to allow the outside hind leg to step in the direction between the two fore legs. The inside rider's leg, however, driving particularly well forward, has to keep the inside hind leg active and on the track of the inside fore leg which, particularly in the case of horses very receptive to sideward-driving aids, requires careful attention. If, in the course of this work, the rider or trainer notices that the horse is beginning to evade with the hindquarters, in other words to sway, the horse must be ridden increasingly forward again by way of checking and of correction, e. g. also on large curved tracks. The horse has to "pull" reliably again.

Also in the case of riding in position, the competent rider - the young rider has to learn to do it in time - will have to arrange and coordinate his application of the aids in a very differentiated way with one and the same horse when riding on different reins, depending on whether he is working on the hollow side or the compulsion side. On the hollow side in the first place he has to avoid too strong bending of the neck again and possibly falling out over the shoulder (aids as in shoulder-fore, see above). On the stiff side he has to exercise influence with both legs more precise-

Riding in position: The poll is almost a little low.

ly, possibly also somewhat more resolutely, in order to prevent the horse pushing inwards with the shoulder and moving outwards with the hindquarters. Also as concerns the rein aids, the same applies as already described above with regard to shoulder-fore.

As in the case of all exercises and movements in which longitudinal bending is important, the rider should not exaggerate his weight aids increasing the weight on one seat bone. This will be applied correctly, and also completely sufficiently, if only the horse and rider feel it, virtually no change should be detectable in the seat and particularly in the posture of the upper body. The increased load on the inner half of the rider's seat comes about solely through the fact that the rider, when repositioning the outside leg to guard, takes back his entire leg, in other words including the thigh, out of the hip. In this way the notorious collapsing in the hip and the consequently incorrect shift of weight never need to happen.

Also in the case of shoulder-fore and riding in position, the rider and trainer must respond positively to any progress the young horse makes in the learning phase, and always be reasonable about how often to ride repeats.

10.3 Shoulder-in

Following the preliminary exercises, shoulder-fore and riding in position, we now come to the actual lateral movements, first of all to shoulder-in. Shoulder-in is the first genuine lateral movement (side gait – in German: Seitengang) and can be commenced and practised by appropriately experienced and good riders even with relatively young horses. Normally this exercise is required in the collected trot, however in the learning phase it can also be ridden at walk or in a somewhat shortened working trot.

The horse moves on three track lines here (> Illustration p. 196). The hind legs continue to step nearly straight ahead and, thanks to even longitudinal bending, also in the ribcage, the shoulder is brought in so far that the outside fore leg steps exactly in front of the inside hind leg. The neck should only be bent marginally more than the horse in the rest of its longitudinal axle. When the movement is executed well, the horse maintains regular rhythm and lively activity in the movement, shows good cadence depending on the degree of collection and quality of its sequence of movement, is reliably on the outside rein and in good self-carriage.

Application of the aids

As in every other dressage-like exercise, the rider will only be able to give correct, and therefore effective, aids if he approaches the task with the correct idea in mind: he must try to ride shoulder-in as if he would constantly like to start riding a volte. The horse is bent around the rider's inside leg, with the outside leg in a guarding function, the weight aid increasing the weight on one seat bone, thus the slightly increased pressure on the inside seat bone already comes about as a consequence of the outside leg, In this case the entire leg rather than just the lower part, is taken back slightly out of the hip. The inside rein flexes the horse, either through taking and yielding or, however, even better by sideways-leading, and the outside rein, which the horse is hopefully stepping onto reliably, permits the flexion and also limits it, however.

So that the horse now does not actually begin the volte, but remains on the track, the rider exercises slightly clearer influence, almost sideways-driving, with the inside leg, although

Riding in position

Travers with correct bending and angle, poll coming slightly too low

In the travers the horse moves forwards-sideways with even longitudinal bending and an angle (between horse and track) of max. 30 degrees. The fore legs move on the track, usually along the long side or middle line; the front legs cross slightly, the hind legs more significantly in the process. Under no circumstances should the horse be bent too much at the neck, its brow should be in the right angle to the long side, or parallel to the short side. In contrast to shoulder-in, in which the horse moves on three tracks, travers and renvers involve the horse moving on four tracks. This ensues from the fact that in these two exercises fore legs and hind legs cross. Nevertheless, it also applies here that the 30 degree angle is the aim and in the learning phase requirements in this respect may only be increased very gradually.

Application of the aids
Before beginning the rider improves the collection and control of the trot by half halts. During the travers

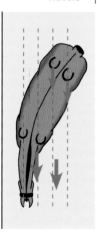

Travers

- the rider's inside leg positioned close to the girth ensures the continuing forward and active forward stepping of the horse's inside hind leg, however it is also primarily responsible for the required longitudinal bending in the ribcage,
- the outside leg positioned somewhat further back in a guarding position, is responsible for the forward-sideways movement and, being opposite the inside leg, also assists in the bending of the ribcage.

- Through this position of the legs, particularly thanks to the outside leg taken back out of the hip, there is slightly increased weight on the rider's inside seat bone, which contributes to the improvement of the longitudinal bending,
- the inside, somewhat shortened rein gives the horse the flexion and can be used in a somewhat sideways-leading function here too,
- the outside, guarding rein yields as much as the bending in the neck area requires, in order then also to limit this.
- In order to improve the weight aid, it can be helpful to imagine pushing the outside seat bone somewhat towards the centre of the saddle (and to avoid collapsing in the inside hip).

Altogether in this movement, the rider should have the idea of sitting in the direction in which he would like to ride, and of taking the horse with him by means of his weight and leg aids. Unfortunately many riders sit too far outwards here and collapse in the inside hip because they have the incorrect concept of having to push the horse in the appropriate direction. The better the horse is already trained, the more counterproductive this kind of application of the aids is, because the ridden horse has learned to follow the rider's weight in order to come into balance with the rider again.

Normally the travers begins, as every exercise along the long side, at the marker at which the hindquarters are then guided into the arena. When practising it is recommendable, however, to take the longitudinal bending with you out of the well-ridden corner, perhaps even to improve it further by means of a volte in the corner, and then to begin, without riding a horse's length straight first. If the preparatory exercises shoulder-fore and particularly riding in position have been done carefully, the travers, at least with a small angle, will succeed immediately.

On the rein on which the horse is somewhat stiffer, in other words does not allow itself to be bent so easily, it will frequently try to escape the required longitudinal bending by becoming more rushed, in order then to move along the wall or the track in leg-yielding style. In this case the rider must improve the longitudinal bending again, e.g. by riding a large volte, ensure the horse comes off from the inside rein by using the diagonal aids – inside leg, outside rein – and immediately before starting the travers, even shorten the tempo a little in order to keep the horse reliably on the aids. The inside leg is the decisive aid in order to ensure yielding in the inside gullet and avoiding pushing in with the inside shoulder.

On the other rein, in other words on the "hollow" or "difficult" side horses, by contrast, tend much more to avoid taking up weight with the inside hind leg by pushing in the hindquarters strongly of their own accord, in other words offering too much of an angle, usually at the same time leaning to a greater or lesser extent on the outside rein.

In this case the rider must, by way of preparation, work more on the horse coming off the outside rein again and also stepping onto the inside rein better. For this purpose it may be enough to give, to yield on the outside rein even once beforehand, usually it is necessary, however, to take and give again clearly with the outside rein, once or several times, whilst the inside rein must always prevent the bit being pulled through the horse's mouth.

When the travers is to begin on this rein, the rider must pay particular attention to a good flow in the forward action on this rein and should not put the outside leg back too far and also not exert too much influence with it.

In the learning phase it is important on both reins only to increase the demands on the horse very gradually and, for example, rather to be happy with a few well controlled steps in the travers than to ride the exercise for so long that the quality of the execution deteriorates.

In order to end the travers, just as ending a volte, the horse is simply ridden straight ahead again, the sideways-crossing is terminated, however without the hindquarters pushing out sideways onto the track.

Practising the travers on a curved track, e.g. on a large circle, is somewhat more demanding. Especially on the horse's compulsion side, this can be helpful and effective in improving the longitudinal flexion and the crossing of the hind legs.

10.5 Renvers

The renvers is the counter movement to the travers, in which accordingly the hindquarters remain on the track and the forehand is brought into the arena. It should not be attempted, however, until the travers has at least started to succeed. Due to the fact that the horse is not ridden towards the track or towards the wall, the danger is even greater that the rider exercises too much influence with the reins in order to prevent the horse form running into the arena for example, in other words leaving the track.

> The renvers may be begun in any of the following ways:
> - **After riding through the first corner of the long side, the rider continues as if preparing to do a simple serpentine loop. As soon as the horse comes away from the track with its shoulder, its flexion is changed and aids analogously as for the travers are applied. Here it is even more important than with practising the travers to begin with just very**

Correct renvers, it would be better if the rider sat slightly more to the right.

Renvers

- little angle and to be content with just very few steps.
- Renvers can also be developed from the second track by means of the hindquarters being brought onto the first track with appropriate bending around the rider's new inside leg.
- A third possibility is out of a turn on the haunches from walk or trot, immediately before finishing this exercise, to continue riding in renvers with the horse which is indeed already correctly flexed and bent. This kind of exercise will only be possible and meaningful with a horse which is already very through.
- The renvers can also be developed out of shoulder-in. For this purpose the horse, after a few steps in shoulder-in, will be flexed and bent to the other side. This exercise can only be done well by a very experienced rider.

In order to finish the renvers the forehand is brought back to the track again in flowing forward movement, and the horse is straightened.

The travers as well as the renvers are usually ridden in the collected trot. As at canter, on account of the diagonal sequence of movement from the outside hind leg to the inside fore leg, horses anyway tend to move somewhat crooked in this gait, these movements should only be done at canter in exceptional cases and by very experienced riders in order to further improve the litheness, the longitudinal bending and the collection or, in the case of horses which have difficulties with half-passes at canter, to prepare them for these.

Mistakes

It is important to avoid the following mistakes in the travers and renvers:

If the horse is not reliable enough on the (diagonal) aids, is not accepting the inside leg and the outside rein reliably enough (frequently on the stiff or compulsion side), then this can lead to mistakes in regularity as well as a decrease in the liveliness of the activity. This occurs particularly when the rider tries increasingly to improve the flexion with the inside rein, also taking the inside hand higher in the process or even pressing it over the crest of the mane. This will only make the horse shorter in the neck, consequently it will be more difficult to flex it, and probably it will also cause tilting at the poll. As always, the only solution here is to go back a stage in order to create the right conditions again through straightening bending work. Furthermore, the turning of the rider's upper body in the direction in which he is riding, which is sometimes required, is exaggerated frequently, thus causing the rider to collapse in the inside hip and usually also pull on the inside rein.

In the classical training the horse should not be bent more in its neck for the lateral movements than in the rest of its longitudinal axis. Unfortunately many riders and trainers try to disguise deficiencies in the bending of the ribcage by increased angling of the neck (and occasionally are even rewarded with good marks for doing so). This incorrect execution will, however, not be able to improve the horse's being straightened, collection and ultimately throughness.

too much angle, no longitudinal bend

very little angle, too much bend in the neck

exaggerated longitudinal bend

Mistakes in the travers, the same applies analogously for the renvers

10.6 Half-passes

Half-passes are forward-sideways movements in collected trot or in collected canter. In the learning phase for rider or horse they can also be ridden in walk. Their sequence of movement corresponds exactly to that of the travers, except that now it has to be ridden along a more or less steep diagonal line. The horse thus moves with regular longitudinal bending, in a good flow(ing style), and, according to its potential of movement and degree of collection, with clear cadence. It moves with its inside shoulder and hips parallel to the long side. In tests half, double half, full, double full and zig-zag half-passes are required. ("Half half pass" means across the half width, a "full half pass" across the whole width of the arena.)

In the zig-zag half-passes a certain number of metres are always required, at canter – from Intermediare II upwards – the precise number of strides is prescribed.

Application of the aids

When the rider and his horse have a fairly sure command of the travers and possibly also the renvers, the half-pass will not present any major difficulties. The rider simply has to imagine that he is riding the travers along a diagonal line. The degree of the angle (the angle between the longitudinal axle of the horse and the diagonal line in question) corresponds exactly to the angle between the track or wall and the diagonal line – according to the parallelism required (> Illustration p.202).

Important for the application of the aids is once again the rider's idea of sitting in the direction in which he would like to ride, wanting to take the horse along with him using the weight and leg aids, and also leading it there with the inside rein. The aids applied are the same as those for the travers:

- **The inside leg positioned close to the girth ensures the continuing regular**

and active stepping forward of the inside hind leg, it is also primarily responsible however, for the required longitudinal bending especially in the ribcage,
- **the outside leg somewhat further back in a guarding position, is responsible for the forward-sideways movement and, being counter-poise the inside leg, also assists in the bending of the ribcage.**
- **Through this position of the legs, particularly thanks to the outside leg taken back out of the hip, there is increased weight on the rider's inside seat bone, which contributes to the improvement of the longitudinal bending,**
- **the inside, somewhat shortened rein gives the horse the flexion and can be used in a somewhat sideways-leading function here,**
- **the outside, guarding rein yields as much as is required for the bending in the neck area, in order then also to limit this.**
- **In order to improve the weight aid, it can be helpful to imagine pushing the outside seat bone somewhat towards the centre of the saddle.**

As in the case of travers, many riders unfortunately also in the half-pass sit outwards and collapse in the inside hip, because the incorrectly

Half-pass at trot with good longitudinal bending and leg crossing

Good half-pass at canter

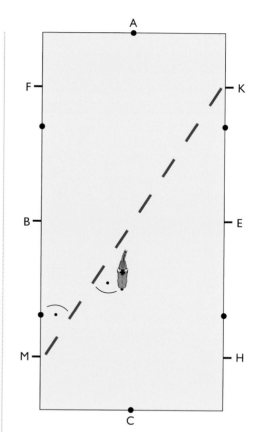

A half-pass is like travers along a diagonal line

believe that they have to push the horse sideways. The better the horse is trained, the more counter-productive the effects of this mistake are, because the horse has indeed learned to follow the rider's weight in order to maintain the common balance.

If half-passes are to succeed reliably and to a good quality standard, it is extremely important that the horse accepts the diagonal application of the aids (inside leg – outside rein), and that the rider comes off from the inside rein. Therefore it is recommendable already in the preparation, e.g. in turns, always to "feel" a little with the inside rein (become light) or to give and take the reins. Becoming light with both hands or giving and taking the reins during the half-pass serves to check the horse's self-carriage, and at the same time rewards it positively for its cooperation.

To introduce the half-pass, the horse is bent in accordance with the direction of movement and, depending on its level of training and sensitivity, the forward-sideways movement is asked for. In the case of very finely balanced tuned horses the mere thought of the rider to begin the half-pass may even be sufficient. In the earlier stages of training the rider has to begin the half-pass by giving a slight impulse to the already bent horse with the outside leg positioned back some-

what, by a slight taking and yielding on the outside rein and sideways-leading with the inside rein. To finish the half-pass the sideways movement is brought to an end by the rider's inside leg in connection with the outside rein, ridden straight ahead and only then, the horse straightened again.

10.6.1 Dealing with natural crookedness in the half-pass

In the case of younger horses, but also in the case of older ones which do not yet allow themselves to be straightened completely, the rider will have to differentiate very clearly in the aids he applies depending on the crookedness of his horse, and whether he would like to ride the half-

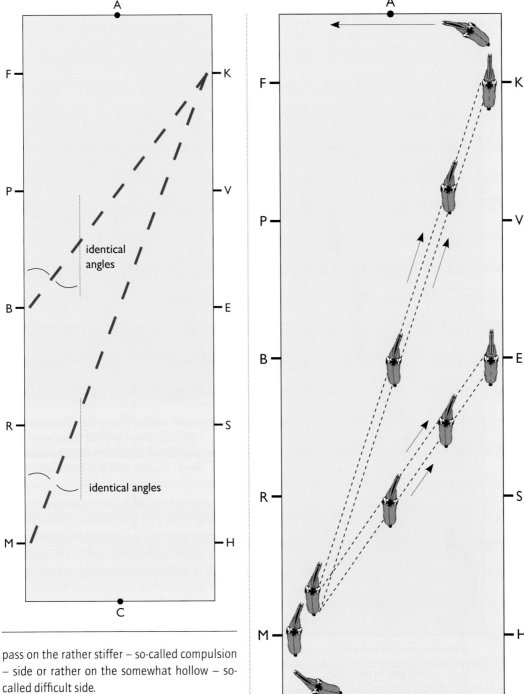

Due to the parallelism required, the angle at which the horse is positioned depends on the angle of the diagonals

pass on the rather stiffer – so-called compulsion – side or rather on the somewhat hollow – so-called difficult side.

In the first case he would be well advised in the preparation to think more about riding in position, possibly even about travers, in order to be able to ride the half-pass with regular longitudi-

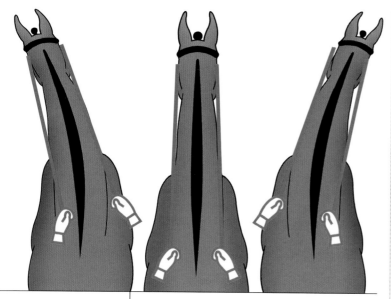

find it easier to keep the horse parallel when starting from the track.

10.6.2 Change in flexion and bend between two half-passes

When changing flexion and bend between two half-passes the application of the aids is changed whilst riding straight ahead and the horse is flexed and bent according to the new direction of movement. The better the coordination between horse and rider, the more through the horse reacts, the more this straight-ahead stretch can be shortened, until ultimately the horse can go straight from one half-pass movement into the other.

In the case of canter half-passes, a command of the flying change is naturally essential. The change of leg takes place in straight ahead, whereby very experienced riders have an individually modified technique. They do not ride the change until they have re-positioned the horse.

As the horse is somewhat narrower in the shoulder area than in the pelvis area, it makes sense always to think of shoulder-fore when re-positioning, in other words to have the idea of guiding the horse's shoulder into the new directions.

If, when changing position, particularly to the stiffer side, the horse does not step onto the new outside rein enough, the inside hind leg can become blocked so that mistakes in rhythm can come about and the horse does not stride through enough in the change at canter.

10.6.3 Mistakes in the half-passes

Apart from the mistakes already mentioned above, the following also occur frequently and some of them are even mutually responsible for each other:

If the hindquarters keep leading again and again, the half-pass first of all has to be started out of shoulder-fore. Attention has to be paid to ensure that the horse "pulls" onto the hand

When the horse is bent the rider can move his hands as far to the right or left accordingly as is possible with the reins still remaining straight and running along the horse's neck to the mouth; this facilitates smooth and fluent changes of flexion e.g. in double serpentine loops or zig-zag half-passes.

rider can think more in terms of riding in position or even shoulder-fore on the straight-ahead stretch. It is also possible to ride a volte, in which the accepting of the leg aids and coming off from the inside rein must be the main priorities.

> **Also in practising half-passes, the good rider and trainer will pay careful attention to ensure that demands concerning the steepness, i.e. the crossing, but also the length of the repeats, are in no way exaggerated. He will observe attentively whether the rhythm, the fluency and flow of the sequence of movement is preserved, and if necessary he will immediately react accordingly.**

Horses which are still learning usually find it easier to begin half-passes from the centre line or the quarter line, whereby however they have the tendency in the last three or four metres before the wall to become rushed and „run" with less bend to the track. This must be prevented by careful controlling of every step or stride with a half halt.

On the other hand, the rider who is still learning – naturally on a suitable "schoolmaster" will

with enough impulsion and that it has sufficient self-carriage, which can be checked well by becoming light with both hands or giving and retaking the reins. Moving the outside leg back too far and exercising too much influence with it is to be avoided.

When changing flexion and bend between two half-passes this mistake occurs principally when riding to the hollow side. Then it makes sense, when changing to this side, to guide the horse with its forehand increasingly into the new direction, as at the vertex of a simple serpentine loop. General speaking, it is important when remedying this mistake to avoid everything which makes the horse short in the neck.

Becoming short in the neck is unfortunately a mistake which occurs so frequently nowadays that it is no longer even seriously recognized as such by many people, never mind anything being undertaken to combat it. Always when more collection is demanded, this mistake occurs more, and such is also the case here with half-passes. Without going into this problem in too much detail here, it must be quite clearly stated that a horse which is short in the neck will certainly not be able to bend as well and will be limited in the swinging through of its hind legs. Therefore it always has to be worked on having the horse well on the driving aids, stepping forward evenly onto both reins, thus "pulling" reliably so that half halts can be given without making the horse short in the neck.

Tilting at the poll will also occur particularly frequently with a horse which is short in the neck. It is cause by technical mistakes e.g.

- by a hand held high on one side, particularly when a double bridle is used,
- by a hand pressing across the crest of the mane – this can be the inside or outside hand
- by faulty yielding on the outside, guarding rein,
- by a curb rein sticking on one side

If the outside leg is not respected enough, either in guarding or sideways-driving function, there is no point in positioning the leg further back, instead it is important to use the spur to reinforce the aid and for this purpose it is not a problem if the front of the foot points slightly outwards whilst the spur is being applied.

- or quite generally, when the horse is not stepping evenly enough onto both reins.

It should be possible to avoid the technically caused mistakes relatively quickly; in the case of the latter one mentioned, however, which is connected with a lack of straightening, more thorough correction has to be undertaken, first of all more emphasis has to be placed on straightening bending work.

→ Contact; impulsion; straightening; riding of turns; flying changesl

Good collection at the canter is a pre-requisite for the flying change.

canter beforehand which is why, in the case of problems in the changes, work always has to be done on improving the collected canter first of all. Nevertheless occasionally there are horses, particularly those with very large transmission, which do surprisingly good, springy changes out of a rather dragging, flat canter.

Application of the aids

Very decisive for the success of the flying change is the correct "timing", in other words the exact temporal coordination of the aids. The aids for the change always have to be given immediately before the moment of suspension in order to make it possible for the horse to change legs during it. The absolutely precise moment to apply them, whether it is in the last three-leg or not until the last one-leg support phase is to be chosen individually as it differs from horse to horse, depending on the sensitivity and particularly the speed of the reactions of the individual horse. In the learning phase it may even differ, depending on whether the horse is being ridden on the left or right rein.

By way of preparation, the rider improves the canter and the horse's alertness by half-halts.

11. Flying Change of Leg

In the flying change the sequence of footfalls is changed in the moment of suspension, e.g. from canter leading on the left leg to canter leading on the right. It is required in dressage tests from (open) medium level upwards. Flying changes in sequences, i.e. regular leg changes after each fourth, third, second or even single canter stride do not feature until tests at advanced level.

11.1 Criteria for a successful flying change

The horse should execute the flying change in regular rhythm. In other words, all canter strides, even the last one before the change and the first one after it should be in clear three-beat rhythm.

The horse should be composed, with good forward fluency, straightened and striding uphill with as good groundcover as possible. It should accept precise but fairly unobtrusive aids promptly and willingly. The quality of the change normally cannot be any better than that of the

- **The outside leg, which has been guarding until now, becomes the new inside leg, i.e. it takes over a driving function and for this purpose is brought forward to be put on the girth. At the same time the previous inside leg is now taken back a little to exercise a guarding function.**
- **By changing the leg position the supple and well-balanced rider will automatically impose more weight on the new inside seat bone; but apart from that he will remain sitting with the upper body as calm as possible.**
- **A slight change of position of the horse takes place just before the change; here the horse has to stride through onto the**

new outside rein so that the new inside hind leg can stride through far enough forwards.

In this connection it is worth giving some consideration to canter aids in general.

My opinion is that in the training of young riders as well as in the training of young horses, the importance of the rider's outside leg is emphasized far too much. Sometimes it is done really according to the motto: "Move the outside leg (as far as possible) … and the canter is there!" And in this case the significance of the inside leg, which has a forward-driving function and as such is responsible for the inside hind leg striding accordingly far forward, is neglected too much. Even when riding in counter-canter, many riders work with the idea that they have to prevent the change of leg by the horse through moving their guarding leg back more significantly. However, it is much more correct to ask for the canter desired at every individual stride with the rider's – as before – inside leg. This has the additional advantage that the horse does not get crooked so easily. When on a straight line at canter the horse is to be held straight better, it is, of course, correct to place more emphasis on the diagonal application of the aids "inside leg – outside rein".

It also has clear advantages for the riding of flying changes, for the refinement of the aids, to increase the significance of the new inside leg in the course of training:

The horse can keep cantering increasingly better on a straight line during the changes, the rider can gradually apply the aids more subtly, which also means his seat becomes calmer. Horses ridden in this way then execute flying changes in sequence in response to very fine aids, they do not forgive faults by the rider so easily, however.

Also in the application of the aids for the flying change, as already discussed in connection with the lateral movements, perhaps it will be advantageous to differentiate, according to the

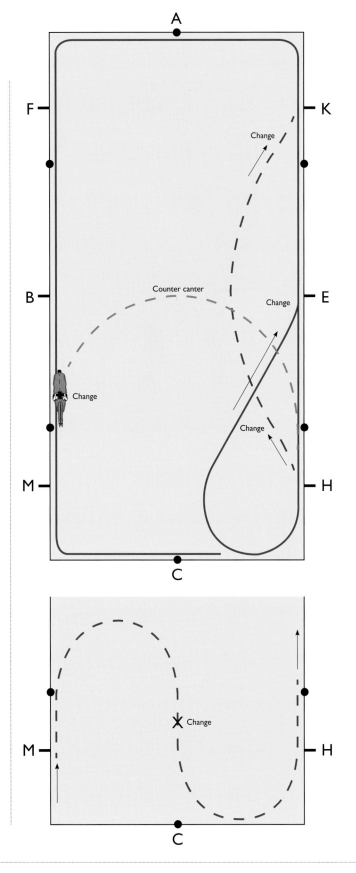

Beautiful forwards-upwards flying change (Rusty with Ulla Salzgeber)

of a syncope. The more calm and regular the sequence in the canter is, e.g. with a well-trained "schoolmaster", the more easily the learning rider will develop a good grasp of the timing.

In order to optimize the learning success for the young horse the canter change should only be trained by an experienced rider until the horse has gained a certain degree of confidence on both reins.

Before proceeding to the different exercise possibilities, I should first like to mention a few important fundamental principles:

- The dressage-like flying change should always be ridden on a straight line. Above all, the rider should never try to demand the change of leg by any kind of abrupt change in direction. Even if – for example to improve the collection – the horse is ridden on a curved track before and after the change (see below) the change itself should always be executed on a straight line.

- In the first exercises it makes sense to practise the flying change onto the rein on which the horse in question canters better, more springy; this is usually relatively clear and easy to determine.

- When learning it is helpful to ride the flying change several times on the same school figure or at the same point of the arena.

- Here also it is very important to exercise care and consideration as far as the intensity and duration of the practice period are concerned. It should never be exaggerated, rather after one or two successful changes the horse should be praised and this work phase terminated.

- It can indeed be worthwhile, after working on the change for a few days, to take a break from it for a while – to give what has been learned a chance to settle.

- Only if, thanks to good feeling and sufficient experience, the rider is in a position to react to the horse's current state of mind and to adapt the intensity of his work and his methods to suit this, is it possible for him to work successfully and effectively.

- If the horse does not react as desired to the aids for the flying change, it should not be pun-

natural crookedness, between the difficult (hollow) side and the compulsion side. If the change is to be made onto the somewhat stiffer side, the new outside guarding leg will certainly have to prevent an evading of the hindquarters somewhat more clearly whilst the inner leg will have to keep the forehand on a good straight line. On the other rein, the rider will have to pay particular attention to ensure that the new outside shoulder does not evade.

The less experienced rider often makes the mistake of giving the aids for the flying change in the same time sequence and rhythm as the aids previously necessary for, asking or accompanying, every canter stride. This is too late, however, so that the horse, if at all, can only react with the fore legs, does not change at all in the hind legs, however – or at best, one canter stride later. This is why he simply has to imagine applying the aid as a kind of interim beat between two canter aids, i.e. significantly sooner. Anyone who plays a musical instrument, or can read music well, can think about it in terms

ished because this can lead to tensions or even blockages caused by fear, which would consequently hinder the horse's spontaneous reactions to the aids for the flying change. Rather exercises such as canter extensions to improve the throughness have to be ridden again, – and in this context also a precise reducing of the pace –, or simple change of leg. Occasionally it can be helpful to support the new inside leg with the whip by touching on the new inside ribcage in order to encourage improved striding forward of the inside hind leg.

- Practising the flying change over a pole or a cavaletti is not recommendable, particularly for dressage horses because it makes uphill striding quite impossible – instead it provokes a late stride behind or a high croup.

11.2 Hints on training

When it is a question of familiarizing the horse with the flying change, the principle applies very strongly that this very demanding stage of training for the young dressage horse can only be optimally structured by an experienced trainer. The question concerning the point in time at which it is most appropriate to start practising the flying change is answered in a variety of different ways. As in the case of all learning, it is also good with horses to take advantage of the better learning ability in younger years. Different horses naturally have different degrees of talent for this exercise. Modern riding horse breeding increasingly frequently supplies us with horses which, thanks to selection particularly concerning ridablility and a very good innate balance, already offer flying changes quite playfully in the first weeks of being ridden. Of course, the good, experienced rider will then accept these.

In order to be able to practise good, dressage-style changes in further training the horse should move with reasonable straightness and collection, particularly as far as cantering work is concerned. It should be able to canter out of walk reliably and straight in response to fine aids at any point, and on both reins. The simple change of leg at canter should already be possible in a very through and precise form. In the case of turns at canter and downward-transitions after canter extensions, a clear taking up of weight should be recognizable and/or feelable.

The first flying changes can be attempted simultaneously with first exercises in the counter-canter. This makes it possible to benefit fully from the young, balanced horse's tendency to prefer moving in true canter. If the horse once changes leg of its own accord in this exercise, it must be corrected immediately and with determination, but under no circumstances it should be punished. Decisive in the flying change as in the counter-canter is that the horse is always reliable on the driving aids, so that the rider has the horse ahead of himself.

It is a matter of opinion what exercises and on what school figures it is best to try the first flying changes, but also a question of the experienced trainer's intuition. An ideal training method for one horse may not necessarily be successful for another horse. And a further point to consider is that sometimes with one and the same horse it may be advantageous or even necessary to use different exercise variations.

11.3 Exercise variations

For all different exercise variations described below (> page 209) an arena or indoor school measuring 20 m x 40 m should be available, in the case of horses with a lot of scope or ground-cover in their canter 20 m x 60 m is preferable.

- After a half-volte back to the track (in the second corner of the long side) the aid to change is to be applied immediately on or after reaching the track, whereby the wall supports the new guarding aids very well, in other words the straight line riding is made easier. Furthermore, the fact that with this method the new outside leg aid is not over-emphasized on one side, but rather also the new inside rider's leg can demand the new inside hind leg to stride forward particularly well (possibly with the support of the whip as described above). This reduces from the beginning the horse's tendency to sway in the change right. Some horses understand the flying change more easily if, out of this half-volte, they are ridden back to the track half-pass-style and then the aid is applied when changing flexion to go straight.

- Experienced, confident trainers prefer, naturally on suitably talented horses, to practise the flying change from the true canter to the counter-canter riding on the second track along the long side. Here the horse can remain absolutely on the straight line, the new inside hind leg can stride through particularly well and there is still enough space to prepare the horse again and repeat the attempt if it is not successful the first time. As the horse canters in the direction of the wall after the change, it usually remains more easily "with the rider" without rushing. Additionally in this variation the counter-canter is also consolidated; the horse's tendency to do an unwanted change of leg will be restricted.

- Another variation – which has proved very successful – is to turn on a 20m half circle at counter-canter and to apply the aids to change on reaching the track. If this exercise is started on the centre circle, it has the advantage of the change taking place onto a straight line again. In the case of horses which initially have difficulty, at least on one side, a whole or even one and a half rounds on the circle can also be ridden in counter-canter before the change, so that the horse is "relieved" so to speak, to be able to change to the true canter.

- **A further good form of exercise to be used here if the horse is starting to anticipate the change because of familiarity of circumstances, is the following:**

After riding through the first corner of the long side, the rider turns in a similar way as when riding the simple serpentine loop. Approximately one to two horse's lengths after leaving the track, where the rider would re-position the horse (change the bend and flexion) if riding a simple serpentine loop, the change is then ridden. Whether the rider rides a transition to trot after a successful change in order to praise the horse, or carries on in counter-canter, depends on the situation and must be decided on the basis of the rider's feeling.

- Occasionally it happens that the horse, particularly in the change on the rein which it finds less easy, tries to storm forward on account of the more energetic application of the aids which is required under such circumstances. In this case it is worth trying the following: creating a large circle and turning the horse on the centre line on a 10 m semi-circle, as in the change through of the circle. This half volte should not be commenced directly at the point of the circle but rather be moved a little more in the direction of the centre of the arena. Then it is possible to ride two or three horse's lengths straight in the direction to the short side and in this direction the change can be attempted. In my experience the rider can keep the horse in front of him better in this way and is able to use the driving aids enough in the change.

Even if we assume that the first flying changes are attempted and ridden by an experienced rider who also has enough feeling to be able to judge himself whether the horse has done the change relatively reliably, it is always an advantage to have a competent helper present, who has a good eye for such sequences of movement and, if necessary, can immediately draw attention to announce the faults. Particularly horses with a somewhat flatter canter sometimes change too late behind, which may be barely perceptible. In order not to train the horse wrongly, in other words not to "programme" any incorrect sequences of movement, it must be assured that the horse only receives praise as a positive award for flying changes which indeed really have succeeded reasonably well but never when late.

When the flying change can be done reasonably successfully on both reins, the next stage is then to achieve more expression by means of reliable uphill movement. Everything which improves the collection and throughness is useful for this purpose. Two particularly useful exercises are described below:

- On a diagonal change line, whereby it makes sense to aim for the circle point as the change point, the canter strides are lengthened somewhat in the first half. Approximately as from the centre line (from X), the horse is collected again by means of careful half halts (well on the driving aids) and then after one, two canter strides the change is ridden as if the rider wanted to extend again.
- With horses which are appropriately balanced and capable of collection, the circle can be reduced as in preliminary exercises for the canter pirouette, whereby the horse then, hopefully without too much hand influence, will take up more load to a certain extent of its own accord. Out of this volte, the rider goes onto the diagonal and, after a few canter strides on the straight line, rides the change again well forward. Possibly subsequently, also on the other rein, the rider can reduce the circle or can go onto a volte in order also to ride the change on the other rein.

In the case of all exercises for the flying change always attention has to be paid to ensure that the horse remains calm. Only then reliable, good quality changes can succeed.

11.4 Faults and their correction

When difficulties occur, it is necessary to look at the prerequisites once again and, if necessary, to undertake corrections:

- The canter stride must be in definite three-beat with a clear moment of suspension,
- the horse must in any case be supple and calm again,
- it must, also in downwards-transitions, remain straight and

- canter in good self-carriage, that is to say well-balanced and with slight contact.

Thus it is not possible, and it also does not make any sense, to prescribe specific methods for the correction of individual faults. If, on the basis of an appropriate "analysis", the cause for the fault can be found, the correction will ensue almost automatically on the basis of what is described above. Normally the preparation for the change has to be improved or done differently before a new attempt with a chance of success can be undertaken.

The horse, for example, can be late with one of the hind legs,

- because it does not stride through enough via the back, or
- because the rider does not come off from the new inside rein enough (lack of being straightened), or
- because the horse is already anticipating the change and does not wait long enough, or
- because the aid is applied somewhat too late, so that the horse can no longer react in time with both hind legs.

A second example here: the horse becomes crooked in the change,

- because over all it is not yet straightened enough in the canter, or
- because it always hesitates in the change, it does not keep enough little "pull" or
- because the rider applies the aid too strongly with the outside leg and too little with the inside leg.

This list could be expanded almost infinitely, the points mentioned, however, should suffice to illustrate the significant aspects.

By way of conclusion, I should like to emphasize once again that normally a younger horse can only learn to do the flying change correctly, without too many unnecessary deviations if taught by an experienced trainer with good feeling.

In the case ◁ of all exercises for the flying change always attention has to be paid to ensure that the horse remains calm. Only then reliable, good quality changes can succeed.

➤ Also with reference to the aids, the same applies with regard to flying changes in sequences as to individual flying changes.

12. Flying Changes in Sequences

In dressage tests from advanced level on flying changes in sequences are required. This means at least three changes in sequence after the fourth, third, second stride or even from stride to stride.

In preparation for this in the most difficult test at medium level three individual flying changes are asked for on a diagonal (on the 60 m arena) – at the beginning, in the centre at X and at the end before reaching the marker.

12.1 Criteria for successful series of flying changes

The criteria for changes in sequences are exactly the same initially as for the individual flying change. They should be regular in rhythm (Takt), calm, fluently forwards, straight, uphill and jumped wide through with the hind legs under the weight. Horse and rider should be so well coordinated that relatively unobtrusive aids are promptly and willingly accepted.

In addition, regular tempo should be maintained, the required number of strides and changes observed exactly and the changes placed symmetrically on the required track.

Application of the aids

Also with reference to the aids, the same applies with regard to flying changes in sequences as to individual flying changes. The fewer the canter strides to be ridden between the changes, the more important it is to keep the horse straight. Good sensitivity for the aids and the ability to accept them willingly and promptly becomes increasingly important.

In the case of four-time and three-time changes the rider can still work on maintaining the quality of the canter in the strides between the changes, indeed even on improving it and preparing the next stride. In the case of two-time changes and of course even more so with one-time changes there is hardly time, however, and therefore care has to be taken beforehand to ensure that, also in the sequences, the horse is reliable on the driving aids. In training, therefore, very special attention has to be paid to this, if necessary the canter changes should be interrupted if the horse hesitates, comes onto the forehand, deteriorates in its uphill movement or other deficiencies emerge. In such a case the canter, with all its criteria as far as collection, has to be improved again first of all.

In order to be able to present exactly the number of changes asked for with the prescribed number of canter strides between them, the rider learn to be able to count these correctly, despite his high concentration on the correct application of the aids.

On the basis of this test it becomes clear again that, precisely as is in the case of the individual flying change, it would be correct for the learning rider to have a reliable horse available for the first exercises, and for the learning horse to become familiarized with the higher requirements of such a test by an experienced rider.

The less this constellation is fulfilled, the more important it is only to increase the demands regarding the length of the sequences and the number of canter strides between the changes only very gradually and not to continue practising them for so long that the horse and rider start to make more mistakes due to lack of concentration.

The simplest method to count the four-time changes, for example, is 1,2,3,4/2,2,3,4/3,2,3,4 etc.; the change then always takes place on 4.

If the rider has enough experience and feeling for the rhythm in question, he will only count the actual changes, not the strides in-between.

12.2 Change from stride to stride (à tempo)

As here the aid for the change is always given already during the preceding canter stride, in the changes from stride to stride the aids for the first change have to be followed very closely by the aids for the second change; there is no time to wait until the first change has taken place. For all further changes the same prin-

ciple naturally applies. This assumes good ability to react and high sensitivity on the part of the horse, and very skilful, and very well timed, application of the aids on the part of the rider.

On account of the short, or even non-existent intervals between the changes, quite particularly of course in the case of the two-time changes and one-time changes, it is impossible or would be disturbing to re-position the horse for each change. Rather it must stride forward straight onto both reins; the contact on the new outside rein should always be somewhat stronger, on the new inside rein somewhat lighter, in order to let the canter stride come through well forwards, particularly with the new inside hind leg.

Changes in sequences, particularly changes from stride to stride, can succeed very well if the application of the aids is so optimally refined that communication between rider and horse can function almost exclusively on the basis of subtle signs.

12.3 Hints on training

Before even attempting flying changes in sequences, it is essential that individual flying changes succeed reliably and with quality all the time and at almost every point.

In order to prevent – as far as possible – any swaying in the changes right from the start, it is advantageous to begin doing these along the long side on the second or third track, normally with a change to counter-canter and a second change back to true canter. Initially the number of canter strides between the changes is not so significant. What is really important, however, is that the second change is not ridden until the horse is reliable on the aids and ready to respond willingly to the aids, but without anticipating them.

With increasing confidence the demands relating to the number of changes, as well as to the set number of canter strides between them, can be increased.

It is a great advantage to have a large arena of 60 metres length or more for these exercis-
es. As a matter of principle the next stage upwards should never take place until horse and rider have a good command of the preceding stage. Changes every three strides should not be attempted until changes every four strides can be done reliably.

The rider or trainer should always observe the quality of the canter very critically in order – in good time – to make corrections by reducing the level of demands imposed, if necessary.

If flying changes in sequences succeed along the long side on a good straight line, they can then also be practised on the diagonal. With regard to the riding of dressage tests, a further requirement is also involved here, that is to say the correct (symmetrical) placement: the middle change, i.e. in the case of seven two-time changes, the fourth change, should take place as exactly as possible at X. That means that, depending on the scope of the individual canter stride with different horses, possibly also the first change has to take place at a slightly different stage after the turn onto the diagonal.

Flying changes in sequences every stride should most certainly not be attempted until the two-time changes succeed reliably and calmly. Initially, again along the long side, only two one-time changes should be asked for, from true canter to counter-canter and back to true canter. If, for example, the horse prefers the change to the left and executes it more easily, one should begin on the left rein with the change to the right and back to canter leading on the left leg. As training progresses, this exercise should be repeated frequently on both reins and the speed of the horse's reactions increased with the exercise. With the gradual increase in demands via three to four and five one-time changes, attention always has to be paid to ensure the work involves enough variety, particularly also involving repeats of medium canter with the relevant transitions. In this process the rider and trainer should always have the various criteria of

Before even ◄ attempting flying changes in sequences, it is essential that individual flying changes succeed reliably and with quality all the time and at almost every point.

➢ Concerning the change from stride to stride, it should be mentioned that there are indeed horses which learn changes every two strides perfectly reliably, however the same horses have problems doing changes from stride to stride, possibly even feel overstrained with this.

the scale of training at the back of their minds, should take seriously any initial signs of tension or even crampedness and take immediate steps to remedy the problem.

The tempo at which one-time changes should be practised has to be considered on an individual basis. Initially it is certainly important above all to have the horse well in front of the rider in relatively calm tempo in order to be able to assure the precise timing of the application of the aids, that the aids do not come too late. With increasing confidence, the changes can and should be ridden somewhat more in forwards, in order to increase the groundcover, impulsion and expression.

Exactly as with the other changes in sequence, increased attention has to be paid to keeping the horse straight when practising on the diagonals.

Indeed, and this also applies to all changes in sequences, it will become very quickly and clearly noticeable if the horse is not straightened enough:

Changing to the rather hollow side, horses usually have an increased tendency to become crooked, to push the hindquarters over, on the rather stiff side it easily happens that the new inside hind leg only strides through in shortened form.

If such deficiencies in execution occur, this should immediately be a reason to dedicate more attention and time to straightening work again, to take more care again to ensure that the horse steps equally well onto both reins.

Concerning the change from stride to stride, it should be mentioned that there are indeed horses which learn changes every two strides perfectly reliably, however the same horses have problems doing changes from stride to stride, possibly even feel overstrained with this. The possibilities to assess this correctly, whether and how success with such horses can, nevertheless, be achieved, as well as correct planning of how to progress, requires considerable experience, good feeling and a lot of patience.

In further advanced training it is worthwhile also practising flying changes in sequences on large curved tracks. In this way experienced riders can improve the striding far through and the straightness in the changes, in freestyle tests the degree of difficulty increases as a result.

Flying changes in sequences, particularly changes every stride, assume a high degree of agility, capacity of reaction and throughness on the part of the horse. Only a rider who sits in a supple way, deep and well-balanced, has quick reactions and is in a position to give precise aids coordinated with feeling, will be able to ride high-quality changes in sequences or even teach a horse to do them.

Flying changes in sequences belong to the lessons which are indeed executed very obediently by some experienced horses, because they lack good activity over the back, however, these horses stride through with too little impulse out of the hindquarters – and this does not achieve a satisfactory result. The competent observer sees that the hind legs only follow instead of actively developing thrust.

Everything which was said about mistakes, their causes and their remedies in connection with single flying changes, applies equally here. Also in practising flying changes in sequences it is of prime importance in daily work to critically observe the quality of each individual change, in order to avoid mistakes becoming a habit and taking place on an automatic basis.

➔ Canter work

13. Canter Pirouettes

Canter pirouettes are turns by the horse around the hindquarters. They are ridden out of the collected canter with flexion and bending in the direction of movement. The inside hind foot turns around a radius (circle) which is as small as possible. For this purpose the highest possible degree of collection is required in the canter, with the hindquarters having to be lowered and to take up more load.

In dressage tests – from advanced level upwards – half and full canter pirouettes are required, in order to increase the degree of difficulty in the grand prix freestyle, many riders present one and a half or even double pirouettes.

The carrying power required for this has to be trained carefully by means of well-considered collecting work in correct, well measured doses for the horse in question; the significance of the time factor here should most certainly not be under-estimated. Of course the different natural disposition, particularly as regards ability and willingness for collection in the canter, plays a decisive role here. The born uphill horse, which accordingly also has good natural balance, has clear advantages here. These are also already important criteria in dressage horse tests at elementary and medium levels (for 5- and 6-years old horses).

For the riding of canter pirouettes and quite particularly, of course, when it is a question of teaching horses to do them, a high degree of ability on the part of the rider is absolutely essential. The rider not only has to sit in optimum balance, above all he must also have a good feeling for the common balance with the horse and for the load-bearing capacity at any particular time.

13.1 Criteria for good-quality canter pirouettes

First of all, in accordance with our scale of training, the regularity of rhythm is to be mentioned. This means in the pirouette the horse should stride through actively "round", evenly and calmly, but not too slowly. It has, however, been ascertained with the aid of slow-motion film that, even with really well-executed pirouettes, the diagonal pair of legs no longer steps down exactly simultaneously, but rather that the inside hind leg touches the ground a fraction of a second before the outside foreleg. This should not be visible with the naked eye, however.

Good pirouette canter, it would be better to let the nose come forward a little.

Yielding at the poll, the horse strides reliably onto the outside rein in consistent good contact so that the longitudinal bending (including flexion) is maintained until the last canter stride.

Thanks to good ability and willingness to collect, with good bending of the haunches, the hindquarters take up more weight and thus enable three canter strides in the half pirouette and at least six in the full pirouette.

Application of the aids

The horse is shortened more with half halts in order to collect the canter in an optimum way:

- **The rider's inside leg is positioned directly on the girth, ensures continuing good activity of the inside hind leg and**

- is responsible for the longitudinal bending, also in the ribcage.
- The outside leg is positioned slightly back in a guarding function; it prevents the hindquarters from evading and, together with the other aids, ensures the forward tendency, also during the turn, as well as the even longitudinal bending and the turning around of the horse.
- Through this position of the legs, particularly thanks to the outside leg taken back out of the hip, somewhat more weight is imposed on the inside seat bone, which also contributes to the longitudinal bending and to the horse's willingness to turn in the appropriate direction.
- The inside rein is shortened somewhat, giving the flexion, and sideways-leading brings the horse into the turn.
- The outside guarding rein yields to permit the flexion, but also limits it and – if necessary – prevents too much bending of the neck, which would disturb the balance and therefore also the horse's willingness to turn.

Altogether every canter stride has to be ridden particularly carefully in the pirouette, just as when cantering on, whereby great importance is accorded to becoming light with the inside rein so as not to restrict the inside hind leg, on which so much strain is imposed, from taking up the weight in any way.

As already mentioned in the lateral movements, for the flying change at canter and the walk pirouettes, which are ridden in a very similar way, depending on the natural crookedness of the horse in question, it will frequently be necessary to apply the aids somewhat differently on the difficult (hollow) side than on the stiffer one, the so-called compulsion side:

On the difficult side the horse will usually tend to want to lead with the hindquarters, in other words to avoid taking up the weight by evading to the inside; furthermore it may try to lean on the outside rein and to bend too much in the neck, which thus means that it cannot be brought around so easily with the shoulder. Of course this problem must be prevented by doing appropriate straightening work in the preparation. During the pirouette and particularly also in the last canter strides beforehand, in the application of his aids, particularly concerning the legs, the rider has to think of shoulder-fore or even "croup-out" and also yield quickly somewhat – prophylactically – with the outside rein.

On the compulsion or stiffer side, horses frequently tend to push into the turn with the shoulder, even to toss about, in order to escape the longitudinal bending. When this happens the hindquarters evade outwards. Here also decisive improvement can only be achieved by means of serious straightening work. During the pirouette and the last introductory canter strides the rider now has to think of riding in position or even of travers, i.e. with the inside leg prevent the forehand from pressing inwards, the hindquarters from evading outwards.

13.2 Training hints

A prerequisite for practising canter pirouettes is very good ability and willingness to collect at canter. The horse has to be able and willing, with appropriate bending of the haunches, to take up enough weight with the hindquarters. The necessary shortening in the canter has to be possible for the rider with subtle aids, particularly concerning the rein aids. For example, the horse must reduce willingly in the down-transition from medium canter and take up more weight with the hindquarters, when the rider drives forward somewhat more clearly out of the seat to the non-yielding rein but also becomes light again immediately in order to facilitate the closing up of the hindquarters.

As soon as the horse has been prepared far enough in its training it will surely also have a command of the canter half passes on both reins, as already required in medium level dressage tests. The reliable, springy striding onto the outside rein is almost more important for the pirouette than it is in the lateral movements. This can be checked particularly well by "reducing the circle" (> Illustration page 221) or the riding of voltes at canter.

If in "riding into the circle " the rider has always avoided exercising too strong influence with the hands, he will, particularly in "reducing the circle", have experienced moments with every correctly trained horse with sufficient natural ability for collection in the canter, in which the horse almost collects of its own accord and begins to stride in a quite perceivably more uphill way. In these moments it is important to pay attention that the horse – with all its willingness to collect and the lighter contact which ensues from this - still continues to stride forward enough onto the hand; only then is it possible to ride the horse out of the turn again at any time, possibly with a simultaneous lengthening of the canter strides. The horse should not become "faster" of its own accord, however, quasi in an attempt to "flee" from taking up the weight.

If the horse accepts this shortening well on the straight and curved track, this is already the beginning of the so-called pirouette canter. Particularly in the case of horses with large canter transmission, great attention has to be paid to this "maintaining lively activity" when collecting, because otherwise a disturbance in the clear three-beat stride can very quickly come about. In the case of horses with less scope in their canter it is particularly important to avoid any rushing or becoming hectic.

In this work the horse requires a lot of strength, which of course can only be developed gradually, to the extent required to do pirouettes in the canter. **The rider and/or trainer have to pay great attention in this training to ensure that the training impulses are not affected negatively as a result of too long repeats or too strong shortening. Depending on the horse's**

temperament this can lead to blockages or even to disobedience.

When then in further training, real "reducing the circle" is ridden (in contrast to "riding into the circle"), this is done in travers-canter, enlarging the circle in shoulder-in canter. With some horses it is necessary to avoid letting the hindquarters lead when reducing the circle, particularly on the rein on which they try to make themselves hollow, because then there is a risk that they may not be able to take up enough weight with the inside hind leg. In this case the rider, as in the case of a walk pirouette, has to think more in terms of guiding the forehand round; he should not take his outside leg back too far in the process. As these horses indeed take the outside rein too strongly or even try to lean on it, the rider must not offer this too much, rather he has to keep yielding with it.

Pirouette at canter with good bend and collection: Rusty with Ulla Salzgeber

Riding the circle progressively smaller at canter

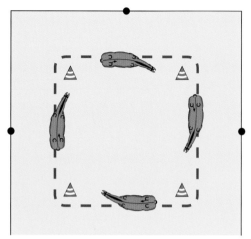

The square volte is also a good way of preparing for the canter pirouette.

Attention has to be accorded to the same aspects on the other rein (riding on the stiffer side) when enlarging: the rider's inside leg then has to be positioned very reliably on the girth in order to maintain the longitudinal bending, also when enlarging, in connection with the guarding outside leg.

With appropriately talented horses it is then only a small step from this correct "reducing the circle" to the working pirouette (a pirouette on a rather larger radius). Decisive, however, is the rider's reliable feeling for what he can already demand of his horse; maintaining the regular and active canter with good impulsion must always have priority above riding the turn on as small a radius as possible.

Already when "reducing the circle", but quite definitely in the working pirouette, it is easier for the rider to place or centre the turn correctly if

he can do the exercise around a helper or a cone. With many horses it may be observed that they then can also carry on cantering more actively of their own accord.

Particularly also riders who, on the basis of their body proportions, e.g. thanks to long levers, are in a position to exercise relatively strong influence, have to be careful not to extend the exercise repeats and the strain involved beyond reason. Overdone and too frequent practising of canter pirouettes imposes too much strain on the horse and can lead to serious damage.

13.3 Exercise variations

When horses have learned to shorten more the canter in the turn, as described above, the canter pirouette can also be practised in the form of a half volte back to the track (> Illustration page 222). Here, rather like "reducing the circle" the turn is done in travers-like style and, depending on the horse's level of training, the whole movement is gradually ridden on a smaller radius. The travers-style, whereby the hindquarters describe a somewhat smaller loop than the forehand, can be emphasized somewhat more clearly on the rein on which the horse is naturally somewhat

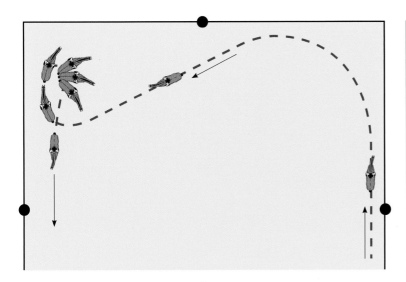

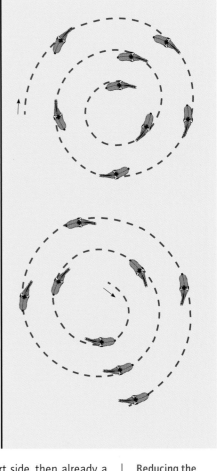

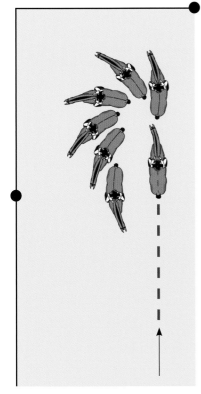

Different exercises for canter pirouettes which help the rider to be able to use less rein influence.

Reducing the circle in travers-like movement, enlarging it with a shoulder-in type movement

better, the wall, by riding the turn out of counter canter. This can either be done in the first corner of the short side in the form of a turn of 180° or in the second corner of the short side, then already a turn of 270° (> Illustration page 221). For many horses these variations are extremely helpful, although they restrict the rider somewhat in his flexibility because he can not ride out of the turn at any point for purposes of correction.

A further practice method, which was already mentioned in connection with turns on the haunches from walk or trot, is the practising of quarter pirouettes on a large square. In an appropriately large indoor school or, even better, arena, a pentagon or hexagon would also be possible, whereby the length of the straight section can be made individually dependent on how the horse "feels" (to the rider). On the rein on which the horse tends to make itself stiffer, the rider should think in terms of "riding-in-position"

stiffer. In more advanced training this exercise can be ridden on the centre line or on the open side of the circle.

Furthermore, good use can be made of the shortening effect of the arena railings or, even

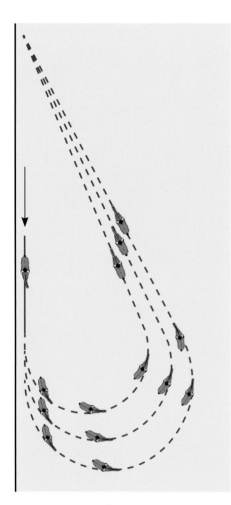

It is possible to prepare canter pirouettes with half voltes and back to the track.

or travers, on the rather hollow side, more in terms of shoulder-fore. This form of practice can be used particularly well when the horse begins to anticipate the turn, or to rush around on the turn.

When practising this very demanding movement of canter pirouette, the assistance of an experienced and critical observer, at least occasionally, is always valuable, even for the experienced rider.

In the case of very eager horses which experience pleasure in working together with the rider, but which lack calmness and composure in the work on pirouettes, it can be helpful in the work pirouette to reduce repeatedly to walk and then to start the canter pirouette again.

13.4 Faults and their correction

Also in the case of canter pirouettes it is not worth trying to find standardized solutions by means of which to remedy individual mistakes. Rather it is a question here of immediately scrutinizing the circumstances whenever difficulties arise and, if necessary, going back several stages to re-establish the pre-requisites. If in this "analysis", possibly with the assistance of a trainer with good powers of observation, or of video recordings, it is possible to find the cause of the fault, the correction solution will be clear on the basis of what has already been discussed. Nor-

mally everything has to be prepared differently or better before any new attempt can promise success.

In order to provide help for this analysis, I should like to mention just a few typical causes of mistakes which occur frequently:

- **seat faults, e.g. not balanced enough influence with the weight aids, possibly due to moving the upper body over too much in connection with collapsing in the hip;**
- **exaggerated use of the guarding leg, sometimes accompanied by too little use – and perhaps also wrong position – of the forward-driving inside leg;**
- **incorrect use of the rein aids, such as too high hands, pressing the inside or outside hand across the crest of the mane, occasionally also hands positioned too low.**

By way of assistance in discovering the cause of mistakes, as far as the training of the horse is concerned, I would always recommend repeated reference to the points of the training scale.

Nearly always when problems occur this will be found to be due to too little time having been given to the horse during training, and unfortunately this also affects even the particularly very talented horses. In daily work it particularly concerns correct suppling work, careful straightening and collecting work, from behind to the front, specifically adapted to suit the horse in question.

➔ Riding of turns; Walk pirouettes

Trotting over cavaletti in good balance

14. Cavaletti Work for Variety

Work with cavaletti serves the purpose of gymnasticizing, particularly in the case of younger horses. It is possible in this way to improve the horse's physical strength as well as its movability, especially with regard to the limbs; at the same time, however, its motoric powers are also trained:

- **this work promotes the regular stepping off in walk and in trot,**
- **animates the horses to stretch, thus improving their suppleness and back activity,**
- **demands more energetic, higher stepping off, thus also improving the thrust and collection,**
- **it trains the balance and sure-footedness as well as**
- **alertness and ability to judge the height and take-off point.**

Caveletti also help to introduce more variety into daily training, in the indoor winter season, for example. They can be used for cantering work as required for jumping.

For the training of the rider the use of cavaletti also has a lot of advantages but, if possible, the young rider should be trained on a horse which is familiar with this kind of work:

- **here he learns to balance in a more elastic way,**
- **also when sitting in the saddle, to relieve the horse's back by leaning forward slightly out of the hips,**
- **and to offer the horse a gentle and constant connection even in stretch position, as well as later when jumping;**
- **generally, this work will improve the rider's seat and train his feeling as a rider.**

For the young rider a varied structure of the riding lessons is almost more important than for the horse. With a little imagination, and thanks to the very varied possibilities of using cavaletti, the trainer can very quickly create "aha experiences" for his pupils, repeatedly arouse enthusi-

A fairly young horse in good stretch posture, it has slightly too much forwards drive, however, and therefore is not swinging through so well with its hind legs; the rider is sitting well - she must try to exert the half halts better before the cavaletti.

This type of cavaletti is easy to handle and very suitable for trotting work.

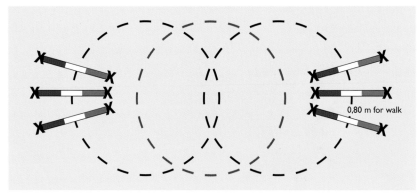

0,80 m for walk

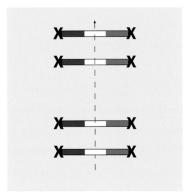

Different ways of setting up cavaletti

asm along the long and not always easy course to be followed in order to learn to ride. Here crampedness and stiffness on the part of the riders can nearly always be seen to disappear almost of their own accord.

Despite all the enthusiasm in connection with cavaletti work, however, the strain ensuing from it should never be under-estimated. Therefore attention always has to be paid to ensure that the work is done in the right proportions – and never exaggerated, particularly at the beginning of this training phase. Any over-strain would be counter-productive.

Such work can only be successful if the right technical prerequisites are fulfilled in the first place:

Cavaletti exist in a variety of different designs. In any case in the lower adjustment with the tope edge of the pole they should be approx. 15 cm high. A length of 2.5 to 3 m is perfectly sufficient. With longer cavaletti horses tend more to veer off the desired track.

The poles of the cavaletti should be in a colour which contrasts with the ground surface, they should be painted white for example.

For pure walking or trotting work cavaletti with rectangular feet are most suitable because they are very practical to handle (see Illustration p. 223 below). Anyone who wants to do cantering work with cavaletti and would like to have the higher adjustment for this purpose, has to use designs with square or cross-shaped feet.

For normal use it is sufficient to have six cavaletti available; for inexperienced horses wings at the start are a useful addition.

Using simple poles instead of cavaletti can only be a poor compromise, because they lie too flat on the ground, do not have the necessary height and do not even receive enough attention after they have been ridden over a few times. Moreover they slip very easily and can lead to uncertainty or even represent a safety risk if a horse steps on one and gets a sprain or a pulled muscle as a result of conflict with the rolling pole.

Good ground conditions are particularly important for cavaletti work. Very deep and very hard ground imposes excess strain on the tendons and ligaments or joints. Above all, however, the surface must be safe to tread on, even and level so that the horses feel safe enough to step confidently and supply.

Even horses which are used to being ridden without leg protection, should wear boots or bandages for cavaletti work. This can prevent the formation of splints, which can be caused by hitting or knocking the cavaletti in attempts which do not succeed.

For normal work the cavaletti are set up initially in a low position and on a straight line. The usual distance for work at walk is approx. 0.80 -

0.90 m, for work at trot on average 1.30 m, and for canter work a distance of 3.20 - 3.50 m would be correct.

Work over cavaletti at canter is less valuable for dressage training because it is impossible here to do an uphill canter with a lowered croup. It is very demanding work, however, which represents an almost indispensable preparation for riding out in the country or over fences; for this purpose the cavaletti are also set up in a higher position, i.e. at a height of approx. 50 cm.

Although cavaletti work promotes suppleness, as mentioned above, within the training unit the horse must first of all have become so supple that it finds a low position, in other words begins to stretch, and can be regulated reliably at working trot. Only when the horse is far enough on it is possible to ride over the cavaletti in a calm but active working pace, can this work commence. If the horse nevertheless becomes tense and hurried over the cavaletti, the rider must react; often it helps to show the horse the cavaletti, to ride along them several times or even to do a transition to walk or even halt in front of them in order to achieve the necessary composure.

In the case of horses and riders whoa are unfamiliar with cavaletti as yet, work begins with single cavaletti which are ridden over at walk. How fast demands can be increased is a very individual matter. Wings positioned at the first cavaletti facilitate the approach; in the case of very cautious and spooky horses an experienced lead horse should help. In normal work 4 - 6 cavaletti can quite easily be set up. Particularly in the case of horses which tend to become hurried the approach should be arranged in such a way that the horse comes out of a turn and is only ridden straight two to three horse's lengths before the cavaletti.

When a certain reliability has been achieved on a straight line, the cavaletti can also be arranged in a large curve (at least approximately 15 m diameter). The desired distance will then always be measured in the middle of the caval-

etti. With this arrangement the experienced rider has the possibility, depending on how the way is arranged, to select narrower or wider distances. In the further work the arrangement of the cavaletti should be changed fairly frequently to ensure increased concentration of the horse. For example, by removing one cavaletti, an extra interim step can be demanded in the middle of the course.

The less experienced rider should shorten his stirrups by one or two holes for cavaletti work. It will then be easier for him to go somewhat into the light seat, in other words to lean slightly forward out of the hips. The hands will go forward accordingly somewhat in the direction of the horse's mouth, whereby the reins may have to be shortened a little in order to assure the elastic but nevertheless still constant connection to the horse's mouth. This kind of relieving, forward seat naturally has to be practised without cavaletti first of all because this seat involves a slight change in the balance, making it somewhat more difficult. In order to be able to be completely in common balance with the horse at the first cavaletti, the rider should take up this seat already a few horse's lengths beforehand. The rider must try to sit very supply, above all also to be able to permit the desired "stretching" of the horse out of the shoulder and elbow joint. Doing a rising trot over cavaletti is less instructional and can only be pleasant for the horse in the case of a very skilful and well-balanced rider. With a trained and well-muscled horse, the rider can also sit in the dressage seat here. If there is any doubt, the horse's reaction will always show if it was correct.

Only if the horse remains calm during this work and the rider is able to continue driving whilst yielding with the hand, the training will be of value.

Normally, as mentioned above, cavaletti work serves the purpose of improving the horse's suppleness, particularly also with regard to the back. Therefore it is very important to select the

Also in ◄ cavaletti work the horse's reactions will show whether the build-up and demands imposed were appropriate.

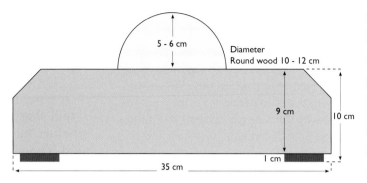

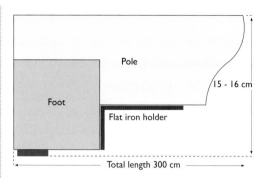

Construction details if you wish to build your own cavaletti

➢ **Only if the horse remains calm during this work and the rider is able to continue driving whilst yielding with the hand, will the training be of value.**

exact individually suitable distances in the walk and working trot. If the distances are too short the horse hesitates, if they are even only a little too long the horse can indeed become stiff in the back.

Only in individual cases can the very experienced trainer successfully pursue other training aims with cavaletti. If, for example, attempts are made to improve the ground cover in the extended trot by means of cavaletti positioned somewhat further apart, in the case of horses which do not have over-average gait qualities, this will very easily lead to them indeed stepping off more strongly with the hind legs, but not being able to swing through enough over the back, indeed even working increasingly further back-and outwards. In principle the same applies regarding the attempt to promote collection through cavaletti positioned closer together or even half-high.

14.1 Summary

In other words, horses with which this work would be feasible, probably do not need it; whereas those which require improvement in these points cannot cope with it – are even damaged by it as a result.

Cavaletti can also be beneficially used in work on the lunge (see Illustration page 224 right). Nevertheless only someone who has a good command of this work and is able to have his horse very reliably on the aids and lunge it precisely on the desired tracks should venture to try it. Only then will it be possible to keep the horse exactly on the circle line and thus to get it going over the cavaletti in such a way as to find suitable distances.

On the other hand the experienced lunger has the possibility of working with different distances without having to do any re-building.

For safety reasons lunging work should always be done only with cavaletti without crosses. Otherwise the lunge could very easily catch in these crosses.

Anyone who would like to inform themselves in more detail about cavaletti work, also in connection with gymnastic jumping, would be recommended to read the book "Cavaletti – Dressur und Springen" by Ingrid and Reiner Klimke.

➔ **Suppleness**

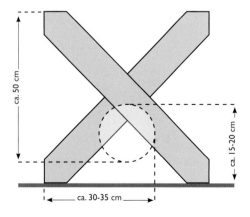

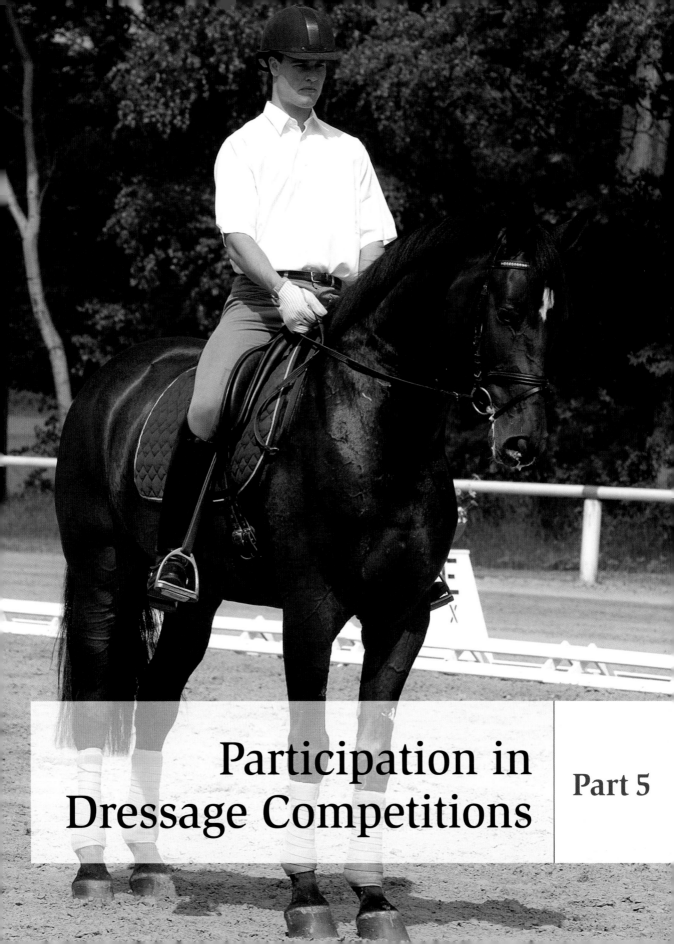

Participation in
Dressage Competitions

Part 5

Exemplary conditions under which to warm-up for a dressage test (Verden)

1. Warming up for Dressage Competitions and Preparation of Movements

The decisive importance of correct warming up is a subject beyond dispute. Anyone who has ever competed at a horse show, remembers competitions in which a better result could have been achieved if better warming up had taken place.

Even if the method of procedure in daily work has to be somewhat different, the same principle nevertheless applies here – that careful, correct suppling is an essential pre-requisite for successful work leading to a sense of contentment with horse and rider alike. If there is a day when time for riding is rather short then the work phase must be abbreviated somewhat, but under no circumstances the suppling phase; the rider then limits himself to so-called "health work".[1]

This naturally applies with regard to all disciplines. Here and now, however – this indeed ensues from our subject matter on hand –, we want to concentrate principally on work with dressage horses. **Simply to clarify the definitions:** Suppling work in both cases is essential at the beginning of riding. Warming up for tests in a competition con-

text includes more, however. Here the horse has to be worked until it is just prior to reaching its highest level of performance ability, which it subsequently achieves in the arena – still with enough energy to complete the test before its performance level starts to fall.

In order to emphasize once again how important I consider warming up to be, I should now like to mention a few examples to illustrate how I normally do this:

- **In the case of every rider whom I am to teach and support, and/or perhaps quite particularly in the case of a rider at medium level and upwards, I should definitely like to observe and influence the suppling work, including riding at walk. I am only able to make exceptions here when I most definitely know that the person in question understands how to ride in accordance with my conceptions and is also convinced that this method is correct.**
  I insist on this in every training course – the time for it simply has to be made available because it always pays off in the long run – particularly also, however, when somebody would just like to present his horse to me once because he has some problem with it.

- **Also in the case of tests such as exam-tests for getting badges or qualifying as amateur instructors, or professional instructors (Pferdewirtschaftsmeister), for which I have constantly been responsible for more than 20 years, I consider supervising, or at least accompanying, the warm-up to be necessary; especially in such stress situations mistakes suddenly occur which the rider actually considered to have been eliminated.**

- **The same applies with regard to accompanying pupils to horse shows, except in the case of very experienced pupils who work correctly and keep a cool head of their own accord.**

In this connection and for the sake of completion, I should also like to mention the inspection of a horse which is being offered for sale. Here also it is very important to see the horse working

---

[1] Health work refers to the following: The horse is carefully suppled and ridden for most of the time in stretch position. The entire work is adapted carefully to suit its exterieur, interieur and level of training off course. It is particularly advantageous as a way of bringing variety into the daily routine, e.g. by hacking out in the country, cavaletti work or some easy jumping exercises.
> Chapter "Suppleness (Losgelassenheit) – First and Final Aim in the Training of a Riding Horse"

228   Riding with *Understanding and Feeling*

right from the first moment, and not just to have it presented after it has been warmed up.

1.1 What should be achieved by warming up before the competition?

Generally speaking, the aim of any warming up is to achieve optimum ability and willingness to perform. On the one hand, it is essential to ensure enough time is available for this, on the other hand it is an advantage which is not to be underestimated – for rider as well as horse – depending on the demands of the test to be undertaken, 30 - 50 minutes are sufficient for this, in other words the aim can be achieved relatively quickly.

Both save physical and, almost more important, mental energy (ability to concentrate).

1.2 How should the warm-up be planned?

What are the factors which influence how much time is required for warming up?
- **Age and level of training of the horse**
- **Physical build (exterieur) and mental qualities (interieur) of the horse**
- **Content and degree of difficulty of the test to be ridden**
- **External circumstances, e.g. ground and surface conditions and weather**
- **Location of the warm-up and competition arena, particularly with regard to distraction factors**
- **Level of training and experience of the rider**
- **When, where and, above all, how was the last work (the end of one work unit to a certain extent represents the beginning of the next one)?**

These points have to be carefully considered and respected every day anew and applied individually to the particular horse in question; only then is it possible to calculate the time required for warming up correctly.

The following schedule can be used as a rough guide here:
- 15-20 minutes suppling work
- short recuperation and relaxation break
- 15-20 minutes for working on the appropriate degree of collection
- 3-5 minutes for the final preparation of rider and horse for the competition
- 5-10 minutes final work, e.g. riding of trot and canter extensions

Before beginning the warm up, it must be clarified of course whether set starting times are indicated for the test to be ridden, whether the timing has been realistically arranged and how precisely it will be observed. If there are no set times, the planning is somewhat more difficult, at the latest from medium level upwards, however, this should not happen.

It is then all the more recommendable, however, to plan in more rather than less time because extra time available can always be filled in with work at walk whereas there is no way of making up time which is lacking.

> **The more demanding the task, the more important it is to avoid riding the horse in such a way that it becomes tired.**

A supple and content horse at trot. The rider should maintain even better contact with hands held thumbs upwards and more relaxed arms!

"Briefing"

Nevertheless, three points should be emphasized again in this connection as being particularly important because careful adherence to them is what indeed makes suppling work successful:

- Good, concentrated work with the horse begins with well thought-out work at walk!
- From the moment the rider mounts, the horse must have the feeling that it is being ridden. Therefore it is essential to control the sequence of movement carefully from the beginning, particularly the basic tempo in the trotting work
- Due attention must be paid to correct, well-considered dealing with the natural crookedness and straightening work every day, also from the beginning onwards; this is absolutely fundamental for the success of suppling work, indeed for the success of all serious equestrian training.

In this phase of work it is essential to combat the tendency, particularly also of young riders, to ride the horse too quickly, or even to ride right from the beginning in a position which is in fact only necessary and sensible at the beginning of the work phase, even if the horse should offer it earlier.

Equally not to be recommended is an exaggerated neck posture ("Beizäumung"), such as unfortunately can be seen everywhere nowadays, and is even sometimes presented "by way of example" by our top riders. This is then described as "deep positioning" (low, deep and round) despite the fact that frequently it is pure forced posture for the horse. Therefore it is absolutely essential to give careful consideration to the subject of "back activity of the horse" in this connection.

Incidentally, in this connection I should also like to mention that, particularly with regard to big, very demanding competitions, very careful consideration should be given to when and how the horse can and must be fed and watered beforehand.

1.3 The warm up

Supplying work

It is certainly not necessary here to describe suppling work again in all possible variations (> Part 3, Chapter 3. "Suppleness").

Arrangement of the work phase

The better the rider knows his horse under competition conditions, the more accurately he can organize the work because he knows which exercises and movements he should ride how in individual cases and how often.

Asking for individual movements shortly before the competitions is indeed of considerable importance, in order not to confront the horse for the first time with higher demands in the test itself. In this connection the following points should be considered and respected with reference to the individual horse in question:

- **Choose the correct order, in order to be able to let the horse relax again if necessary!**
- **Should the movement be ridden in exactly the same connection as it is to be ridden in the test, or is it better to ride it differently?**
- **In the case of movement faults, e.g. with flying change at canter or with halting, punishing the horse immediately before the test makes even less sense than otherwise. Naturally there is nothing to say against an immediate and also resolute correction, which nevertheless should always be directed towards treating the root of the problem.**
- **When warming up the rider should not try to correct the horse's fundamental problem points too much, as this can easily lead to disagreements.**

In spite of very careful consideration and planning, the good rider will repeatedly "listen to" and "explore" his horse to be able to sense and recognize any deviations from its normal form as early as possible, to analyse them and adapt his warm-up riding accordingly; if necessary he will even abstain from participating in the competition.

The question of whether the entire procedure of suppling and/or warming up should in fact always be organized in exactly the same way, has to be answered quite differently with regard to each individual horse. A certain degree of variety should always be provided also in the daily warming up at home in order, above all, to show the horse repeatedly that it must indeed accept the aids promptly and willingly, but it must also wait for them.

As, of course, no rule exists without an exception, – and our sport is particularly rich in examples of this –, mention should also be made here of horses which are ridden best in a competition in a "cold state", so to speak. It is, however, not correct to claim that they are being ridden without any warm up whatsoever because in such cases the warm up has in fact taken place in thorough form several hours beforehand. Immediately prior to the start such horses are only briefly, but very calmly, suppled up.

I can only recommend this procedure with certain reservations. On the long term every horse, if possible, should be schooled in such a way by his rider that normal warming up before a competition is possible. The physical and psychological cost, and ultimately also the wear and tear, at the end of the day are less.[1]

→ **Riding at walk; suppleness; straightening; riding of a test**

2. Riding a Dressage Test in Training and at a Horse Show

Everyone who is committed to dressage riding, whether as a rider or trainer, will have experienced the following:

You ride a horse which has sound dressage training and already does all exercises and movements quite reliably in daily work, at elementary level for example. In order now to prepare the horse for its first elementary-level dressage test at a horse show, you take test book and ask someone to read a relevant test aloud to you. In this process you will probably realize that it actually makes a very considerable difference when you have to ride the lessons and movements required in one complete test and also at clearly stipulated points of the arena. This well-known effect naturally occurs to an even greater extent in tests of the higher levels. For this reason it is very important to ride through and to practise concrete tests regularly on an arena with the described dimensions and points.

Before we progress to the elementary level 2 test (German test book) and take this through in detail, I should like to make some general pre-

---

[1] In the case of horses which are used to being worked in the morning, at a show naturally it makes sense to ride them for a while in the morning also when they are not scheduled to compete until the afternoon.

16.	(A-F-M)	(The collected canter).
	M	Half volte left 8 metres returning to the track
17.	(B-F-A)	(The counter canter).
18.	A	Simple change
19.	(K-H)	Medium canter.
	H	Collected canter.
20.		(Transitions from collected canter to medium canter and from medium canter to collected canter).
21.	C	Collected trot.
	M-X-K	At medium trot diagonal change of rein.
	K	Collected trot.
22.		(Transitions from collected canter to collected trot, from collected trot to medium trot and from medium trot to collected trot).
23.	A	Down centre line
	X	Halt. Salute.
		Leave arena at medium walk on long reins

manding exercises in a dressage test at elementary level. It can only be done correctly if the horse carries itself sufficiently and is reliable on the rider's driving aids beforehand in the counter-canter, thanks to good, reliable collection and elevation. Then the contact will also be correspondingly light so that the horse can take up weight with the hindquarters in the half halt and does not come onto the forehand. In the test three to five clear steps at walk should follow, before cantering on again, this time on the left (see above). In training the horse has to be ridden consistently at walk for as long as is necessary until the horse starts to step calmly again, without trying to anticipate the canter aid. Also here, it is again quite decisive that the rider makes positive demands with the driving aids and does not try to prevent premature cantering on with the reins.

The counter-canter on the other rein and the next simple change are ridden analogously to the first one, under consideration of the horse's natural crookedness.

- Also in the case of the subsequent medium canter on the long side from K to H, a decisive criterion is the horse's being straightened, as was the case beforehand in the collected pace. However in the extension it requires a considerably higher degree of throughness in order to keep the horse straight and on the track from the lengthening to the shortening of the pace. As already explained above, in the case of the medium trot, the rider has to control every canter stride and under no circumstances allow the horse to start taking the initiative. The shortening can then only succeed with throughness and appropriate taking up of the weight with the hindquarters if the horse has been sufficiently schooled with regard to its ability and willingness to collect in the training sessions. If too strong and too long non-yielding rein aids are given here, the horse cannot close up with the hind legs, instead it will come onto the forehand, possibly even fall out (to trot). Each individual canter stride has

to be carefully and specifically asked for with the rider's legs, particularly the inside one.

On account of horses' tendency to become crooked at canter, particularly when extending and shortening again, the rider always has to think in terms of shoulder-fore. This means he has to have the idea of driving the horse forward so reliably onto the hand that it can come away slightly from the outside edge of the track with the forehand.

It is important to avoid two frequently occurring mistakes here: firstly the rider should not try to push the horse's shoulder over with his outside hand because this would shorten the neck and provoke tilting in the poll; secondly, he should, however, also not try to push the hindquarters out with the inside leg positioned slightly further back because otherwise the horse would press over towards the rails of the arena and have problems with its balance, possibly also involving restriction in the activity of the inside hind leg.

- If the collected canter is again done in good self-carriage, the transition to the collected trot will succeed precisely and fluently. In order to already prepare the medium trot, every step has to be accompanied by a light half halt, well ridden with the driving aids.
- The medium trot on the diagonals with the transitions has already been discussed above. Here, however, it is started on the other rein therefore a differentiation should again be made for the turn, depending on whether this is approached on the horse's stiffer side or rather hollow side. (see above concerning movement 3)
- The same also applies for the last riding up the centre line with the left turn. (Concerning halt > Part 1, Chapter 4.4.2)

Good luck! I wish you success and plenty of enjoyment practising as well as competing at horse shows!

➔ Transitions; warming up as well as all exercises and movements mentioned

Breaking in –
Basic Education for Horses

Part 6

1. Imprinting Experiences

When young horses are broken in it is important to consider that particularly this first period of familiarization with new tasks, and perhaps also new people, has a very imprinting effect – either in a positive or in a negative sense. It must be clear to the responsible horse-lover that this task belongs exclusively in the hands of competent riders and trainers.

Only a person who has many years of experience in the saddle and in dealing with different horses can train the young horse with an appropriate level of understanding and give it an optimum basic training. Additionally, this person must have the feeling and also be willing to assess the individual horse correctly and deal with it appropriately.

"The Principles of Riding" issued by the German Equestrian Federation include a very good list of the principles to be observed by the trainer – also when instructing riders, moreover.

The training has to: [1]
- take place according to a well thought-out plan,
- progress systematically from an easier to a more difficult level,
- be correctly structured from a methodical point of view,
- show continuity,
- be varied and diversified,
- take into account the change between work effort and relaxation,
- be characterized by comprehensibility and consistency,
- exclude uncontrolled emotions on the part of the rider,
- involve regular checks of training progress,
- take into account the individuality of every horse,
- lead to the external and internal balance of horse and rider.

The right attitude and conception of what one intends to do is decisive. One has to be quite clear about the fact that the horse's later ability and willingness for work depend on how content and comfortable it feels in hand and under the saddle. In order to do justice to this, the trainer has to think carefully about what psychological aspects have to be taken into consideration in dealing with the horse and in its training.

The horse understands the human as a fellow being, but it will only follow him if the hierarchical order is properly clarified. In order to gain the higher position in the hierarchy, the rider has to apply his intellect as well as his willpower; his manner in dealing with the horse must be characterized by confidence and assertiveness. Whenever the horse makes a mistake, the rider must question his own action, ask himself whether the horse was really able to understand him correctly or whether the demands he imposed on it were too high.

When handled correctly, the horse will very quickly gain confidence in the human being and feel safe and secure with him.

Thanks to the work done by breeders over the last 50 to 60 years, and their orientation according to riding horse qualities, we now have wonderful, motivated horses available with a high degree of willingness to perform. For the rider this means that he can assume appropriate basic ridability and, following good training, high throughness values. On the other hand, however, the demands on the rider are higher concerning balance of the seat, fineness in the dealings and subtlety, sensitively in the application of the aids.

Quite frequently a skilled and able rider is available but on account of his youth he may not yet have enough experience, and perhaps also not yet enough calmness, composure and consistency, to be able to act correctly in difficult situations. For this reason it is essential also to involve an appropriately competent helper and trainer by way of compensation.

[1] s. The Principles of Riding

2. When is the Right Time to Start Breaking-in and Training?

Normally training of a horse under the rider should not be started before it is three years old. In this context careful consideration must also be given to the frequently very different conditions of the individual horse regarding physical build, growth and constitution.

Because in the case of horses – as also in the case of human beings – the ability to learn, particularly concerning the motorics, decreases as they get older, the start of training should only be postponed until later in exceptional cases.

With individual horses it makes sense, after the end of the third grazing season, in other words at the age of approximately two and a half years, to undertake a phase of familiarization of the horse with the saddle and bridle as well as with the rider. If, over a period of four to six weeks, the horse is acquainted with the bridle, saddle and rider, the benefits will be felt one year later when it is being broken in, the effort involved is most certainly worthwhile. Particularly in the case of early familiarization, which may be compared to a young child attending preschool, it depends very much on the competence of the trainer. Only if the trainer has a good eye and feeling for the young horse, will the work be of value and without problems for the horse.

3. Getting used to the Bridle and Saddle

Even if it is not always the case, it should be assumed that the young horse has been reared competently. This includes having learned since its earliest days to respect the human being and knowing that it can feel safe and secure in his care.
The following should be possible:
- leading and tying up in a headcollar
- grooming and hoofcare
- putting on a rug
- allowing to run loose on both reins with attention being paid to the person holding the whip

When the horse is to be familiarized with the bridle and saddle, it is best for this to be done by a person with whom the horse is familiar, or at least for such a person to be present.

If this has not already been done beforehand, the horse must now become accustomed to standing alone in its box, at least for a few hours at a time, because it will also be alone when it is first backed and broken in.

Putting on the bridle should not represent a problem for a horse which is used to a headcollar. The bit has to be put into the mouth carefully. A few grains of oats or a little treat can be helpful here.

If the horse is sensitive at the head and around the ears, it may be a good idea to make the bridle a bit larger before putting it on and then afterwards to shorten the cheek pieces to the right length. Under no circumstances should the bridle be kept on the horse for too long in the larger size because otherwise it would be encouraged to play with the bit. The bridle has to be of an optimum fit. In the case of horses with a small sized mouth a loose ring snaffle of medium thickness, i.e. 18 millimetres, is to be recommended. In order to avoid playing with the bit and tongue, a well-fitting noseband should be used right from the beginning, normally an ordinary or flash noseband not fastened too tight.

With the many large horses which exist today, first exercises in putting on a bridle are to be undertaken by a tall person who can reach the head well and with whom the horse not can immediately discover that by taking its head up high it can evade the task in question.

Being tied up and groomed is something a young horse should become familiar with and learn to enjoy.

A young horse on the lunge under the rider

be ensured that the horse is concentrating and is not distracted by other horses or external disturbances.

The saddle which is placed on the horse's back should be of a suitable fit for the young horse with its withers which may not be distinctively formed as yet. A general purpose saddle with a well-fitting numnah has proved most successful, particularly as breaking in is done with slightly shorter stirrups. A suitable girth can be found easily by visual judgement, and it should enable easy closing. In the case of very sensitive and ticklish horses smooth leather girths, which are somewhat narrower in the elbow region, and have rubber inserts on one side, have proved successful. It is essential that a second person is available to help when putting on the saddle and tightening the girth.

Occasionally there are horses which do not have a well-developed girth position and with whom there is therefore a danger of the saddle slipping backwards. In such a case a breast-plate has to be used, at least in the initial stages.

4. The First Time as a Riding Horse

The first tacking up has taken place successfully. Now the equine pupil will become accustomed to lunging and will be backed for the first time by the rider. The following section describes how the trainer should proceed.

When tacking up has been done successfully, the horse can be lead onto the lunging circle and familiarized with lunging. A helper should be available to help lead the horse for the first time. Later it is best for the trainer to hold the lunge and whip himself with the helper remaining nearby.

Because the horse already knows the whip holder and the whip from running loose in the arena, after the girth has been tightened the trainer can get the horse moving on the circle with a lunge and whip. It is good if the horse remains at walk first of all and the trainer can move slowly on a somewhat smaller circle at a certain

Taking the bridle off a young horse must also be done with great care: When the head piece has been brought forwards over the ears, the bridle should still be held well upright so that the horse has time to spit out the bit. The left hand may need to help a little here. Under no circumstances may the bridle be simply pulled off the head because otherwise the bit will knock against the horse's teeth.

If the horse has learned to tolerate a rug, putting on a saddle and fastening the girth will not pose a problem. First experiences with putting on the saddle should take place outside the box, ideally in an open or closed lunging circle or in a partitioned outside arena or in an indoor school.

In these exercises, just as when backing the horse and in the first mounted exercises, it must

Attaching the lunge…

…to the snaffle ring

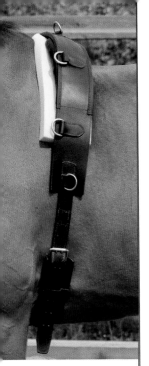

Foam rubber underlay ensures the lunging girth will sit well and remain firmly in position.

distance parallel to the horse. No side reins are used for the first exercise, the reins are unbuckled or attached to the „help strap" on the saddle (small strap attached to the gullet of the saddle).

The lunge can be attached in a variety of different ways for this work (see photos on this page):

• To a cavesson, which has to fit exactly and be buckled tightly, because otherwise it will slip around the horse's head.

• To a well-fitting headcollar: the lunge is attached to the rings at the side of the headcollar so as to avoid exerting direct influence on the horse's mouth.

• If an enclosed outdoor or indoor lunging circle is available so that the horse has no way of breaking out, a good system is to attach the lunge to both rings of the bit via a somewhat longer connecting strap, without the horse's mouth being irritated in any way.

• If a buckle is attached to the end of the lunge, the lunge can also be buckled through the snaffle ring and the noseband.

Even if the horse is not yet shod, protection boots should be used at least on the fore legs, in order to protect against knocks.

The stirrup irons are attached firmly by means of the stirrup leathers (see photo p.244), so that they do not slip down and knock the horse under its belly when it is trotting or cantering. To what extent the horse can be lunged at trot or canter is dependent on the horse as well as on the situation and has to be decided by the experienced trainer.

On no account should the horse be made fit on the lunge over a period of several days before backing work with the rider has been started.

The act of backing usually works quickly and without problems in the case of well reared horses which have not been spoiled by any bad experiences.

In addition to a suitable rider, two or three helpers should also be available the first time a horse is mounted: the trainer holds the horse on the lunge and stands on the left side, slightly in front of the horse's shoulder. One helper stands on the right side, holds the horse's bridle with the right hand and with the left hand helps the rider into the stirrup, when the moment of mounting comes. A second helper, if necessary the trainer holding the lunge, helps the rider to the horse first of all and then properly onto it.

Already when putting on the saddle and in between times when changing the rein during lunging, the saddle should be touched repeatedly and moved sideways on the horse's back to test how the horse will react when it is backed. In the case of smaller horses, a taller trainer can put his arm over the saddle, exert a little pressure and perhaps even pat the horse a little on the right side.

Attaching the lunge…

…to the snaffle ring

…to the snaffle ring and noseband

…to the snaffle ring and second (lower) noseband

…to the cavesson

This is a secure way of fixing the stirrups whilst lunging.

Prior to the first backing the horse should be lunged first of all in order to let off superfluous energies. This time the stirrup irons can be already pulled down into riding position.

4.1 The first mounting

The two helpers who are holding the horse should pay attention that the horse remains standing and does not jump sideways or rush away. First of all, the rider will only be lifted up to the horse to test how the horse reacts when the rider appears behind and above.

It is assumed that with some horses the instinct to flee is activated more by the rider appearing above it than by the rider's weight. The second or third time the rider is raised so far that he can already lie somewhat over the horse and let his full weight rest on the horse. If this can be done without any tension – with constant praising and being given the occasional treat to munch – the rider can be raised properly into the saddle. For this purpose all participants have to be so skilful that the rider can slide gently into the saddle, make himself rather small in order to relieve the horse and avoid giving the horse a fright with his right leg behind the saddle. If the horse remains standing calmly during this practising phase, without tensing up too much, the rider should then slide skilfully out of the saddle again, praise the horse liberally and practise the whole procedure two or three times.

If this mounting and dismounting can be done without any significant tension, then the next important step can be undertaken: the leading off.

4.2 Leading off

Even if the horse stands very calmly when mounting and dismounting, the first step, the first movement with the rider in the saddle is often a difficult moment because balance problems can very easily occur here. This is why the rider must be skilful and well-balanced with a good command of the light seat. In order to avoid this moment of tension with the first leading off, some trainers try to raise the rider into the saddle whilst the horse is being led at walk.

In the further procedure the horse is stopped several times and led on again. Only when this is possible in a reliable and calm way, the rider can help with a light click of the tongue, and when halting, with the voice, and the trainer approaches the centre of the circle, allowing the lunge to get longer, does it make sense to start thinking about the first trotting steps under the rider. At the latest when this is starting, the rider has to take the reins in his hands in order to be able to exercise influence on the horse.

How quickly this work can proceed, when trotting work on the other rein can start, and over how many days the work has to be distributed, has to be decided on an individual basis.

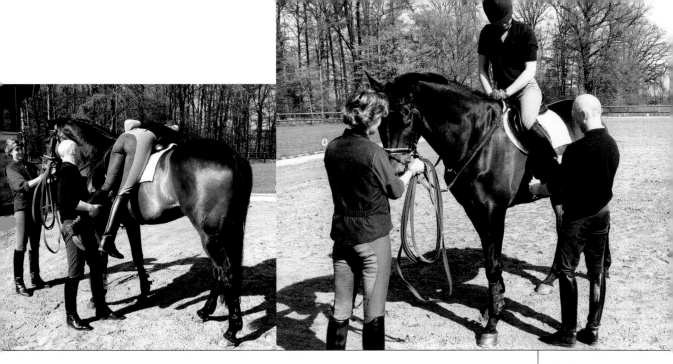

In order to do these things in the right proportions the trainer needs a good eye for horses and also as much experience as possible with their basic training. In addition to all calmness and care which should be exercised in this phase, attention should also be paid to consistency and regularity (daily practice). It is normally not particularly beneficial to delay real riding for too long. In the case of well-reared, unspoiled horses this training phase until first riding on the lunge should not last for much longer than three to five days.

4.3 Riding without the lunge

When the trainer can let the horse off the lunge in order to allow the rider to ride initially on an enclosed circle, later in an indoor school or on a well fenced-in arena, whereby he can use the lunging whip from the ground to help drive the horse, is not something for which a general rule can be applied. At this stage at the latest, the rider should carry a little jumping whip with a swatter to use on the shoulder as an auxiliary driving aid because the young horse is not very receptive to the leg aids yet.

An important further step in the breaking-in phase is the first canter under the rider. Under no circumstances should this be forced. It may be assumed that every horse offers the canter when it feels supple and balanced enough to have the confidence to canter.

If the rider is working with the young horse without a lunge in an indoor school or a fenced-in arena, the trainer, possibly with a helper, can provide support in driving and in changing the rein by means of always very carefully taking up the right position on the arena and moving correctly, as in lunging or letting the horse run loose.

In this phase it can be a good idea also to have one or two other – experienced, if possible – riding horses in the arena which can be used rather like lead horses. Constant riding behind a lead horse should be avoided right from the beginning, however, because otherwise it will become difficult to ride the horse independently later on and it will always try to hang on behind another horse.

"Controlling" with assistance

In this assistance of the trainer or helper from the ground as mentioned above, just as in the case of lunging or letting run loose, it is a question of making full use of the horse's natural reactions. A good horse trainer proceeds in a similar way in dressage performances by liberty horses in the circus.

Sitting on a
young horse
for the first time

At the beginning
a lead horse can
be very helpful.

A few examples here: **In order first of all to keep the horse in regular forward movement, in other words to increase the horse's understanding of the driving aids, the whip holder has to move in such a way that he always has the horse slightly in front of him. For this purpose he moves in** an oval area on the arena or in the indoor school (➢ Illustration page 248). The narrower the arena is, **the more carefully he has to avoid standing in the horse's way. The throughway between the trainer and the wall or rails must not appear too narrow to the horse. This precise effect may be used beneficially in order to assist with the change of rein** (> Illustration page 247).

If the rider and groundman work together well in these exercises, within a few days the horse **will learn to allow itself to be „controlled" by the rider alone.**

This learning process can only be successful under a well balanced rider who is in a position to coordinate his weight, leg and rein aids as well as the use of the jumping whip confidently and with feeling.

In the further course of this learning process, the training aims and sections are under specification of the first three points of the training scale, "rhythm" (Takt), "suppleness" (Losgelassenheit) and "contact" (Anlehnung). If the trainer and rider have managed so far to avoid unnecessary tensions or excessive strain, there should now be no serious hurdles left in the way of a successful and also relatively fast training and bringing on of the young horse

A partial aim in this phase is an increasingly reliable control of the tempo. Particularly at trot a situation has to be achieved whereby the rider, from as near to the beginning as possible, can choose and determine the suitable basic tempo. The better this succeeds, the sooner the horse becomes balanced, feels at ease and supples up.

The most important prerequisite here also: equestrian feeling and the ability always to sit in balance.

The rider has to sit in balance with the horse and therefore avoid sitting behind the movement, even if a spontaneous lengthening takes him by surprise, or of coming ahead of the horse's movement in the case of sudden shortening. The same also applies for the sideways stability in the case of unforeseen deviation from the track. Thanks to this balance and suppleness of the rider, he can establish a constant and gentle contact to the horse's mouth with a hand which is independent of the seat. This improves the horse's confidence and increases its willingness to accept the rein aids.

How rider and trainer proceed in the daily work, whether the horse is still lunged or is allowed to run loose before it is ridden, has to be

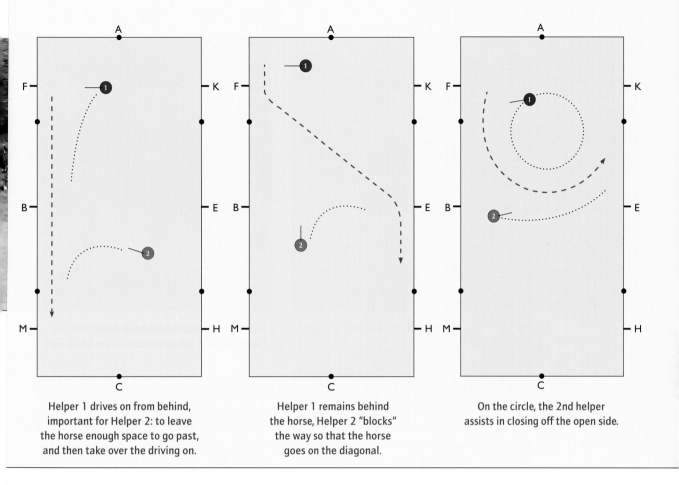

Helper 1 drives on from behind, important for Helper 2: to leave the horse enough space to go past, and then take over the driving on.

Helper 1 remains behind the horse, Helper 2 "blocks" the way so that the horse goes on the diagonal.

On the circle, the 2nd helper assists in closing off the open side.

decided on an individual basis and made dependent on the way the horse is kept (if it was out at grass beforehand, for example).

At this point I should like to express an important thought with regard to the understanding of rein aids:

As soon as possible the horse has to learn, in other words be conditioned accordingly, to "pull" in a positive way. That means that the rider, when the horse hesitates and does not go forward enough, indeed drives more, possibly also with the jumping whip, and is supported by the whip holder, but that he also keeps the elastic connection to the horse's mouth very constantly instead of pushing the hands forward and let the reins hang loose. Vice versa, when the horse goes forward more, he has to yield repeatedly, and on no account to start pulling or holding

on tight thus conveying the feeling to the horse that it is being held in. (see chapter: How does a horse learn "this little positive pull")

If everything has worked positively until now, the horse has offered the canter and horse and rider can move in balance on a large track, it is quite definitely time to involve some hacking out or at least riding on a large outdoor arena. This offers the horse more variety, also regarding ground conditions and other circumstances relating to the countryside.

If training can only take place in the indoor school or on a dressage arena, cavaletti or poles should be used.

Depending on how "spooky" the horse is, work is done first with one cavaletti on a straight line with wings. A lead horse can possibly be of assistance here. How fast the requirements concern-

Presentation of young horses in a class for 3 and 4 year old horses

es, this simply contributes to a more harmonious overall impression.

The better and more systematically the young horse is broken in and trained, the further and more attractively its muscle system will have developed and the more reliably balanced it will also already be under the rider. The more supple it moves under its rider, when it therefore steps trustingly and contentedly onto the calm hand, the more impulsion and composure it will have during the competition. Naturally this all has a positive effect on the evaluation of the basic gaits, but also of the conformation (e. g. on account of the better muscle development and development of the top line) and of the overall impression including the temperament.

When these connections are taken into consideration in the preparation and presentation of the young horse, the judges can evaluate everything in an optimum way. In trotting work the working trot in the individually suitable basic tempo is of prime importance; lengthening or extending the steps is only required in short repeats. Exaggerated forward riding makes as little contribution to achieving optimum marks as a selected basic tempo which is too hesitant. In both cases, on account of a lack of suppleness, particularly also in the back, the horse will not be able so well to swing through forwards actively with the hind legs, in other words to develop real impulsion (Schwung).

Unfortunately there are always a few riders who believe they can achieve the best trotting marks for their horse with toe flicking ("in front a lion, behind a mouse"). At the most, however, they may occasionally succeed – with a stiff and tense back – in achieving spectacular action of the fore legs. The competent observer will not allow himself to be deceived by this, however, but will recognize that the horses – irrespective of their actual level of training – are raised artificially at the poll, i.e. with the hands, and on account of the very restricted back activity, show little genuine impulsion (thrust from the hindquarters) and little ground cover.

then that he is in a position to exercise influence with aids which are independent of the seat. He has to have a particularly elastic and smooth command of the rising trot, at canter he must be able, also out of a forward seat, to keep his horse well ahead of his aids and at walk to permit and to go with the horse's nodding movement with a fine hand out of an elastic shoulder and elbow joint on the long rein.

As far as these above-mentioned points are concerned, very tall riders are somewhat disadvantaged. Obviously in such a competition it is of benefit if rider and horse are of matching size because, particularly in the case of smaller hors-

Correct presentation in hand at walk

This is how a horse is positioned correctly. The reins should be approx. three hands' widths longer.

This form of riding and presentation has a particularly negative effect on the further training of these young horses: They have no chance of developing to their full potential, but rather will be damaged physically as well as psychologically.

Apart from some short repeats, rising trot only is demanded in such competitions. Therefore riders should not use too long stirrups. When extending at trot on the long side an effort must be made to allow the horse to develop this, – it has to "pull positively", i.e. want to extend. This will then particularly be the case when the driving aids are applied with a good sense of rhythm and without too much strength and pressure and, when extending, the rider sits somewhat in the forward seat rather than too heavily into the saddle.

Similar criteria apply concerning the canter. The better the horse is on the rhythmically and feelingly applied forward-driving aids, the rider has it in front of him and also in the extensions gives it the opportunity to develop, the better it will already canter uphill within the scope of its possibilities and the less it will come onto the forehand (onto the head) in the process.

As a matter of principle, the walk should be presented on the long rein (> Part 3, Chapter 2. Riding at Walk), not with given loose reins, however. This, furthermore is also how it is required in the Notes for the Judging of Classes for Young Horses (issued by the German Equestrian Federation). Whether a horse can be optimally presented at walk depends, more than in the other basic gaits, on how it supples up. The better it has already learned in the short period of training to feel at ease under its rider and to step trustingly onto the hand, the better it will also step at walk in active, regular rhythm but with composure. It can then, in fine contact to the rider's hand, coming out of the shoulder and elbow and going along with the horse's movement, show the natural nodding movement and, from a supple back, develop the possible ground cover. Also at walk, any possible lack of lively activity can only be improved by feelingly applied driving on alternate sides, a short, resolute impulse with the leg can also help sometimes. Constant, laborious and very vigorous driving will, on the contrary however, rather have the effect of the horse

Tips for the Presentation in Classes for Young Horses

• What indeed applies to all other competitions at horse shows, should be adhered to particularly with regard to classes for young horses, that only horses which are in a good general condition of health and care should be presented.

• Even although opinions may differ concerning the beauty aspects of a plaited mane and tail, if this is done well, it indeed enables a much better evaluation of the neck and top line as well as the hindquarters and croup formation.

• Also practising of presentation in hand under competent supervision with appropriate assistance is reflected in an improved presentation and usually higher scoring. Similarly to under the saddle, the horse should show itself to be attentive and interested, simply make a better impression. In the presentation of the horse in hand it has proved beneficial to ensure that the horse shows itself to be alert and with appropriately well developed posture of the neck, but also with the relevant face, i.e. large eyes and pricked ears when it is lined up in front of the judges. In this part of the presentation, some riders carry a twig with leaves on it, the noise of which serves the purpose of making the horse more alert. A helper can possibly also be of assistance, holding a whip and standing slightly back. For removing the saddle, brushing or rubbing down, and possibly also for some clever driving from behind, it is highly recommended to have the support of a competent helper.

• During the examination of the basic gaits under the rider this skill is also reflected by always observing a suitable distance to the horse in front. Depending on the situation a rather larger, or occasionally also, as described above in connection with the walk, a rather shorter distance can be of advantage.

hesitating even more. If it tends to be over-active at walk, first of all the distance to the preceding horse must be kept cleverly short, almost as a brake, because a greater distance encourages the horse to become even faster and more rushed, because it does not want to get left behind. Furthermore, in a fine coordination of driving and restraining aids, a calmer, a little slower movement has to be positively demanded rather than a more rushed movement being prevented by exclusively restraining aids.

After presenting the horses at trot, canter and walk, the judging of the conformation and also the correctness of the gaits, the presentation in hand takes place. This is actually a complete subject in its own right, therefore I should just like to make one short statement here: presentation in hand also needs to be practised in order to be able to position the horse in an optimum way – always open[1] – in front of the judges at the decisive moment.

Unfortunately bad weather conditions sometimes prevent a horse from showing itself in its best light and thus achieving a reasonable score. It quite often happens that young horses supple up badly or even stiffen and hesitate on account of rain and a cold wind. Also ground which is too hard or too deep causes considerable difficulties for some young horses. For all these reasons it is therefore perfectly normal that one and the same horse may achieve very different scores at different horse shows.

Every responsible trainer must always bear in mind that even high quality horses can only be successful in later years – in competitions at higher level – if excessive demands are not imposed on them as three and four year-olds, if they are not entered in too many competitions, and also never forget in these competitions that they are indeed youngsters still in the process of growing.

➔ Basic gaits; suppleness; breaking in

---

[1] Open means that the fore and hind leg on the judges' side are positioned a little wider than the legs on the other side

Anyone who has read this book as far as here has proved his serious interest, commitment and feeling for riding.

All the more I hope that I have succeeded in showing,

- how suitable for horses correct training and riding according to the principles of the so-called classical theory is,
- that the theoretical content of these principles is not grey but rather logical as well as interesting and their implementation indeed makes riding easier, and
- that understanding and feeling in the same measures are important and mutually complement each other.

I wish all readers plenty of aha-experiences with their horses, pleasure in the increasingly harmonious partnership in daily riding, the sporting success which might possibly be an aim, particularly however the satisfaction of being able to reach the aim in question in a way in which the horse can also maintain its pleasure in working together with the rider, its willingness to perform and its "personality".

Michael Putz

The author Michael Putz, born in 1946, began his riding career at the age of 11 years. Already at 22 he took over the independent management of a competition and training yard.

Parallel to this he studied law for a number of semesters and then completed a course of studies to qualify as a teacher for primary and secondary schools at the University of Erlangen/Nuremberg.

From 1977 to 1980 he worked as a rider (Bereiter) for Dr. Josef Neckermann and was in charge of his competition and training yard. Michael Putz is a successful rider in all disciplines up to advanced level, "Pferdewirtschaftsmeister" (qualified Equestrian Manager) and holder of the "Goldenes Reitabzeichen" (gold riding badge), has several decades of experience as a trainer and judge at all levels of training, in dressage as well as jumping.

Michael Putz was Executive Director of the Westphalian Riding and Driving School in Münster/Wesphalia. Since 2001 he has been working as a freelance trainer. He gives individual lessons, runs courses for professionals and amateurs and since 2002 has spent a number of periods in New Zealand in order to instruct judges, trainers and riders in practice and theory.

Furthermore Michael Putz is co-author of the German Guidelines Volumes 1 & 2 "Principles of Riding" and "Advanced Techniques of Dressage" published by the German Equestrian Federation. (FN), author of some equestrian books, of numerous specialized articles in equestrian magazines, an independent equestrian assessor for the law courts, a member of many equestrian committees, working groups and associations as well as a respected editor for the FN Publishing House.

Photographs/Illustrations

Photographs

Arnd Bronkhorst Photography, Garderen/NED
page 147 r., 210, 219

Dirk Caremans, Hemiksen/BEL
page 125

Hugo Czerny, München
page 253 as well as back cover

Werner Ernst, Ganderkesee
page 188 (taken from PSI-Katalog 14)

Bernd Eylers, Hude
page 103 (taken from Hengstprospekt der Hengststation Ludwig Kathmann)

Karl-Heinz Frieler, Gelsenkirchen
page 6

Thoms Lehmann, Warendorf
page 7; page 27 (3), 44 l., 61 u., 106 ru., 162, 178 (5) (> page 27 all taken from Deutsche Reitlehre – Der Reiter. Deutsche Reiterliche Vereinigung (Hrsg.). Warendorf 2000. page 81, 126 l., r., 135)

Löhneysen, Georg Engelhard
page 81 (taken from Löhneysen, G. E. Della Cavalleria. Hildesheim 10. Reprint 1977.

Neddens Tierfotografie, Wuppertal
page 174 r.

Peter Prohn, Barmstedt
page 11, 14, 15 (3) lo., mo., ru., 17 (2) ro., ru., 19 ru., 20 (2), 21, 23 (2), 24, 25 lo., 26, 28, 30, 31, 33, 38 ro., 39 ro., 41, 44 r., 48 ro., 51, 52, 53, 55, 57, 58 (2) r., l., 59 (2) l., m., 61 (2) o., m., 63, 66, 79 l., 83 (4) Nr. 1,2, 3,5, 87 ru., 88, 91, 93 (2), 95 l., 98, 104, 106 (3) lo., lu., ro., 107, 108 (2), 110, 111, 113, 114 l., 116, 124, 128 (2), 133, 137, 138, 139, 142, 143, 144, 146, 147 l., 148 (2), 157, 166 (2), 167, 173 (2), 174 l., 176 (2), 180, 183, 184, 186, 187, 192, 194, 195, 196 (2), 198, 199, 201, 205, 208, 217, 220, 223 ro., 227, 229, 232, 241, 242, 243 l., 244 l., 248, 249 r., 250, 251 (2)

Karin und Michael Putz, Erlangen
page 8, 15 ro., 16 (2) r., 17 (3), lo., m., 18 (2), 19 o., 22, 25 ro., 35, 38 (3) lo., 39 lo., 40, 42 (2), 43, 45 (3), 48 lo., 49 (2), 50, 58 m., 59 r., 60, 65, 70, 71 (2), 72, 74, 75, 78, 79 r., 80, 81, 82, 83 Nr. 4, 85, 87 ro., 89, 90, 94, 95 r., 105, 114 r., 117, 118, 119 l., 123, 126, 131, 132, 149, 152, 153, 158, (2), 175, 181, 202, 207, 223 (2) lo., ru., 228, 230, 239, 243 (4) r., 244 r., 245 (2), 246, 249 l.

Norbert Schamper, Telgte
page 50 l. (taken from Deutsche Reitlehre – Der Reiter. Deutsche Reiterliche Vereinigung (Hrsg.). Warendorf 2000. Seite 104 oben.)

Ute Schmoll, Wiesbaden
page 43 lu., 62, 64, 68, 69, 252

Björn Schröder, Berlin
page 150 (taken from PSI-Katalog Nr. 27)

Illustrations

Illustration page 84 (taken from Kapitzke. G. Das Pferd von A-Z. München. 6. Auflage 2003.)

Gerrit Kreling, Waldalgesheim
page 29, 56, 145

Ute Schmoll, Wiesbaden
Illustrations based on: Richtlinien für Reiten und Fahren Band 1. Grundausbildung für Reiter und Pferd. Deutsche Reiterliche Vereinigung (Hrsg.). Warendorf 2000 und Deutsche Reitlehre – Der Reiter. Deutsche Reiterliche Vereinigung (Hrsg.). Warendorf 2000.
page 16, 24, 37, 43 (2), 47, 81 (2), 88, 91, 92 (2), 96, 104, 105 (2), 107, 119 r., 120, 127, 137, 138, 139, 140, 161, 162, 163 (5), 164 (3), 165 (3), 166 (2), 170, 171 (2), 172, 179, 180 (2), 182, 185, 193, 195, 196, 197, 198, 199, 200, 202, 203 (2), 204 (2), 205, 206, 209, 220, 221 (3), 222, 224 (3), 226 (3), 247 (3), 248

German National Federation (FN)
FN-Training Series, Part 3
Basic training of horse and rider
Dressage – The Scale of Training

DVD, Disk Typ DVD 5,
approx. 30 minutes
Language: German/English
ISBN 978-88542-843-5

German National Federation (FN)
FN Training Series, Part 6
Training of the rider
Show Jumping
for Advanced Riders

DVD, Disk Typ DVD 5,
approx. 30 minutes
Language: German/English
ISBN 978-88542-836-7

German National Federation (FN)
FN Training Series, Part 8
Training of the rider
Advanced Dressage Riding,
Novice and Elementary Level

DVD, Disk Typ DVD 5,
approx. 45 minutes
Language: German/English
ISBN 978-88542-868-8